Sex Education

Rationale and Reaction

Edited by
REX S. ROGERS
Lecturer in Psychology, University of Reading

CAMBRIDGE UNIVERSITY PRESS

Published by the Syndics of the Cambridge University Press
Bentley House, 200 Euston Road, London NW1 2DB
American Branch: 32 East 57th Street, New York, N.Y. 10022

Library of Congress Catalogue Card Number: 73-89764

ISBN: 0 521 20477 1 hardcovers
        0 521 09858 0 paperback

First published 1974

Printed in Great Britain by Alden & Mowbray Ltd
at the Alden Press, Oxford

To Karina with love

The right rule is simple: until a child is nearing the age of puberty teach him or her no sexual morality whatever, and carefully avoid instilling the idea that there is anything disgusting in the natural bodily functions. As the time approaches when it becomes necessary to give moral instruction, be sure that it is rational, and that at every point you can give good grounds for what you say.

BERTRAND RUSSELL, *The Conquest of Happiness*

Contents

Preface

Sex education is a growing social and educational phenomenon. Unlike other innovations such as 'New Mathematics', however, its introduction into curricula has broader implications – for it reflects and, in turn, influences a change in contemporary values. Such changes are seldom totally comfortable, either for the members of society experiencing them or for those whose lot it is to implement them. Concern about the issues raised by sex education, as much as the growth in the demand for it, seem responsible for the ever-expanding literature on the subject.

In this book of readings, I have tried to avoid the format of a lot of good advice but little hard fact. I have concentrated instead on a more empirical approach, using research findings wherever possible to illustrate the grounds for sex education, its spread in the educational system and the effects it has. In doing this, I hope I have provided a text useful to all those involved in sexual instruction. No apologies, in a field dominated by North American and Scandinavian literature, are made for a certain bias towards the work of British writers.

In a controversial field like sex education, it is perhaps worthwhile pointing out that a book of readings, however much it indicates an editor's judgement of what is important, cannot take a stand on issues in the same way as would be expected of a single individual's text. One function of the commentaries in the present book is to provide some perspective and, as such, is obviously open to criticism. One reaction I would like to anticipate relates to my use of the expression 'sex education' itself. It is, in my view, little more than an umbrella phrase – useful as a rubric because it guides the reader (more effectively than do the alternatives) as to what range of phenomena are being considered. Synonyms, such as 'sexual instruction', have been used where a need existed to lighten the load of textual repetitiveness.

As always in the production of a book, thanks are due to many hidden hands: Professor Hilde Himmelweit under whose aegis and guidance my own research (p. 251) was conducted; Dorothy Dallas and Alan Harris who gave much constructive criticism on earlier drafts; and, by no means least, to Wendy Davies who spent many long hours trying to turn it into something readable. Errors, biases and omissions are mine alone.

University of Reading

REX S. ROGERS

Acknowledgements

The publishers and editor are grateful to the following for permission to quote copyright material from their publications. The numbers correspond to the numbering of the chapters. The source of each article is given in full at the foot of the first page of each chapter.

(1) *New Society*; (2) *Journal of Moral Education*; (3) and (12) Longman Group Ltd; (4) IPPF, London; (5) *New Statesman*; (6), (7) and (15) Health Education Council and *Health Education Journal*; (8) Williams and Wilkins Co.. Baltimore, Maryland; (9) The Society for Research in Child Development, Inc.; (10) Phi Delta Kappa, Bloomington, Indiana; (11) *The Practitioner*; (13) Allen Lane, Penguin Books Ltd; (14) Granada Television Ltd; (16) Grampian Television Ltd; (17) B.B.C. Publications, London; (18) Health Education Journal; (19) National Council on Family Relations, Minneapolis, Minnesota.

SECTION A
Sex Education: Theory, Practice and Perspective

Overview

This first section concentrates on the clarification of what we understand by sex education and on how society has come to bring such instruction into the normal scholastic framework. At the most basic level, a concern with sex education must stem from the recognition that human socio-sexual development is a *learning*[1] process (see Fig. 1). Such a view has not always been held for, in the past, sex has tended to be seen as an innate 'animal passion'. Our present more environmental thinking is a result of both clinical and experimental studies of the way in which specific learning opportunities affect sexual behaviour. Indeed one of the few points of agreement between the two sides of the 'permissiveness' debate is that man's sexual expression depends on his socialisation – society being seen by both as having the power to produce sexuality that is 'responsible' or sexuality that is 'free'.

It is appropriate, therefore, to begin with a paper which speculates on the exact role that learning plays in sexuality. In Chapter 1, Wright poses the question 'Sex: Instinct or Appetite?'. By this he means to contrast the view that sex is a drive which man merely learns to channel (rather as we do in 'potty training') with the view that sex is a taste (other examples being things like food preferences which are environmentally determined and have little to do with real hunger). The latter view, which Wright favours, calls into question the Freudian notion of a sexual drive (libido) which could be 'dammed up' and so produce psycho-sexual disorders. Nevertheless, it justifies sex education in another sense by pointing out how malleable the sexual appetite is.

It will not escape the reader's attention that there is a sting to the tail of Wright's article, a felt need for sex '. . . to be linked with affection, tenderness and awareness of the feelings of others'. This is, in fact, a very commonly set objective for sex education and one towards which the editor feels both sympathy and unease. Neither

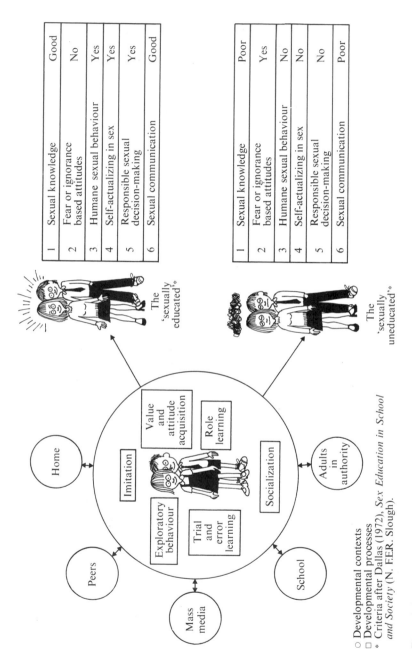

1	Sexual knowledge	Good
2	Fear or ignorance based attitudes	No
3	Humane sexual behaviour	Yes
4	Self-actualizing in sex	Yes
5	Responsible sexual decision-making	Yes
6	Sexual communication	Good

The 'sexually educated'*

1	Sexual knowledge	Poor
2	Fear or ignorance based attitudes	Yes
3	Humane sexual behaviour	No
4	Self-actualizing in sex	No
5	Responsible sexual decision-making	No
6	Sexual communication	Poor

The 'sexually uneducated'*

○ Developmental contexts
□ Developmental processes
* Criteria after Dallas (1972), *Sex Education in School and Society* (N. FER. Slough).

Figure 1. Socio-sexual development

the decision to establish a clear linkage between the provision of information and the tutoring of ethical skills and emotional sensitivity, nor the imposition of deliberate separation of these aspects of sex education is without its problems. Integration is very dependent on the individual teacher's possession of the wherewithall to avoid 'indoctrination' – i.e. the imposition of a *particular* morality onto sexuality. If he fails in this then his value either as a source of information or as a mentor is compromised. Separation, while it avoids (perhaps dodges) this problem, raises other difficulties. Most obviously, those of facing the pupil with a 'clinical' or 'plumbing' approach to knowledge on the one hand and a moral education that is attenuated by its abstraction from the concrete and factual on the other.

My own view is that some kind of compromise is possible – the straight presentation of facts pertaining to sexuality wherever they arise 'naturally' in the curriculum (biology, health education, social studies, domestic science); plus the coverage of sexuality within a *broadly conceived* scheme of moral education (i.e. one that does not place emphasis either on particular areas like sex or on particular ways of construing morality).

Many educationalists, however, take the position that sex education has to be seen as a highly integrated endeavour. Such a view is skillfully presented by Harris (Chapter 2). Arguing from the perspective of moral education (a recent and burgeoning area which now boasts its own journal), Harris attempts the unenviable task of seeking to clarify the terms of reference of the sex educator. The value of such statements of position can be better understood by considering the current status of sex education. Numbers of well-intentioned people (e.g. teachers, health education officers, producers of teaching aids and those specialising in family life education and moral education) are all engaged in what can be broadly labelled sexual instruction. The chances are high, however, that the umbrella of 'sex education' hides a diversity so wide that it includes approaches in direct conflict – a state of affairs I have tried to illustrate in Table 1. In such a situation, there are many advantages which accrue from the generation of well-formulated statements of specific positions such as the view expressed in Chapter 2. For one thing, they create backcloths against which our own attitudes can be seen with more clarity. Further, when we have formal statements, it becomes possible to generate debate about their

Table 1. *Variables in formal sex education schemes*

(1) Underlying value-assumptions	(2) Curriculum definition	(3) Overall aims
Often not explicated. These tend to 'move with the times'	The content of most sex education schemes fit into one or more of the following rubrics:	Often linked to (1). The following is adopted from Dallas (1972) *op. cit.*
Who benefits? 　recipient 　society 　government 　parents Ethical basis 　Christian 　humanistic 　pragmatic Moral tone 　restrictive 　permissive	**Biological emphases** Medicine 　V.D. 　contraception Biology 　facts of life 　animal analogies Psychology 　sex is com- 　munication 　varieties of 　gratification **Sociological emphases** Education 　preparation for 　menstruation 　child molesters Sociology 　relativism of morals 　our own system's values Law 　age of consent 　sexual offences Aesthetics 　enjoyment of sex 　love states Morality 　why we have sexual 　morals 　education for moral 　development Societal costs 　population control 　illegitimacy	Adequate know- 　ledge Attitudes not 　based on fear 　or ignorance Humane sexual 　behaviour Self-actualising 　in sex Responsible 　sexual 　decision-making Adequate sexual 　communication

(4) Specific aims	(5) Locus of contact	(6) Implementation techniques	(7) Assessment and evaluation
Where the major effects are to be expected	Where the poten- tial recipients are to be reached	How the aims are to be achieved	How aim achieve- ment is to be gauged

Attitudes
  changed
Knowledge
  gained
  errors corrected
Behaviour
  changed
  improved
	Places of work
	Hospital/clinic
	Home
	Clubs
	School
		Individual or
		  group approach
		Sexes mixed/
		  segregated
		Group
		  discussions
		Lectures/classes
		'Expert' speakers
		Films/T.V./
		  Audio-visual
		  aids
		Practice (if
		  appropriate)
		Follow-up
		  facilities
		Role-playing
			Formal examination
			Questionnaire/test
			Subjective assess-
			  ment
			Behavioural effects

7

underlying assumptions and so refinements in conceptualisation can emerge. Finally, when we have explicit aims, we can set about satisfying ourselves that they are, in fact, being achieved.

The moral educator's approach *in practice* is well illustrated in the extracts from McPhail *et al.* in Chapter 3. This material is from the companion rationale to the ambitious 'Lifeline' moral education project of the Schools Council. The selections cover both the general structure of the courses and some examples from the unit specifically focussed on sex. By referring to Table 1 of this Overview, the interested reader can trace the particular structure that the moral education position imposes on sex education and contrast it with the type of scheme that would result from a more biological orientation. A good example of the problematic issues raised by the moral education approach to sexuality can be found in the 'Consequences' material where the situation is posed '. . . tries to kiss his girl-friend while driving'. My own reaction to this is that it has nothing to do with sex but a lot to do with good road sense! This can be seen by substituting '. . . tries to do yoga exercises while driving'. In either case the innocent in logic is left with the faulty deduction:

Kissing a girl (yoga exercises) while driving can
cause accidents
Accidents are bad
Hence, sex (yoga) is potentially dangerous.

Although sex education does not have to be seen as an exclusively school-based venture (we could, for example, look to home, youth services or the ordinary mass media as other channels), there are good grounds for regarding the educational system as the major source of information. This stems from the unique role of the school as the single agent to which everybody in society has (at least in theory) equal access. It is also often true that it is easier to change the habits of institutions than those of individuals – so that to see all schools giving sexual instruction is a viable goal[2], whereas to see all parents instructing their children is not.

It is therefore of great importance to explore the current situation in British schools. An adequate understanding of the weaknesses and strengths of the current position seems a necessary pre-requisite to the planning of sex education courses, the development of better teaching aids and the improvement of provisions for instructing teachers in putting the topic across. In this context, the paper by

Burke (Chapter 4) is of great value for it reviews the attitudes and activities of educationalists at both the central and local government levels. In addition, the author discusses the role played by non-governmental bodies and reviews some of the few researches in the area. The valuable appendices include some examples of curricula.

Despite a very obvious need for such data, we lack exact information about the extent to which sex education is included in individual school curricula. As Burke's paper makes clear, many L.E.A.s have developed sex education schemes; others have not. Even where schemes are promoted or external aids like schools broadcasts are available, the very autonomy of individual schools insures that levels of implementation vary greatly. A very good guide to current attitudes and practices is given in the article by Harris (Chapter 5). The information is not based on a random sample but a sufficiently large number of schools were sampled to yield information that must be fairly typical. Any complacency from those favouring sex education about the present situation is likely to be shattered by the finding that, despite an ever lowering age of physical development, over half of junior school heads felt that girls should not be informed before the event about menstruation or that half the primary schools never mentioned mating, conception and pregnancy.

Among the points raised by Harris in discussing his findings is the importance of better teacher-training in improving our efforts in the sex education field. No single institution seems better able to affect change in the whole current pattern of sexual instruction that the Colleges of Education. Yet, in 1964, a survey by Norman Greaves (Chapter 6) revealed that the adequacy of teacher-training in this area is very doubtful. More than half the schemes lasted less than six hours and they were seen not so much as covering how to teach sex education as 'primarily . . . for the personal benefit of the students in forming their own set of values . . .' One of the functions I hope the present publication will serve is to provide material that will prove useful to Colleges and Departments of Education in designing courses intended to help trainee teachers in the aims and techniques of sexual instruction.

In Chapter 7, Gill, Reid and Smith provide some broader perspectives on sex education: a review of typical press comment (Gill *et al.* concentrate on the Scottish press – the editor's own informal reading south of the border has shown much the same pattern), and a study of parental views. The average parent sampled accepted the need for a positive attempt at sex education (see Chapter 11 and Chapter 18 for further confirmation of parental approval). Additionally, about half of the parents mentioned school as a preferred agent of instruction. Some effects of seeing Grampian Television's 'Living and Growing' series (Chapter 16) on parental attitudes were also examined. These last statistics suggest that confidence in school as an agent of sex education and acceptance of the need for sex education may be enhanced by parental exposure to potential teaching aids.

The work of Masters and Johnson has popularly become almost synonymous with sexual research. It is fitting, therefore, to end this section with an extract from their writings (Chapter 8). In the paper selected they talk not about their more famous pure research but about the counselling side of their work. The term 'sexual re-education' seems to fit this well as the therapy is concerned in part with rectifying the effects of inadequate or maladjustive early learning. It is obviously tempting when one considers the prevalance of distressing psycho-sexual disorders like impotence and frigidity to wonder how far the frequency of such problems could be reduced by adequate sex education. As is noted in Section C, however, such evidence is very hard to collect and the question remains unanswered. Nevertheless, the success of Masters and Johnson-type therapeutic techniques are powerful evidence that a broad-based sex education programme (including factual information, attitude manipulation, practice and counselling in relationships) can have major behavioural consequences.

NOTES

1 Not to be confused with saying that it has been *taught* in the sense of imposed on a passive organism by an all-powerful environment. Modern psychological thinking about learning sees it as more like the whole process of seeking out food and then digesting it. Equally, this view recognises that such learning ultimately represents an *interaction* between the given (genetic factors – including sex gender) and the acquired (all those elements of sexuality derived from the socialising community).

2 It also, of course, means a generation of up-coming parents who have at least the *knowledge* with which to instruct *their* children.

1 Sex: Instinct or Appetite?

DEREK WRIGHT

Sex is usually thought of as one of the instincts, and as such classed with hunger and thirst. It is notoriously difficult to define precisely what an instinct is; but in everyday usage it refers to an urge which directs behaviour and which is generated by a biological need. On the analogy with hunger and thirst, it follows that deprivation of sexual satisfaction should lead to an increase in need. So when someone apparently does not go in for sexual activity, we are left wondering what he does about this need. Healthy living, we presume, requires regular sexual 'outlets'. When this is not possible we expect the sex urge to find more indirect and devious ways of expressing itself.

Until recently psychologists themselves held a similar view to this. Behaviourist psychologists classed sex as a primary drive and they assumed that the principles which govern behaviour instigated by hunger will also apply to sexual behaviour. Freud's view of sex is similar. He defines 'libido' as 'psychic energy' – the tension or excitation that is seeking discharge through behaviour. At any particular time, according to Freud, libido exists in a finite quantity and it originates in internal bodily processes. It differs from other instinctual energies, he says, in that it is highly displaceable, and easily repressed, sublimated or diverted into forms of behaviour which have no obvious connection with sexuality. This highly mobile quality of the libido enabled Freud to discover its presence in creative art, science and so on.

In the last decade or so, there has been a burgeoning of research in this field, much of it directed towards the biology and physiology of sex. Discrepancies have emerged between the way sex seems to act, and the way hunger or thirst do.

Admittedly, the determining influence of genetic structure has

Derek Wright, 'Sex: instinct or appetite?' This article first appeared in *New Society* (22 May 1969), pp. 791–3..

been demonstrated in the sexual behaviour of several animal species. Thus, in mice, genetics seem to account for differences in the number of times the penis is inserted before ejaculation is reached, and in the amount of time before the sex drive is recovered after ejaculation. Again, in monkeys, erection of the penis and ejaculation can be produced by electrical stimulation of the brain.

Such research shows how important the inbuilt biological factors are. But their influence is neither simple nor direct, particularly in human beings. Sexual arousal depends much more on external stimuli than hunger or thirst does. Even the hormones that are secreted by the glands seem only to make sexual arousal possible when appropriate stimulation occurs, rather than themselves induce it directly. There is evidence, too, that once a pattern of sexual behaviour is well established in an animal, it tends to become 'autonomous', i.e. it becomes a little bit less dependent on its biological basis. Rats castrated as adults will nonetheless copulate when the relevant stimuli, such as a female on heat, are there.

Most important is the evidence of evolutionary development in sexual behaviour. The higher up we go in the phylogenetic scale, the more the cortex (the upper brain) is involved. In lower species, what external stimuli will release sexual activity is largely determined by the innate genetic structure of the animal; in man, however, they are heavily conditioned by culture and circumstances. The Harlows showed that monkeys which were grossly deprived of social contact virtually lacked sexual activity when they became adult. Psychiatric observation suggests that human sexual behaviour is subtly shaped by the nature of the social attachments formed during a person's development.

In man, as in lower species, secretions of hormones bring the body to functional readiness at puberty; but the relation between hormonal balance and sex drive is obscure. Some studies have found that women who are undergoing androgen therapy report enhanced sexual interest, but the evidence is meagre, and for men it is quite inconclusive.

Wide individual differences are observable in sexual interest. Whether a person has sexual intercourse often or less often, he can adapt fairly readily to either situation without his general efficiency being affected. In Michael Schofield's survey of the sexual behaviour of adolescents* less than half the boys reported enjoying their first

* See Chapter 12 [Ed.].

experience of sexual intercourse (despite the fact that apparently the great majority reached orgasm) and less than a third of the girls. It did not appear to be a particularly thrilling event for either sex.

Thus, it is misleading to see sex in human beings as a simple response to a biological need. It is much closer to the truth to think of it as an acquired appetite or taste. Professor F. A. Beach, one of the most distinguished of researchers into sexual behaviour, makes the point forcibly:

No genuine tissue or biological needs are generated by sexual abstinence. It used to be believed that prolonged sexual inactivity in adulthood resulted in the progressive accumulation of secretions within the accessory sex glands, and that nerve impulses from these distended receptacles gave rise to sexual urges. Modern evidence negates this hypothesis... What is commonly confused with a primary drive associated with sexual need is in actuality sexual appetite, and this has little or no relation to biological or physiological needs... Sexual appetite is... a product of experience, actual or vicarious. The adolescent boy's periodic preoccupation with sexual matters is traceable to psychological stimuli, external and phantasied, and is not dependent upon his recently matured reproductive glands. His erotic urges stem more from socio-cultural factors than from those of a strictly physiological nature.

This approach to sexual motivation has been taken up and elaborated at length by others (by K. R. Hardy and R. E. Whalen, notably). This analysis assumes that there are two basic mechanisms physiologically given. The first, labelled the 'sexual arousal mechanism', refers to the fact that touching the genitals brings pleasurable arousal. As this stimulation gets more intense, the second mechanism takes over, namely the convulsive upheaval of orgasm (which is termed, for the male, the intromissive and ejaculatory mechanism).

Now the mechanism of orgasm is stereotyped and largely involuntary. But the sexual arousal mechanism, in human beings, is very changeable and conditionable. Through conditioning, the arousal which stimulation of the genitals brings can be evoked by touching other parts of the body and above all by imagination and other thought-processes. The context in which sexual stimulation occurs will determine the other emotional responses that become associated with it. It is worth mentioning that Albert Bandura and Richard Walters (in their study, *Adolescent Aggression*) found that youths who had a history of conflict with their parents, associated sexual arousal with aggressive feelings. Among other youths, sexual arousal was coupled with tender feelings.

The final link in learning sexual behaviour takes place during adolescence when a boy or girl discovers that when arousal reaches a given pitch it triggers the second, orgasmic mechanism. As this link grows firmly established, sexual arousal, from being a pleasurable state in itself, becomes a foretaste of something much better. Hence it may thereafter be felt to be frustrating if it is not concluded with orgasm.

Once sexual arousal is thus associated with imagination and with the mind, cultural influences (whether friends, art, comics, advertisements or entertainment) can condition one to feel sexual arousal even *before* the relevant stimulus takes place. A boy will learn to expect that holding the hand of a girl his own age will arouse him sexually, though he knows that the hands of his aunts have no such magic. The fact that one can induce or reduce sexual arousal by taking thought means that it is at least partly a matter of volition, not compulsion. The cookbooks on sexual technique recognise this when they recommend that a man who wants to delay orgasm during intercourse, in the interests of his partner's pleasure, should divert his mind to other, non-sexual matters.

Sexual appetite, then, is a habit by which one has *learned* to expect pleasurable arousal and orgasm in certain kinds of situation. (The innate component is the *capacity* for arousal and orgasm.) The emotions and imaginings that accompany sexual appetite – tenderness, shame, aggression, or whatever – are inseparable from it. D. H. Lawrence fulminated against 'sex in the head'. But if sex in the head were somehow eliminated, sexual desire and behaviour would largely disappear. For human sex is sustained and directed much more by stimuli the individual has learned to perceive as arousing, and by his own self-directed imagining, than by physiology.

Though we haven't the evidence to be sure, it seems that those religious people who take vows of chastity and consider masturbation a sin, achieve a life in which sexual arousal is minimal, and the orgasmic mechanism falls into more or less permanent disuse. And they are none the worse for it. On the hypothesis that sex is a biological 'need' like hunger or thirst, one has to infer complicated processes of repression and sublimation to account for this. But on the appetite theory we can suppose either that sexual arousal has not been conditioned much to stimuli other than direct touching of the genitals, in the first place; or that through the discipline of their way of life, these people have undergone a massive de-conditioning so that arousal now comes from very few stimuli other than directly tactile ones. At the same time, their commitment to their beliefs makes them mentally restructure many stimuli which would 'normally' arouse them, so that they evoke other kinds of emotion. A priest may habitually *see* attractive women as children of God in need of forgiveness, rather than as potential bed-mates.

Whether or not one goes the whole way with the theory that human sexual behaviour is basically an appetite that is learned, there's no doubt it is a much needed corrective to the theory of biological need. It is in harmony with much everyday observation, and it has certain social implications.

According to the moralists, our present-day society is obsessed with sex, and in their view of course this is a bad thing. Certainly novelists, film makers, dramatists and advertisers (not to mention dress designers) now have great freedom to exploit stimuli that are sexually arousing. Defenders of this freedom commonly base their case upon the 'biological need' theory of sex. Their argument goes something like this. Sexual stimulation cannot make people any more sexually motivated than they are by nature, because the strength of each person's sexual drive is biologically determined. On the other hand, freedom of sexual expression in society will tend to disinhibit those in whom the sexual instinct is repressed or suppressed. But this is beneficial because healthy living demands that our basic instincts should be satisfied. If we bottle up our sex energies, they go bad on us.

The 'appetite' theory leads to a rather different assessment. What we are doing is cultivating our sexual appetites by steadily extending the variety of stimuli that provoke sexual arousal, and by sustaining this arousal through filling our minds with sexual imagery and thought. Biology may set limits (both upper and lower) to how far we can develop these appetites; but within these limits the possibilities are wide. As a society we appear to have decided to maximise them.

Obviously it does not follow from the appetite theory that it is wrong to cultivate our sexual appetites. That must be decided on other grounds (though it does seem silly to cultivate them freely, and at the same time deny them satisfaction). A case could be made for saying that, provided we take suitable measures to control birth, sex is a better appetite to cultivate than others like power or the itch to interfere in the lives of others. But the point is that our defence of sexual freedom will have to be on other grounds than biological need.

A more important issue raised by the appetite theory is the nature of the emotions we judge appropriate to sexual arousal. A glance at the various cultural influences at work – from advertising and novels to religious tracts and sermons – suggests a whole string of emotions that are currently associated with sex: desire for social status and success; aggression and cruelty; pride in skilful performance; self-contempt, fear and guilt; aesthetic feeling; delight in the forbidden; inferiority; curiosity; and even mystical experience. And there are some influences (Kinsey?) which tend to separate sex from any other kind of emotional response and make it a thing apart from other aspects of living.

If sex is to be fully human and personal, then it ought to be linked with affection, tenderness and awareness of the feelings of others. This, one may suppose, is the normal outcome of a warmly affectionate and reasonably permissive upbringing. In any case, the more sex is associated with fear, guilt, aggression and the rest, the less it will be integrated with affection. Rather than lament the fact that sexual appetite is now being encouraged, we might more profitably spend our time trying to ensure that the emotions that are integrated with it are the ones we approve of. To condition sexual arousal to moral feelings of guilt and obligation may destroy the ties with affection as effectively as conditioning it to cruelty or disgust.

We hear much of the 'public concern' over the sexual morality of the young. Yet when you listen to what the young themselves have to say, in surveys and personal conversations, you find that a great many of them are in fact rejecting traditional morality precisely in order to maintain and affirm this coalescence of sexual desire and affection. As they see it, to hedge sexual behaviour but not affection with rules is to push the two apart. For me, this attitude revives the faded hope that one day we may have a society in which the social influences surrounding us all conspire to tie sex and affection inextricably together.

Then perhaps the moralists and the press will give up writing about it, because nobody will be interested in reading what they have to say.

REFERENCES

Beach, F. A. 'Characteristics of Masculine "sex drive" '. In *Nebraska Symposium on Motivation* (University of Nebraska Press, 1956).

Beach, F. A. (ed). *Sex and Behaviour* (Wiley, 1965).

Hardy, K. R. 'An appetitional theory of sexual motivation'. *Psychological Review,* vol. 71, no. 1, 1964.

Whalen, R. E. 'Sexual motivation'. *Psychological Review,* vol. 73, no. 2, 1966.

Bandura, A. and Walters, R. H. *Adolescent Aggression* (New York, Ronald Press, 1959).

Schofield, M. *The Sexual Behaviour of Young People* (Longmans, 1965).

Harlow, H. F. and M. K. 'Effects of various mother-infant relationships on rhesus monkey behaviours. In *Determinants of Infant Behaviour,* IV, edited by B. M. Foss (Methuen, 1969).

2   What does 'Sex Education' Mean?

ALAN HARRIS

Current disputes of the sort raging about Dr Martin Cole's film* or about the content of sex education in general, tend to be pointless because everyone involved has a different set of assumptions or prejudices about the aims of sex education (or, in some cases, because they simply have not realized that sex education *could* have aims). But unless some measure of agreement can be reached in this area it is clearly futile to argue about the means by which these aims could best be achieved. There could be no agreement about how to teach people to swim, for example, if everyone disagreed about what was meant by 'swimming'. In this article, therefore, I shall try to do two things: first, to clarify the concept of sex education; and second, to see what implications this analysis has for teachers.

In the first place, I want to take the word 'education' seriously. Education is not identical with such processes as instruction, training or indoctrination. It is not just the teaching of facts, or the imparting of skills. It is quite incompatible with such an aim as making people behave in a certain way. Education aims at *initiating* people into worthwhile activities concerned with learning and understanding. Sex education, therefore, cannot (logically) be only the giving of certain facts, or only training in relevant skills (whatever those might be). Nor can it involve imposing a particular attitude toward 'sexual morality'. What it must achieve, if it is to be judged by the same criteria as other areas of education, is the maximum possible degree of knowledge and understanding concerning sexual behaviour. Furthermore, this knowledge and understanding must not (to use R. S. Peter's terms) be *inert* in the sense that it makes no difference to the way in which the pupil conducts his life.

Alan Harris, 'What does "sex education" mean?', *Journal of Moral Education*, vol. 1, no. 1, pp. 7–11.

* 'Growing Up' [Ed.].

The ultimate aim of education, I would argue, is the promotion of personal autonomy. *The more educated a person is the better he is able to make a responsible and informed choice between possible courses of behaviour. The more aware he is of these possibilities, the more freedom he has in the way he conducts his life.* Concepts such as 'generosity', 'altruism', 'unselfishness', and even 'love' make no sense at all except in the context of autonomy, for any sort of 'moral' behaviour (as opposed to sub-moral behaviour such as 'acting on an impulse' or automatically obeying rules) involves the making of choices which are concious, rational, and free.

The person who gives money to a charity is not acting altruistically if he is forced to do so at gun-point or if he has a blind compulsion to give, or if he has no thought of the purpose of his gift. One would praise him if (a) he was free *not* to give, and (b) he understood the consequences (for other people) of giving or not giving – if, in other words, he was acting autonomously.

(If readers still doubt that 'autonomy' is an overriding goal in education, I suggest that they pause at this point and try to think of any process which could both [a] properly be called 'educational', and [b] have the effect of limiting the development of personal autonomy.)

Now among the conditions for being autonomous are those concerned with the ability to satisfy one's needs; and since these needs often conflict with each other one has a further need – namely, the ability to resolve these conflicts as effectively as possible.

To take some examples at random: (1) We need to survive physically – the more effectively we can satisfy this need the more autonomous we are in this respect (e.g. we need to know what comprises a good diet, how to keep fit, etc.). *Physical education* and *health education* cater for these needs; the more effectively we can use our bodies the greater the range of choice of physical activities we have, and therefore the more autonomous we are.

The more effectively we keep healthy, again, the more choice we have in how we spend our time.

(2) We need relationships with other people (with our parents in the first place, with friends, employers, husbands or wives, with our own children). The more capable we become in participating in such relationships, the more effective is the choice we have in forming relationships which we value.

The role of the school here is to provide education in personal relationships, though this not the place to expand on what such education involves.

(3) We need knowledge, to be able to find things out, to store and use information. The better we are at finding things out, the more autonomous we are (and the less we have to rely on other people) in how we make judgments, choose our career, entertain ourselves, etc. Education in all the forms of thought, mathematics, history, science, aesthetics, and so on, should, as education, make us more autonomous in that we learn to think mathematically, or whatever, for ourselves.

(4) Lastly, we need to resolve conflicts between other needs, to be able to evaluate them. But it falls short of being autonomous if we simply choose arbitrarily how to resolve conflicts, if we 'resolve' our conflicts by doing 'just what we feel like doing' or 'what the rules say' or 'what the Church says'. The role of the school here is to provide moral education.

If the arguments so far are acceptable, what then is sex education? What exactly are sexual needs, and how can education help us to satisfy them? What is 'sexual autonomy', and how can education help us to achieve this state?

In fact, is 'sex education' an intelligible concept? My own feeling is that it is just as intelligible as 'physical education'.

We all have sexual needs, and sex education should in principle render us more able to satisfy them. It should open up a wider range of possible forms of behaviour, and therefore give us greater autonomy of choice. Provisionally, then, the aim of sex education is *to help people to satisfy their sexual needs in the fullest possible sense.* To stop short at teaching people basic anatomy would be as strange as stopping maths at the stage of counting to ten. To 'give' people the attitude that sex outside marriage is always wrong (or never wrong) would be as strange as teaching that Ptolemy was 'right' about the universe. Education aims at autonomy, and the greatest possible degree of informed, responsible choice. *Sex* education should enable people to be aware of the full range of possible sexual behaviour and values, so that they can meaningfully choose how they themselves will behave.

However, sexual needs can never be considered in isolation, because (a) they often conflict with other needs, and (b) they are, essentially, cooperant needs, i.e. they usually involve relationships with other people. A 'sexually educated' person must logically be one who understands how to resolve the conflicts between sexual needs and others, and who is able to understand and take into account the needs of other people. Therefore, he needs to be 'morally' educated as well; otherwise he cannot possess sexual autonomy.

Readers who wish to pursue the philosophical problems inherent in these issues should read basic works such as *Freedom and Reason* (R. M. Hare, OUP) and *The Logic of Education* (Hirst and Peters, RKP). *Moral Education* by John Wilson (Heinemann) is also particularly useful, and in this book he introduces an analysis of what it means to be 'morally educated'. Unfortunately I cannot do justice to his arguments here; I can only borrow his analysis and adapt it to my own purposes, which is to make a similar analysis of the concept of being 'sexually educated'.

I suggest that the following components are all logically necessary tasks in sex education. How they could best be carried out must be left to the imagination of individual teachers.

(1) We should foster the attitude that in sexual relationships, as in all other relationships, the feelings and needs of other people are equally important as our own. All is not fair in love and war. (If the word 'foster' here sounds dangerously like indoctrination, I can only say that without this attitude people would not need to think morally at all.)

(2) We should foster insight into the sexual feelings and needs (both conscious and unconscious) of other people. We should also foster a person's ability to have insight into his own sexual feelings and needs. Without such insight one cannot possibly hope to know how to avoid hurting people, making them jealous, resentful, and so on. One therefore lacks autonomy in the sense of being able to achieve desired relationships.

(3) We should teach, to an appropriate level, facts about human biology, intercourse, contraception, venereal disease, and so on. Insofar as a person lacks information that he may need, he is to that extent less autonomous. A girl is not 'free' to avoid having a baby if she has intercourse and does not know about contraception, or to avoid getting VD if she cannot recognize the symptoms. We should also teach about the sexual mores of our own society, and of other societies, so that pupils are free to take these into account in their expectations of other people.

(4) We should teach people how to communicate about their

21

sexual feelings and needs. A person who is unable to make his more subtle needs felt, or to understand the expressed wishes of his partner, is to that extent less autonomous (because that less free to exercise choice). It is in this area, perhaps, that our schools are least effective. The pupils are set no example, for the most part, by either their parents or their teachers; small wonder they remain inarticulate and adopt the language and sentiments of TV commercials or girls' comics.

(5) We should teach people how to get to the stage of forming their own moral principles based on 1–4 above. If they adopt someone else's principles rather than formulate their own, they are to that extent less autonomous.

(6) We should foster people's ability to be alert and sensitive to situations where they ought to stop and think. This is particularly important in such an emotional area as sexual relationships. People often adopt an altogether different set of principles in sexual relationships from those they would adopt in, for example, business relationships. Or to be more accurate they abandon moral principles altogether, and are to that extent less autonomous.

(7) We should help people to have confidence in their own judgments, if we have no reason for supposing that these are unsound. It is particularly important that we should give this support to teenagers, who, being less experienced in many ways, are more vulnerable to external pressures (such as those toward chastity for its own silly sake, or those toward a fashionable, sloppy sort of liberalism which is just as inconsistent with personal autonomy as driving a car with no steering wheel or brakes).

I have no space here to expand on the practical measures which would help to realize these aims (I have more to say about this in *Thinking about Education,* Heinemann). But I hope that the main implications are clear enough.

In the first place, it is high time we adopted a wholly positive approach to sex education, instead of grudgingly throwing a few titbits of information in an atmosphere of moral gloom.

And in the second place, we should be as scrupulous about setting children on the road to sexual autonomy as we are about offering them the chance of becoming original scientists, mathematicians or engineers. At present, the situation of sex education is rather like that of astronomy in the time of Galileo: hedged around with taboos and superstitions, and conducted by a process of tight-lipped indoctrination.

Detailed consideration of the seven aims stated above should lead to the conclusion that sex education can never be a 'subject' on the timetable, taught by 'experts'. For one thing, most people who would regard themselves as 'experts' on sexual behaviour would never be allowed into the teaching profession at all, if Lord Denning had his way. But to be serious, it should be obvious that sex education is a function of the entire curriculum.

Specific elements will be taught in biology, general science, or health education; physical education, in the modern sense, is directly relevant as it helps the body to become a more controlled and expressive instrument; literature, creative writing, discussion in English, social science, RE, should all contribute to the insights, understanding, and expressive skills demanded by aims 2, 4, and 6. Everything that John Wilson describes as necessary for moral education is also necessary for sex education: I would refer the reader to the practical suggestions he makes in Section One of *An Introduction to Moral Education* (Penguin).

But most of all, what we need in the first place is not so much a scheme of practical suggestions for teachers; it is a change of heart, a fresh and sympathetic approach to the whole problem – the positive approach that I mentioned earlier...

3 Moral Education in the Secondary School

PETER McPHAIL *et al.*

In moral education, theory which is not specifically related to practice is about as much use as a mirage to a man in need of a compass; on the other hand practice which is not guided by relevant theory at best leads to stumbling and painful progress, at worst to confusion and despair. We have in consequence firmly resisted any idea that we should produce one book of theory, which would gather dust on school and college shelves, and another practical book which would lie around, dog-eared, in staff rooms.

What we have attempted to do is to relate rationale and method within one volume hoping that the one will illustrate and support the other. We do not necessarily expect that those initially interested in rationale will immediately read through all the chapters concerned with method; nor that teachers and students seeking in the first place for practical guidance on how to use materials in school, will first sit down and work through what is said about rationale. What we do hope is that everyone, whatever his point of departure, will sooner or later look at those chapters which are not of primary concern to him; and, moreover, that all readers will arrive at a stage (if they have not already reached it) where moral education is seen as a field where theory and practice, rationale and method are mutually interdependent.

'Lifeline' – a programme of moral education for the seventies.

It is tempting, having developed a programme of moral education for use in schools, to claim that ours is a definitive approach. Mindful, however, that one of the most necessary attributes of moral educators is, if not humility, then at least lack of self-righteousness, we do not believe that the methods we propose are necessarily exclu-

Reproduced by permission from Schools Council's *Moral Education in the Secondary School,* by Peter McPhail, J. R. Ungoed-Thomas and Hilary Chapman (Longman Group Ltd., 1972), Chapter 5 and part of Appendix.

sive of other ideas and techniques. Indeed, it seems to us that moral education is a field which cannot but benefit from a variety of approaches, provided only that they are professional and directed to the needs of boys and girls. Furthermore, even within the context of our programme we do not wish to give the impression that there is anything sacrosanct about the material we have prepared. What we would like to see is teachers using the methods we propose, going on to develop their own materials geared to the needs of the pupils in the particular schools and areas where they are working...

There are, nevertheless, various claims which we do make for the programme, the first and foremost being that it works in practice. It has been extensively tested while being developed, in a wide variety of schools. In all, prior to publication it has been used by upwards of 20,000 pupils. As a result we, and the teachers involved, are satisfied that it is viable and has a real contribution to make. We also believe that although we have been working in an area about which there has been much public concern the programme we have produced is the first systematic, professionally developed attempt to show how, within the context of a modern curriculum, boys and girls can be helped to develop a style of life which is in practice both personally satisfying and considerate of others.

We have called the programme 'Lifeline' because we are concerned with educating for life and wish to suggest that our materials may offer help to schools. As we have already mentioned there is evidence of an urgent need for assistance in this area; and further, any scheme of moral education should offer a sense of direction and continuing support. 'Lifeline' therefore seems to us to suggest in one word the general aims of our approach.

Overall the 'Lifeline' programme consists of a variety of different materials and methods. Although individual parts of the programme can be used separately, each piece of material in fact has its part in and contributes towards a coherent and consistent pattern (see Fig. 2).

First, of course, there is this book, *Moral Education in the Secondary School*: it is intended for all those interested in moral education, from the student and practising teacher who wants practical assistance, to the parent, educational administrator, head teacher or any other person wishing to see how in practice or theory moral education can be related to school curriculum and organisation. Next there are the three sets of curriculum material: 'In other people's shoes', 'Proving the rule'? and 'What would you have done? These form the heart of the programme and are intended primarily for ages twelve-plus to fifteen-plus. This curriculum approach is itself designed as a whole, with its own interrelationships. Finally, since we are aware that curriculum material alone can be ineffective without institutional support, we have looked at ways in which the school organisation can encourage moral behaviour. 'Our School, a handbook on the practice of democracy by secondary school pupils', has been prepared to suggest ways in which moral behaviour can be encouraged throughout the school.

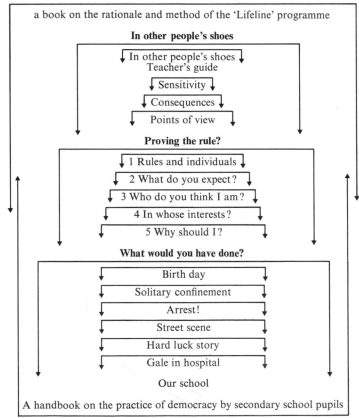

Moral education in the secondary school

a book on the rationale and method of the 'Lifeline' programme

In other people's shoes

In other people's shoes
Teacher's guide

Sensitivity

Consequences

Points of view

Proving the rule?

1 Rules and individuals

2 What do you expect?

3 Who do you think I am?

4 In whose interests?

5 Why should I?

What would you have done?

Birth day

Solitary confinement

Arrest!

Street scene

Hard luck story

Gale in hospital

Our school

A handbook on the practice of democracy by secondary school pupils

The curriculum approach

The three major sets of curriculum material are interrelated by their 'situational' nature, and by the objectives and themes which they have in common. Although the complexity of the incidents differs between 'In other people's shoes', 'Proving the Rule?' and 'What would you have done?' all the materials are based on the use of actual situations. This characteristic of the curriculum approach derives from our belief that, to quote Tillich, 'we all know that we cannot separate ourselves at any time from the world to which we belong'. Tillich had in mind primarily adults when he made this statement, but it is even more true of boys and girls than of their elders that they are conscious of living in a world which cannot be escaped, and which presents an unavoidable challenge. Consequently, it is our opinion, that any educational attempt to deal with morality other than through the 'situation', the actual and the concrete, is likely to fail because it would be evading personal experience, which is the medium through which problems of morality are felt and perceived.

The overall objective of the programme, as has been argued in earlier chapters, is to help pupils to adopt a considerate style of life. If the material is to have a reasonable chance of success, teachers using it need to bear in mind two essential factors. First, they must be aware of the importance of motivating pupils so that they become involved and increasingly committed to the idea and practice of taking others' needs, interests and feelings into account as well as their own. Secondly, they must direct their work with pupils to encouraging them to put moral values and attitudes into practice; any moral education programme which remained simply classroom bound and academic and did not point the way towards the living of a good life would, to all intents and purposes, be a programme not of moral, but of amoral education; what is required in fact, to use Tillich's words again, is a 'courageous participation in the "situation"'. (In terms of the diagram illustrating the curriculum approach, Fig. 3, teachers need to use as necessary guidelines the dimensions of 'Motivation for caring' and 'Caring in action'.)

The major part of the material itself derives directly from research with secondary school pupils (. . .) which showed which are the main areas of adolescent concern in the field of personal, interpersonal and moral problems. Consequently, in the first instance, the material

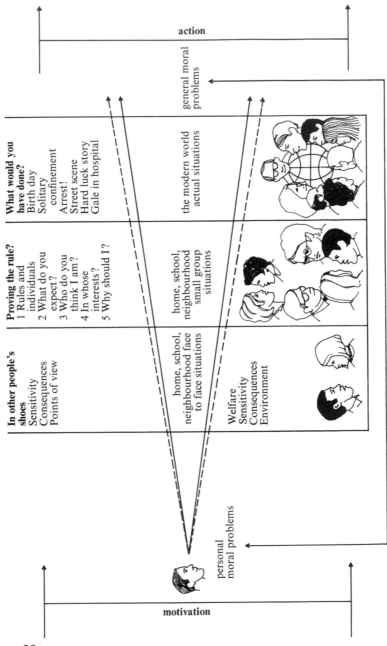

Figure 3. *The curriculum approach*

28

action

general moral problems

What would you have done?
Birth day
Solitary confinement
Arrest!
Street scene
Hard luck story
Gale in hospital

the modern world actual situations

Proving the rule?
1 Rules and individuals
2 What do you expect?
3 Who do you think I am?
4 In whose interests?
5 Why should I?

home, school, neighbourhood small group situations

In other people's shoes
Sensitivity
Consequences
Points of view

home, school, neighbourhood face to face situations

Welfare
Sensitivity
Consequences
Environment

personal moral problems

motivation

is concerned to secure a working out by adolescents as individuals of those moral problems which are critical (and therefore motivating) for them. Secondly, as the programme develops it leads pupils on from considering personal problems towards thinking about more general moral problems. The two, that is the personal and the general, are not perceived as being separate or different in kind, but inescapably linked, for in many ways it is true that the moral dilemmas which afflict society are simply the moral dilemmas which face the individual, only writ large. (In terms of the diagram this link between personal and general moral dilemmas is indicated by the linked phrases 'personal moral problems' and 'general moral problems'.)

The main themes which run through all the materials are initially stated and developed in the 'In other people's shoes' material. These themes are concerned with method and situation. The method themes deriving their main description from the first two titles of 'In other people's shoes' are 'Sensitivity' and 'Consequences'. 'Sensitivity' is a title for the various ways and means of encouraging sensitivity to others; while 'Consequences' is a title for the various ways and means of encouraging awareness of the moral and social consequences of the way one behaves, or particular actions which one takes. In general, to become morally educated it is necessary to become sensitive to others, to learn to think about what consequences one's actions may have, and, further, to be inclined to act upon the understanding which derives from increased moral awareness. (In terms of the diagram the two method themes are indicated, to begin with, as materials within the 'In other people's shoes' part of the programme. They are also indicated as two diameters running through all three parts of the programme, 'In other people's shoes', 'Proving the rule?' and 'What would you have done?')

The second two themes concerned with situation are 'Welfare' and 'Environment'. Each of the situations in the programme occur in circumstances which encourage consideration of the welfare of the people involved, and the relationship between them and their social, physical or economic environment. An effective moral education needs to encourage awareness of and concern for welfare and environment. (In terms of the diagram the two 'situational' themes are indicated as two outer diameters running through all three parts of the programme.)

As to the plan of the materials themselves, they progress from simple towards complex situations. So in the first part, 'In other people's shoes', the two sections (*a*) 'Sensitivity', and (*c*) 'Points of view' are nearly all concerned with 'situations' essentially involving only one or two people; and set in the familiar surroundings of home, school or neighbourhood. The second part, 'Proving the rule?' which is divided into five booklets, also deals with 'situations' set in home, school or neighbourhood surroundings, but instead of one or two people being involved the series is concerned with personal and social identity, relationships within groups, and conflicts between different groups of people. Finally the third part, 'What would you have done?' which is divided into six booklets, deals with 'situations' which actually happened, set in the context of the modern world (1900–70). The situations here are more complex and set out at greater length than the situations in 'Proving the rule?' just as in turn the 'Proving the rule?' situations are more complex, and set out at greater length than the 'In other people's shoes' situations. (In terms of the diagram the progressively more complex plan of the materials is indicated by the widening of the angle between the two sets of diameters as they pass through the three columns of materials. Within the diameters the settings and social nature of the three different types of situation are indicated. The titles of the materials themselves are shown at the start of each of the three columns.

The three sets of curriculum materials are considered separately, with particular reference to method in subsequent chapters. ... Any of the materials can be used individually, without necessary reference to other materials in the programme. However, since they are designed as a whole they would obviously benefit from being used in conjunction with each other. This raises the problem of how the 'Lifeline' programme in particular, and indeed moral education in general, is most appropriately related to curriculum and timetable. ...

The Project is firmly commited to the view that any adequate sex education programme for secondary schools must be based on the realisation that sexual activity cannot be isolated from the needs, feelings and interests of the individuals involved, and that sexual problems, V.D., contraception and childbirth occur within a complexity of personal and social relationships.

The 'Lifeline' programme contains situations which are relevant to sex education; these can be extended and developed by those who have a particular interest in this field of education.

INTRODUCTORY SEX EDUCATION THROUGH 'SENSITIVITY',
'CONSEQUENCES' AND 'POINTS OF VIEW' MATERIAL

Some examples of situations particularly relevant to sex education
which were cited by adolescent boys and girls as posing problems
about what to do.

(1) *From 'Sensitivity' material*

a You are very attracted to a girl/boy but she/he ignores you.
b A boy or girl of your own age, with whom you are friendly,
appears to be very upset for some reason unknown to you.
c Your mother herself adopts teenage fashions.
d Your father brags about how good he was at games when he was
young.
e An adult has drunk too much at a party which you are attending
and is over-hearty or over-familiar towards you.
f You are kissing on the top deck of a bus when the conductor
threatens to put you off at the next stop.

(2) *From 'Consequences'*

Outline what could happen when someone:
a sleeps with casual acquaintances;
b tries to kiss his girlfriend while driving.

(3) *From 'Points of view'*

a A girl in her teens is trying to run the house while her mother is in
hospital but her younger brother refuses to wash up because he says
it is woman's work.
b You have a girl friend of whom you are extremely fond and she
seems to care a lot about you. You suggest that you go off for a long
day's picnicking and walking in the school summer holidays. She
seems reluctant to agree and you can't think why, as you know she
enjoys walking.

FURTHER SEX EDUCATION THROUGH 'PROVING THE RULE?'

(1) *From 'Why should I?'*

'My dad said I had to be in by eleven,' said Vicky to Eddie at the
club one Friday night. 'I can't stay 'cause he'd go up the wall if I
was late and . . .'

'Eleven o'clock!' interrupted Eddie. 'That's ridiculous!'

'Yeah, I know, but it's not all daft, is it? You never know who you're going to meet when you're walking home late, do you?'

'Well, I'm with you, ain't I?' replied Eddie.

'How's he to know that? You're not that reliable, are you?' Vicky pouted and took a sip of her Coke.

'O.K., O.K.,' said Eddie. 'Don't let's fight about that, but we're just starting to enjoy ourselves and you say you've got to go home just because of your old man.'

Vicky put down her glass and said angrily, 'Don't you think I mind? I shall be glad when I leave home ... and school for that matter. Do you know something?' She leaned towards Eddie confidentially, 'We had to stand outside in the freezing cold at break today, just because they have this daft rule at school about staying out of the buildings at break except when it's literally belting down with rain.'

'There's a point in that,' said Eddie. 'If they let everybody stay in, the whole would get smashed up.'

'Huh!' said Vicky, 'If we wanted to smash things up, we could do it just as easily outside as inside ... windows and that.'

'I don't know about that. It's the desks and things. They think they're the bloody crown jewels. But you can see the point of it.'

'You sound like me dad. Every time I say. 'What's the point of a rule like that?" he just says, "There must be a reason or they wouldn't have it, would they?" Suppose they said you had to stand on your head three times a day? My dad would say, "There *must* be a reason",' replied Vicky sarcastically ...

4 Sex Education in the United Kingdom

SUE BURKE

This report on sex education in Britain outlines some of the most important activities and developments. As in all matters relevant to the attitudes and behaviour of youth and the future of society, it is a field where many agencies, both governmental and non-governmental, have expressed interest and concern, and, in some instances, have been actively involved. Interest in family life and sex education is expressed by educationalists, as well as by medical and welfare personnel, although the former are most frequently in contact with, and are therefore particularly aware of, the variety and complexity of the problems facing all young people today.

Because activities in sex education are concentrated in the educational field, it will be helpful to describe briefly the educational scene in Britain. The structure of the education system is such that specific activities in a particular school are left to the discretion of the head teacher of that school, who is expected to adjust recommendations from Central and Local Government to suit the needs of his own school community. As a result of the autonomous organization of each school, there is wide diversity in sex education activities, as in many other spheres, in different parts of the country. However, each school is answerable to a Local Education Authority, which in some instances attempts to influence the head teachers of the schools of its area by producing reports and circulating recommendations. There are 163 Local Education Authorities in England and Wales. Each of these is responsible to the Central Government, and is expected to promote national education policies at the local level, as well as undertaking general administrative functions in the organization and co-ordination of the educational institutions in a particular area.

Sue Burke (ed.), *Responsible Parenthood and Sex Education* (IPPF, London, 1970). A report prepared for an International Planned Parenthood Federation Working Group held in Tunisia, November 1969.

The information included in this report is arranged under the following headings:

I   Action at the Central Government level
    Statements and reports
    Curriculum development
    Public examinations
    Schools broadcasting

II   Action at Local Education Authority level
    Specific schemes
    Teacher training

III   Surveys

IV   Action at a non-Governmental level
    Educational organizations
    Medical organizations
    Religious groups
    Other groups

V   Young people's attitudes to sex education

VI   Comment

Appendices

I. Action at a Central Government level

STATEMENTS AND REPORTS

A succession of reports and pamphlets have been produced from Central Government agencies indicating an awareness of the urgent need to educate young people in personal relationships including the sexual aspects.

The 1944 Education Act, which reorganized the British education system, contained the following statement, which is generally accepted as including sex education:

... it shall be the duty of the local education authority for every area, so far as their powers extend, to contribute towards the spiritual, moral, mental, and physical development of the community ...

Before this, in 1943, the Board of Education, later to become the

Ministry of Education, produced a pamphlet entitled *Sex Education in Schools and Youth Organizations.* This drew the attention of Local Education Authorities to the need for special courses in sex education for teachers and youth leaders. It contained the suggestions that student teachers in training colleges were often in need of personal guidance themselves, and that *ad hoc* courses in sex instruction for mature teachers and youth leaders would provide the most suitable guidance '... for this difficult and delicate task'.

Since 1956 a number of important Government Reports have made reference to young people's need for adequate sex education, moral education, and education for personal relationships. These include the Crowther Report 1959, the Newsom Report 1963, the Plowden Report 1967, among others. In addition to these which were produced by the Ministry of Education and later the Department of Education and Science, other Central Government reports are noted and summarized in Appendix 1.

In 1956 a Ministry of Education pamphlet entitled *Health Education* was published which states that there are grounds for believing that '... a better understanding of the reproductive processes in man, of the nature of sex and sexual behaviour and the basic facts about population...' may help many people to achieve more rational conduct in their sex lives and in family relations.

The Crowther Report, entitled *15 to 18*, was presented to the Government in 1959. It deals with the needs of 15 to 18 year olds at a time of changing social and industrial conditions. Most of its recommendations are concerned with the balance and relevance of school curricula. It emphasizes that changes are needed in the education of adolescent girls, particularly among the less able to whom marriage is of great importance, particularly at the present time when the age of marriage is getting younger. It points out that 'To preserve the family in the future a conscious effort is needed by way of the educational system, on a much greater scale than has yet been envisaged.' At the same time authors of the report recognize that sexual problems are not confined to marriage, and suggest that there should be opportunities to discuss sexual ethics in the school. They also suggest that these and other needs of the individual could be dealt with during an extra compulsory year at school, thus raising the leaving age to sixteen years. New courses of relevance to the demands of the real world would have to be devised for the extra year.

The education of young people, aged 13 to 16 years old, of average or less than average ability, is discussed in a report entitled *Half our Future* (the Newsom Report), presented to the Ministry of Education in 1963. It is important to note that this category of pupils comprises over half of the school population. Many references to and recommendations on personal and social development of these pupils are made in the report. Certain specific objectives are stated, which include the need to develop both a sense of responsibility towards other people, and an internalized code of moral behaviour. The authors of the report suggest that the overwhelming influence in the lives of young people of this age is the sexual instinct. One of the main recommendations in the report is that: 'Positive and realistic guidance to boys and girls on sexual behaviour is essential', and that such guidance should include biological, moral, social, and personal aspects. Other recommendations include: that sex education schemes in schools should be paralleled by advisory programmes for parents on the physical and emotional problems of their children; that religious instruction has a role in helping boys and girls to find a firm base for sexual morality, based on chastity before marriage, and fidelity within it; that married teachers handle the problems of sex education more easily than others; and that, taking the broadest interpretation of sex education, opportunities should be created for boys and girls to meet members of the opposite sex in a helpful educative environment.

The Plowden Report, *Children and their Primary Schools,* was presented to the Government in 1967. The authors state that sex education is a parental responsibility though often avoided. They suggest that each school should have a definite policy on sex education, made in consultation with the parents; that children should understand the biological nature of reproduction; that any confusion with excretion should be clarified at this early stage; that use of correct scientific terms should be encouraged; that all questions should be answered truthfully; and that ethical aspects of sex education should not be avoided. It is also suggested that the best person in the school, to deal with these various matters, is the children's usual teacher, but it is recognized that some teachers will not feel comfortable in this situation. The authors of the report request that teacher training colleges should note this point. They also make an interesting comment on children who show '... an unhealthy interest in sex ...' which, they suggest, is probably not an uncommon phenomenon and should not be dealt with harshly.

An interesting report, known as the Cohen Report but entitled *Health Education,* was produced by the Central and Scottish Health Services Council in 1964. In it several recommendations and comments are made on the content of health education courses in schools, which it is noted should include '. . . more education where it is most necessary . . .', citing sex education as one example. The authors of the report suggest that health education syllabi in schools should aim at giving a child knowledge that will equip him to face the social and health problems he will meet in the future and should include the social implications of relationships between the sexes, and the social and health problems of adolescence and adulthood. A series of recommendations are made in the report including a request that the Minister of Health should draw the attention of the Minister of Education to the content of the report. It is also recommended that there should be close co-operation between Local Education Authorities, Public Health Departments, and the Central Government on the subject of health education; that the Government should foster the training of special health educators since those teaching the subject require such training in addition to possessing certain personal qualities; that health education should be included in the school syllabus; that the Government should promote training in health education for doctors, nurses, and teachers, although it is pointed out that such people will not be able to use their training unless they have co-operation and support from the Local Education Authority, and the head teacher, the doctor, the health visitor, and the inspector of the school.

In the reports mentioned above, and others noted in Appendix 1, calls are made to Local Education Authorities and to the Central Government to take a greater interest in the field of sex education, in one or more of the following ways:

by encouraging increased activity under various sections of the curriculum in schools;
by encouraging special training for teachers;
by increasing co-operation with parents.

CURRICULUM DEVELOPMENT

In 1964 the Schools Council was set up by the Government to carry out research and development work on curricula, teaching methods, and examinations in schools. One of its main objectives is to maintain the independent responsibility of each school to develop its own curricula and teaching approach, based on the needs of its pupils. With this in mind the Schools Council has produced a number of working papers on a wide range of topics, either as a preliminary to investigating new activities or approaches, or to encourage local developments in the educational field, or to report on existing progressive activities. Some of the papers contain information of relevance to the field of sex education. For example, two papers consider the implications of raising the school leaving age to 16 years as recommended in the Newsom Report (see page 36). In the initial paper fields of enquiry are outlined, existing work of relevance is noted and reviewed, the Schools Council's programme of work is outlined, and recommendations are made to the schools, to develop teaching programmes relevant to the need of young people who will have no education after 16 years, and who will probably resent having to stay at school for an extra year. The second paper describes some experimental school programmes and curricula in the humanities subjects, and suggests that the main emphasis of the school curriculum should be man and society, commencing with the individual in society and culminating with the function and role of the community. It is suggested that central teams, such as those involved in the Nuffield Foundation Projects (see below), can provide information and take initiative in specific fields of curriculum development. The information and techniques developed can be passed on to local groups of teachers and others to test and modify in their schools.

As a result, the Nuffield Foundation and the Schools Council have jointly sponsored revision of the content of school courses, particularly in the science field. It is expected that the curriculum recommendations made by the various project groups will gradually be incorporated into future school syllabi.

One of the project groups, the Secondary Science Project, will produce a collection of materials and curriculum suggestions which teachers can use in planning courses for children of average and less than average ability, in a wide variety of schools. This material is at present on trial, and publication is expected in 1971. It includes material for teaching the anatomical, physiological and behavioural aspects of the whole life cycle of man, and will contain suggestions for work on contraception, venereal disease and population problems. Film loops which can be integrated into this work have been made, covering such topics as human growth, hormones, world population problems and solutions. Another Schools Council and Nuffield Foundation project is the Resources for Learning Project, which is experimenting with a programmed learning course in sex education. A further project is the Humanities Curriculum project which is currently testing teaching methods and materials with 14 to 16 year olds of average and less than average ability. The premise behind this project is that work in the humanities will help pupils to develop an understanding of the controversial areas of universal human concern. It is intended to develop a new approach to handling such controversial issues through the technique of discussion, so that pupils are not influenced by the teacher's own views, and to a large extent take responsibility for their own learning. Collections of material have been made which are used to provide evidence during the discussions. Material in these collections ranges from printed extracts of fictional and non-fictional prose, poetry and drama, to photographs, cartoons, advertisements and tapes of songs and interviews. Two of the nine subjects selected for experimental study are the family and relations between the sexes. Another curriculum project is the General Certificate of Education Biology project. As a result of this project a series of five textbooks and five teachers' guides have been produced, to be used during a five year course for 11 to 16 year olds. Human sexuality is referred in years one and five of the course, but no mention is made of venereal diseases or contraception.

In addition to the papers mentioned above the Schools Council has also prepared a paper called 'Counselling in Schools' (Schools Council Working Paper No. 15, published 1967, by Her Majesty's Stationery Office) on counselling and guidance, demonstrating the breadth of the modern concept of curriculum. In it counselling is defined as the guidance of young people in personal, educational and vocational matters. At the time of publication of the working paper five university departments of education and one professional institution were concerned with training school counsellors. It is clearly stated in the paper that, when considering the scope of counselling in schools in Britain, those employed in the field should be prepared to cope with all types of problems experienced by pupils in relationships with home, friends, school and community, as well as with the pupils' employment problems and other difficulties.

School counsellors should also influence curriculum content, and should aim towards the adjustment of a school programme to the demands made by the community.

This section reviews the content relevant to sex education of the syllabi of a selection of regional examinations boards. The syllabi used in many schools, particularly for more able pupils, are orientated to the requirements of public examinations. The following short outline, and the contents of Appendix 2, give some indication of the relevance or irrelevance of public examination syllabi, and therefore school syllabi, to pupils' needs.

The Certificate of Secondary Education examination (CSE) can be taken just prior to leaving school at 15 or 16 years of age by less academic pupils; a group constituting about three-quarters of the total school population. The CSE is quite an innovation and only a proportion of the school leavers take this examination. The CSE syllabi tend to be more oriented to the demands of everyday life than the GCE syllabi (see below). For instance the CSE syllabi of the Metropolitan Examinations Board include: in biology, a simple account of reproduction in the mammal, with particular reference to the human being; in social studies, close relationships, including the family today, changing roles of men and women, relationships with the other sex, marriage, morals, rules of conduct, loyalties and responsibilities; in religious knowledge, a section on Christian obedience mentions, under the heading 'Personal Life', general behaviour and going out, use of leisure, the opposite sex (sex, marriage, divorce), and right choices.

Appendix 2 includes a table indicating the content of the 1969 Ordinary level General Certificate of Education (GCE) syllabi of eight examining boards throughout the country which might be relevant to sex education in the broadest sense. The GCE examination is taken at 16 years of age by pupils of above average academic ability. Four out of eight of the biology curricula of these examination boards include a note that all descriptions of mammalian physiology should make special reference to man. All the syllabi include reproduction in mammals. Therefore it must be assumed that only four of the syllabi are intended to cover human reproduction. Only one religious knowledge syllabus out of eight has any reference to values in the modern world. Only one examinations board offers an examination in Sociology at Ordinary level, and the content of this includes aspects of human behaviour, the family, and population (see Appendix 2).

The University of London Examinations Board syllabi for 1970 and 1971 include some relevant content in biology, human biology, and religious knowledge. More details are given in Appendix 2. This appears to be one of the most progressive Boards as regards the relationship of syllabus content to young people's everyday problems and needs, but even this is rather limited.

SCHOOLS BROADCASTING

The British Broadcasting Corporation plays a recognized role in education and provides both radio and television programmes for schools, and for education of the individual. Its policies for school programmes are laid down by a Council consisting of representatives from teachers' associations, Local Education Authorities, and the Department of Education and Science, among others. For a number of years, programme series covering aspects of sex education have been produced. The policy in schools television includes 'the provision of material of clear relevance and interest to a child's needs and interests', presented in such a way as to stimulate further discussion. It is felt that current trends in secondary schools 'towards more active bringing of social and personal problems into discussion make the evidential material which broadcasting can supply especially welcome'. Radio and television programmes for schools are supplemented by teachers' guides and well illustrated pupils' booklets. Recent examples of programmes relevant to sex education include:

(1) 'Looking Ahead' – a radio series for school leavers intended as preparation for their lives in the future. About six programmes were devoted to sex education. The topics covered in these programmes included physical and emotional development, personal matters, falling in love, starting a family, birth, parental responsibility, and making choices. In many instances, views of and comments from young people were included.

(2) 'Health and Science' – a series of radio programmes on health education. This series included programmes on growing up, put in the context of parental care in animal groups and in different human

41

societies; on changes at puberty related to hormonal changes; on survival in the context of the welfare state and free health services; and on diet and accident prevention. The final programme in this series was on reproduction, and included heredity, male and female physiology, childbirth, and rearing a family.

(3) Reproduction and Growth – a series of broadcasts, lasting for one term, for children aged 10 to 13 years. This series included an elementary explanation of cell types, asexual and sexual reproduction culminating in vertebrate, mammalian, and human reproduction. Other programmes dealt with environmental influences and the population explosion.

(4) In autumn 1969 a new series of radio-vision programmes on sex education for 8 to 11 year olds will be broadcast, which will involve use of filmstrip to the accompaniment of a recorded radio commentary.*

The BBC also provide further education programmes for the general public. One series entitled 'The Science of Man' consisted of eight programmes on reproduction and birth, and four on heredity; each of these topics being dealt with in detail. A similar depth series on education is planned for autumn 1969 and some programmes will certainly be devoted to discussing sex education. The series is intended for parents, teachers, and others concerned about or involved in education.

Commercial television companies under the auspices of the Independent Television Authority also produce programmes for use in schools. For example, the Granada Television Company has produced a series of television programmes entitled 'Understanding' for 15 and 16 year olds.† This was designed to encourage responsible discussion on various aspects of sex, marriage, family life and friendship.

Another series produced by an independent television company, entitled 'What's it all about', was prepared for young people of over 14 years of age. Each programme in this series presented a realistic situation relevant to the life of a young person today, and was intended to provide a basis for discussion. In each film a representative of a particular welfare or other agency, or a member of the medical profession, discussed the situation depicted, and suggested some of the sources from which information could be

* See Chapter 17 [Ed.].   † See Chapter 14 [Ed.].

sought. The film topics included unmarried mothers, early marriage, illegitimacy and adoption, housing, family roles, and leisure. Another television company produced a late night documentary for parents called 'What shall we tell the children', when young mothers discussed their problems and feelings about giving their sons and daughters information about sex, and young people, children, and teachers indicated their opinions or knowledge on the subject.

II. Action at a Local Authority level

In an effort to review the policies of Local Education Authorities in the field of sex education, a letter of inquiry was circulated by the IPPF to all Chief Education Officers in England and Wales. This resulted in sufficient responses to make the following generalizations about policies in sex education which tend to fall into one of three groups:

(1) Schools are encouraged to incorporate sex education into the normal curriculum.

(2) Schools are encouraged to use the normal curriculum, and to call in agencies such as the local Health Department or the Marriage Guidance Council.

(3) The initiative for sex education in schools comes from the Local Authority Health Department, which in some instances employs Health Education Officers for this function.

Since category 2 includes Health Departments, it is apparent that among respondents local Health Departments play an important role in promoting sex education in schools.

Several Authorities also arrange in-service training for teachers responsible for sex education. Examples of such schemes are outlined below (see also page 48). About twelve Local Education Authorities have published documents or reports on sex education, education for personal relationships, or health education in schools. Recommendations and comments from a selection of these publications are outlined below. Summaries from other publications of Local Education Authorities can be found in Appendix 3.

SPECIFIC SCHEMES

At the initiative of the Education Officer, the *Gloucestershire Association of Family Life* was formed in 1961 to consider whether further steps should be taken to help young people to understand the problems of personal relationships between the sexes, and to obtain a happy relationship in their own lives. The Association consists of representatives from the Local Education Authority, from schools, and from voluntary organizations. The Association has developed a training scheme for teachers and youth leaders from schools and youth groups throughout Gloucestershire. This scheme is run by special staff and is intended to prepare those responsible for educating young people in personal relationships and family life. It is emphasized by the Association that the scheme covers a much broader concept than sex education, and that it includes moral education, and all aspects of personal relationships. The Association considers that this type of education should be given in three stages in secondary schools (in Britain it is compulsory for children to attend secondary school between the ages of 11 and 15 years) and that the first stage should be incorporated into the first year at secondary school. This stage should deal with the physiology of human reproduction, laying emphasis on the wonder of life, and the importance of the family. Investigations in schools throughout Gloucestershire indicated that many schools were already giving this information. The Association felt it sufficient to organize annual one-day conferences for teachers responsible for giving this information. It has been suggested that this first stage should take place during the last year at primary school, partly because of the earlier onset of puberty among children today. The Association feels that primary school girls can be advised about menstruation and hygiene by a health visitor but that education for personal relationships should begin when the child first attends secondary school as this is often thought of as a first step towards adulthood. The second and third stages of the Association's scheme are concerned with physical and moral aspects of growth to maturity, and are designed to be given to children over 14 years of age. It is felt that those teachers giving this information require certain personal qualities, so a strict selection procedure has been adopted, which involves teachers attending a 24-hour selection conference when group discussions, open meetings, and private interviews with a psychiatrist and a head teacher take place. At the end of the selection conference candidates may be accepted immediately for this work or may be asked to return to a later selection conference, or may be recommended not to undertake this kind of work. Those selected attend a residential training course for 3 days, which includes instruction in child development, communication techniques, teacher-pupil relationships, and teaching aids.

Wiltshire Local Education Authority adopted a similar scheme in 1963. In this scheme, before a school embarks on a programme, or as a new group of pupils becomes involved, parents are informed and sometimes are invited to a meeting to hear details of the programme. Head teachers are also encouraged to enlist the help of school doctors and health visitors who have already been involved in this type of work so that their contribution can be complementary to the scheme and not in conflict with it.

A second part of the Gloucestershire Association for Family Life scheme is aimed at training workers among young adults. This part of the scheme is similar to that conducted for school teachers, but it involves the selection and training of group leaders. Candidates come from all walks of life, those suitable are selected, in the same way as teachers, at one-day selection conferences. Those selected attend a series of training sessions on group discussion, human development and behaviour, family relationships and community responsibility. The trained group leaders are then available to speak at courses, and give lectures, when requested, to organizations which are usually parent-teacher associations, church organizations, or youth clubs, or at homes for unmarried mothers. Some of the group leaders run a Youth Advisory Service where anonymous help is available to young people requesting it.

Some of the responsibility for sex education in schools in the *London Borough of Croydon* is taken by members of the Health Education Section of the Public Health Department of the Borough. Three or four trained health educators are employed by the Health Department to organize or assist in health education programmes, including sex education, in both primary and secondary schools. In primary schools the health educators approach is quite formalized, aiming at 8 to 11 year olds, and involving co-operation with the children's parents. As part of the primary school programme two evening meetings are held at each primary school in the Borough. The first of these meetings is for parents only, and is to present information on the courses which are being given in the school, as well as providing the parents with an opportunity to discuss the problems their children must be prepared to face while growing towards maturity. Films and other teaching aids which are used during the children's lessons, are demonstrated during the first meeting. A second evening meeting is held for parents and children together, to provide them with an opportunity to discuss what is being taught at the school, and to encourage a helpful atmosphere for further family discussions. The health education and sex education programmes of a primary school are usually incorporated into nature study classes, and may be given either by one of the professional health educators from the Health Department, or by the usual class teacher. The suggested content of the sex education programme includes information on families, parental care, new babies, and growth and development in all kinds of animals and in man. The introduction of elementary social studies into primary school courses will provide further opportunities for family life and sex education. The health educators of the Croydon Public Health Department will test this possibility during 1970. The secondary school sex education programme of the Croydon Health Department is defined by no set policy. If a secondary school requests assistance one of the health educators will take a particular class, and show films and slides, in order to stimulate discussion with the pupils. The health educators of the Croydon Public Health Department also prepare and circulate syllabi on community health or a similar subject, which include sessions on venereal diseases, growth and development, the basis of adulthood, and the family.

The *City of Oxford Local Education Authority* has appointed a health education adviser, who has produced sets of notes to give teachers guidance on education in personal relationships. The notes include suggestions on class discussion topics, and lists of useful films, books and other teaching material. In addition to these notes, six model lessons for sex education in primary schools have been produced by the health education adviser. Information in the model lesson notes includes simple information on male and female reproductive anatomy, on fertilization and pregnancy, on birth and puberty, and introduces the use of a correct vocabulary at a very early stage. Teachers in the City of Oxford Local Education Authority were circulated with the information and notes mentioned above, through each school in the area.

The Committee of the *City of Birmingham Local Education Authority* set up a working party of representatives from teachers organizations, the local Public Health Department, and the local School Health Service. In 1967 the findings of the working party, which were based on a series of surveys and many discussions, were published in a report entitled 'Sex Education in Schools'. Copies of this report were sent to every school in the Birmingham area. The report contains suggestions for sex education work programmes for children of different age levels, and for children of different interest groups and abilities (Appendix 4). It also includes recommendations on the training of teachers and counsellors, and the suggestion that a counsellor should be appointed to work within a group of secondary schools in the area. A further suggestion from the working party, as noted in the report, is that conferences of head teachers and other representative teachers should be held in every school district in the Birmingham Local Education Authority area, in order to discuss the proposals for a more co-ordinated and explicit approach to sex education, but it is added that sex education work is not compulsory, and that any teacher who so wishes can opt out of the scheme. As a result of the working group proposals included in the report, in-service training courses in sex education have been organized for teachers at the City of Birmingham College of Education. Participants in the training courses are recommended by the head teacher of the school in which they teach. The course lasts for 12 days, and involves attending a three-day full-time introductory session, and attendance at weekly intervals after this.

The *City of Newcastle-on-Tyne Education Committee* appointed a curriculum study group to draft a health education syllabus for use in the City's schools. The study group report was presented in 1968. It recommended that at primary school level efforts should be made to encourage parents to take responsibility for informing their children of the 'facts of life', but suggested that, with parents' approval, some supplementary teaching could be provided by the schools. It was suggested that the supplementary teaching should deal with parental care, families and new babies, and the relevant physiological information, including simple explanations of conception and birth, in order to show how life is handed on. It is pointed out in the report that changing morality today necessitates a new approach to sex education in secondary schools, and that the new approach adopted should incorporate time for discussions on human relationships. After considerable discussion it is concluded that the inclusion of contraception in new courses cannot be avoided, particularly with the rising number of illegitimate births and shot-gun marriages, and an increasing incidence of venereal disease. However, it is also stated in the report that '... to indulge in premarital sexual intercourse . . .' should be a choice of mature judgement, and that although teaching should not be indoctrinal, adolescents should be persuaded 'not to jump the gun' in this matter. It is specifically noted in the report that members of the curriculum study group do not support the contention that sex education leads to sexual experimentation. The report includes suggestions for a sex education course in the context of health education (see Appendix 4) with the stated view that no pupil should leave secondary school without having the opportunity to discuss the topics to be covered during the course which it is recommended should be allocated at least one period a week in the school timetable.

An interesting scheme was reported from *Lancashire* in 1966. In this scheme, the Assistant Medical Officer of Health and a representative from the Lancashire Education Authority, working on the principle that parents are the best people to give children information on sex, approached parents through several different sorts of school. Initially a series of evening meetings for parents were held at various primary and secondary schools, with the aim of determining reaction to the introduction of sex education programmes into schools in the area. Various films were shown which it was intended to use later in the school programmes. As a result of these meetings it was suggested that the film should be shown again to groups of parents with their children, because it was felt that this would help parents to overcome difficulties with terminology and lack of knowledge. Most parents found these sessions helped them to raise the subject much more freely with their children. An interesting development which emerged out of this scheme was a series of meetings held for parents who accompanied their very young children to a parent craft club. At these meetings films and tape recordings of typical family scenes were used to demonstrate how sex information can be given to children in an easy and natural way. It was reported that this was felt to be the most important programme in the whole scheme.

TEACHER TRAINING

In Britain, teachers are trained in one of two ways. Either suitably qualified school leavers, at the age of 18 years, go directly to a teacher training college, where they specialize in one or two subjects, and also study teaching methods and techniques, and educational theories, over a period of three of four years. Or, university graduates attend a one-year training course, in order to obtain a Certificate of Education. The general tendency is for those trained at teacher training colleges to teach in primary schools, and for those having university degrees to teach in secondary schools. Further training is available for experienced teachers, who, after five years of teaching may study for a diploma or certificate in educational guidance or counselling. One such course outlines its aims as follows: 'Those trained should be able to recognize and deal with the needs of individual pupils and help each student in his progress through school or college, to help him gain a better understanding of his strengths and limitations, identify his interests and help him plan his vocational goals realistically'. It also adds the point that modern conditions have necessitated a broader and deeper specialist approach to the needs of young people. In addition to the courses mentioned an increasing number of in-service training courses are being organized by local education authorities. Some examples of these have been described previously in this report (pages 44 and 47).

As in the case of schools all establishments concerned with teacher training are to a large extent autonomous and decisions about curriculum content are left to the teaching staff of the institutions. Some examples of the curriculum content relevant to sex education in a selected sample of the different types of teacher training course available, are detailed in Appendix 5.

To give some indication of the amount of training in sex education given to student teachers a survey produced the following evidence on the situation in 1964.[1] All establishments involved in teacher training were sent a questionnaire, which achieved a 66% response rate. Of those replying to the questionnaire, 38% ran formal courses in sex education with an increase of 20 such courses since 1958. There appeared to be a preference among the majority of respondents to include sex education in the wider context of other courses. 71% of the courses provided were intended to provide personal help to the students themselves, who are often found to be very ignorant on these matters. Only 32% of the establishments providing relevant courses, made any attempt to prepare students to teach sex education, although half of these stressed that the course provided was intended to help the student at a later stage in his or her career. 90% of the establishments concerned with teacher training felt that the courses they were providing were adequate, but many said that they had difficulty in finding a suitable person to undertake this aspect of training. In 21 cases college staff and outside agencies were used, in 19 cases college staff only were involved, and in 11 cases outside agencies only were used. The National Marriage Guidance Council accounted for half the instances when outside agencies were used, and medical practitioners accounted for most of the remainder.*

III. Surveys in the field of sex education

To give some indication of the extent of sex education given to young people, the following paragraphs outline some survey findings.

In 1964 a survey into the sexual behaviour of young people was carried out under the auspices of the Health Education Council (then the Central Council for Health Education) (see page 59) by its Research Director, Mr Michael Schofield.†

The survey findings which were based on a random sample of 1,873 young people indicated that there were marked differences in the amount of sex education given to boys and girls. Of the girls 86% said that they had been given some sex education in school, in comparison with 47% of the boys. It is interesting to note that, among the boys, there were marked differences in the information given according to type of school attended. State schools appeared to neglect their duties, and only 43–44% of the boys attending these schools had been given any type of sex education, whereas 71% of boys attending private schools were given some instruction in this subject. The figures quoted above give no indication of the quality of the sex education given, however Mr Schofield did attempt to investigate this. He found that most girls were given biological (excluding man), or physiological (including man) information, but in only 18% of the cases did this information include a description of intercourse. About 20% of the girls were given some form of moral education at school in comparison with 74% of the girls who said that they had been given moral advice by their parents. Boys attending state schools rarely received more than biological or physiological information, although 1 in 3 of the boys attending private schools and receiving sex education were given information which included a description of intercourse. It is worth noting that in most cases schools and parents do not appear to have given young

---

* See Chapter 6 [Ed.].   † See Chapter 12 [Ed.].

people advice on venereal diseases or contraception. Mr Schofield commented that:

The difficulties of providing viable education about sex are immense; much of the moral code is based upon religious thinking which teenagers do not accept, and many of the arguments against premarital intercourse, when unsupported by moral exhortations sound weak to many young people... But there is also plenty of evidence from this research that teenagers are anxious to be informed about sex and want sex education providing it is given with an assurance backed by knowledge and with a proper understanding of their particular problems.

There have been several localized surveys into the amount of sex education undertaken in schools. One of these was organized by the City of Birmingham Education Committee in 1965 as a preliminary to their report 'Sex Education in Schools' (see page 47). A questionnaire was circulated to all primary and secondary schools in the Local Authority area, which inquired into the extent of sex education provided in each school, emphasizing that the information should include 'details of sex education in its truest and deepest sense, based on an education in human relationships and personal responsibility', and commenting that instruction in biology and personal hygiene was only a small aspect of the whole subject. The survey revealed some interesting facts. It was found that staff of junior schools shrink 'from undertaking much positive sex education' though they deal with the questions which arise. Only 12% of the schools dealt with menstruation for the girls, and it seemed to be preferred to leave responsibility for this to the parents, although little effort is made to co-operate or encourage them in this role. Replies from staff of secondary schools indicated their view that factual and background information on sexual matters should be given to the pupils during the last years at junior school. It was also apparent from replies to the questionnaire that most secondary school staff felt it to be important to provide young people with advice and guidance on emotional development, including love, courtship, marriage, home life and parenthood, and chastity. Most of the surveyed schools stated the necessity to discuss promiscuity, adultery, illegitimacy and venereal diseases, and many believed that information should be given on family planning and birth control, although 50% of these were not willing to give details on principles and methods of contraception. About 45% of the schools surveyed encourage parents to play a role in sex education, and about 4% of the schools had experienced difficulties as a result of this.

In 1967 a survey[2] among teachers in 400 primary and secondary schools throughout the country showed that about 60% of the teachers thought that periods in the school timetable should be allocated to moral education other than religious education. Of these teachers three-quarters thought that moral education should include teaching about sexual morality. Most of the teachers surveyed, thought that moral education should be taught by teams of teachers, and should not be the responsibility of one individual.

In 1966 the findings of a survey of adults' additudes to sex education were published by the Gloucestershire Association of Family Life (see page 43). Most of those questioned in the survey were women who were members of Women's Institutes, Mothers' Unions, or Mothers' Clubs. The findings of the survey revealed a very positive attitude among these groups of people indicating that 63·7% feel that sex education is important in encouraging sensible attitudes, while only 13·2% feel that it has little effect. It appeared from answers to questions about sex education that many adults are unaware of what is being attempted in this subject. Many of the respondents in the survey, particularly those from parent-teacher associations, would like more details of the work being done in sex education in schools. Several respondents in the survey expressed concern about the selection of a teacher to undertake this work.

IV. Action at a non-governmental level

There has been no shortage of comments from non-governmental organizations on the need for sex education, although the comments have tended to be confined to educational, medical or religious groups.

EDUCATIONAL ORGANIZATIONS

In November 1968 the *Association of Headmistresses* published a report entitled 'Sauce for the Goose' which draws attention to the work being done in girls' schools, in 'an era of intense sexual self consciousness', in response to advances in the effectiveness of birth control, and the weakening of former moral standards. It is suggested that such work should be obligatory in the education of both boys and girls. The authors of the report point out that girls should not have to carry unequal responsibility in sexual matters which results in over-emphasis of their own sexual significance. Reference is also made in the report to the importance of the personality of the teacher responsible for this type of teaching and it is suggested that the married woman who returns to teaching after rearing a family is an asset in this type of education.

MEDICAL ORGANIZATIONS

At a conference in 1964 the *British Medical Association* stated that it attached great importance to the role of teachers in framing the attitudes of the young, and that it intended to draw this to the attention of colleges of education.

'Adolescence and its Problems' was the subject discussed at a symposium organized by the *Royal College of Practitioners* in September 1967. At one of the seminar sessions on 'Adolescents and Family Planning' a speaker, Dr Faith Spicer, suggested some reasons for increases in premarital sexual activity and unmarried pregnancies, and for the general tendency of avoiding the use of contraception and seeking advice. With these being the prevailing conditions among young people she believes that sex education is valuable and important; that it includes, not only anatomical detail, but also learning about the whole conflict of love and sexuality from parents and siblings; that it should contribute to an ability to discuss feelings and behaviour with people who are trained in discussion; and that schools must support any training given by parents, and must help the child to communicate and work out his feelings in discussion, and where necessary should arrange individual counselling sessions.

In 1967, at a *Royal College of Midwives* symposium on Preparation for Parenthood, midwives were informed of some of the approaches to work with young people which could influence them in their roles as prospective parents. In his opening remarks to the conference, Sir John Peel, President of the Royal College of Obstetricians and Gynaecologists, said that education programmes for young people should include information on the pleasure and desirability of parenthood to the individual and the associated responsibilities to the nation. He felt that this information should be soon after puberty.

RELIGIOUS GROUPS

In 1963 a group of *Quakers* published an enlightened essay entitled

53

'Towards a Quaker View of Sex', in which they put forward the belief that in this era of changing conditions there should be greater understanding of the sexual problems of the individual and a more flexible approach to sexual matters. In the essay they also offered the opinion that the traditional approach of the Christian Church to questions of morality should be replaced by a deeper, more creative and constructive morality. The authors intended that the ideas raised in the essay should help those having personal sexual problems or facing such problems in the lives of others.

In 1964 the *Church of England Board of Education* produced a pamphlet entitled 'Sex Education in Schools'. This was based both on correspondence with 300 schools, and on comments received from Local Education Authorities on the contents of a note on sex education. Through the pamphlet, the Church of England Board of Education called on all schools to accept responsibility for some sex education at the present time when so many parents do not feel able to face this responsibility, but it also recommended that schools should establish full co-operation with parents and should encourage parents to educate their own children in sexual matters. The authors of the pamphlet also suggested that physical facts of sex should be related to marriage and family life, and to the pattern of society; that moral education should not be authoritarian, but should be designed to help the child reach its own moral decisions; that the relationship between religious morality and sexual morality should not be overstressed; but that in all sex education the child's need for security should not be ignored. The Church of England Board of Education has no overall policy on sex education but several of its constituent bodies, including the Youth Council and the Children's Council have undertaken some work in this field. The Youth Council co-operates in diocesan schemes concerned with sex education, and the Children's Council offers advice on suitable teaching aids and literature for use in sex education.

Another constituent board of the *Church of England* is the *Board of Social Responsibility* which, like the Board of Education, has no definite policy in sex education, however, its Committee of Diocesan Moral and Social Welfare is in touch with sixteen local moral welfare councils which participate in schemes for education in personal relationships, in co-operation with Health Departments, Marriage Guidance Councils and social workers.

The *British Council of Churches* produced a booklet in 1966

Newman University Library
Phone 0121 476 1181 ext 1208

Customer ID: 475X

Items that you have borrowed

Title Sex education rationale and reaction
ID 0007690 2

Due: 06 March 2020

Total items 1
Account balance £0.00
14/02/2020 11 38
Borrowed 3
Overdue 0
Reservation requests 0
Ready for collection 0

Thank You for using Newman Library
https //libguides newman ac uk
library@newman ac uk

entitled 'Sex and Morality'. This booklet consisted of a statement, prepared by a joint church working party, which presents the Christian case for abstinence from premarital sexual intercourse. The booklet also contained extensive discussion on the basis of morality in the changing social and cultural scene, and presented the working party's recommendations, which included: that courses on human relationships should be organized for seconded teachers, which could lead to a recognized qualification; that all religious knowledge teachers should take part in such training schemes; that courses in human relationships should be included in the curricula of all schools; and that the local Council of Churches should co-ordinate the activities of all those individuals and organizations having special responsibility for individual's activities in the local community.

The *Catholic Marriage Advisory Council* has seventy centres in Britain, and through these provides a marriage counselling service, a medical advisory service, and an educational service. Within the latter, selected educational counsellors work with the staff of a school in the planning and running of courses in family life education for the pupils. At the same time, parallel courses are arranged for parents and teachers. Courses for pupils are aimed at developing an understanding of the implications of manhood and womanhood, and the idea of marriage as a life vocation. However, considerable emphasis is placed on work with parents which, it is felt, necessitates both good organization and efficient planning. An advice sheet on arranging such occasions has been prepared for schools, together with notes on parents' needs and difficulties. In this, it is suggested, that two meetings should be held for parents; one before the pupils are given a family life education course, and one as a follow-up at the end of the pupils' course. It is also suggested that programmes for these meetings should be largely based on group discussion, giving the parents, the teachers, and the Catholic Marriage Advisory Council representatives an opportunity to exchange ideas and opinions on such topics as the value of the proposed school course, the parents role in the total scheme, and the reactions of the children to the course.

OTHER GROUPS

The *National Childbirth Trust* is a voluntary organization aiming to dispel fears associated with childbirth, which believes that it is

55

vitally important to family life to recognize that childbirth can be a satisfying experience. For this reason it believes that a healthy attitude to reproduction must be encouraged through sex education given in schools, and that both boys and girls need education in the understanding of the physical and emotional aspects of childbirth. At the National Childbirth Trust antenatal classes, teaching is based not only on techniques of breathing and relaxing, but also on giving information which provides the woman with a language through which she can accept her own physical experience as part of the normal pattern. Where this occurs, sex education can begin within the family, which, it is generally agreed, is the ideal. The National Childbirth Trust is in contact with the problems facing teachers who are responsible for sex education, through members of the Trust who are already involved with the subject in schools. To assist these teachers, study days are organized, at which teaching aids are demonstrated and discussed, and when information is shared.

One organization which has been closely involved in family life and sex education is the *National Marriage Guidance Council*. Both the Government and local authorities have recognized and commended its work. The Council undertakes to select marriage guidance counsellors using strict procedures. Selected candidates attend a series of short residential courses over a period of two years, and during the same period are expected to attend practical and case-study discussion at least once a fortnight. At present, the work of counsellors is entirely voluntary, and once qualified, a counsellor is expected to serve a minimum of three hours a week, dealing with both marriage counselling and youth work. Work in schools is co-ordinated from each local marriage council office by an education secretary, who informs the local education authority of the services offered, with the request that all schools in the area be notified of these. Schools then contact the local office when they require assistance. However, before accepting an invitation to visit a school a counsellor stipulates certain conditions: a counsellor is not prepared to give a single talk on sex to a large group of children, and requests that, if at all possible, a series of discussions be arranged with groups of 10 to 15 pupils at the most. It is also preferred if a series of discussion sessions with pupils' parents can be arranged concurrently. A similar approach is used with other youth groups, and similar conditions are required.

To give some idea of the scope of the Marriage Guidance Council's work among young people figures for 1968 indicate:

8,318 sessions were held in schools
1,322 sessions were held in youth groups
1,848 sessions were held with parent teacher associations.

Recently there has been a trend among counsellors from the Marriage Guidance Council towards greater contact with teachers in schools and trainee teachers in colleges. In some cases counsellors have been requested to arrange group discussions, with the staff of a school, on family life and sex education. In other situations, counsellors have been asked to assist in teacher training colleges. This aspect of the Council's work is increasing in amount, and is considered to be very important.

Other organizations and groups of people have also seen the value of counselling methods to help young people deal with personal problems. In 1963, officials of the Marie Stopes Family Planning Clinic realized that there was need both to help young people with their sexual problems, and to provide birth control advice to the unmarried. A project scheme was organized at the Clinic, consisting of weekly consultation sessions for unmarried clients. This scheme was so much in demand that it was decided to offer a grant for the establishment of a centre exclusively for young unmarried people: thus the first *Brook Advisory Centre* was opened in London in 1965. Since then an increasing number of similar youth advisory centres have opened throughout the country, including nine more Brook Centres. The Brook Centres' aims are as follows: to provide birth control advice to the young and unmarried; to provide professional help to those with emotional, sexual and birth control problems; to inculcate a sense of sexual responsibility; and to mitigate the suffering caused by unwanted pregnancy and abortion. The counsellors and other staff working in these centres have found that, although young people come initially for birth control advice, they often require professional help with emotional problems.

Other youth advisory centres have been established by enlightened groups of people, and organizations, in several places including Southampton and Merseyside. The increasing need for such centres is becoming more widely recognized. This recognition, together with the provisions made under the 1967 Family Planning Act obliging local authorities to reconsider their policies on financing and otherwise supporting local family planning facilities has encouraged one London borough to open an advice centre with counselling facilities for young people. Young people are referred to the centre from their schools and colleges, or by social workers, or voluntary organizations in contact with young people in difficulties. The staff of the centre aim initially to provide practical advice, on an informal basis, which often results in the provision of counselling facilities in connection with other problems. The policy of the centre also includes the aims of improving sex education programmes in the borough's schools, and, of increasing the knowledge of the general public on relevant and related matters. It is envisaged that the centre will, in the future, be part of a network of help-services which will deal with the many different needs of adolescents, by providing preventative solutions to many of their problems.

An increasing number of university and college administrations are finding it necessary to provide advice and counselling facilities for the students although, in some instances, the student body provide and sometimes run their own service. Teachers and other educational administrators are also realizing the need for counselling services in schools. Often, the problems arising during counselling situations are concerned with sexual and emotional problems, although other personality problems may emerge.

FAMILY PLANNING ASSOCIATION

In the past, the *Family Planning Association*'s activities have been mainly concerned with clinic services. However, a sex education committee has been formed by the Association which now regards the subject as a priority in its work. All FPA branches organize talks and film shows and participate whenever possible in local sex education activities. In order to launch an integrated, full-scale sex education drive throughout this country, the FPA has initiated an 'Every Child a Wanted Child' campaign. This is a fund-raising campaign which aims to raise the money necessary to provide the trained speakers, audio-visual aids, books and pamphlets which will be needed so suit different audiences and age groups. Teach-ins, brains trusts, lectures, exhibitions and other events are also planned as part of the FPA's future work.

The FPA 1969 Annual Conference devoted considerable attention to sex education. One of the speakers at the Conference was Michael Schofield who talked about 'Sex and Birth Control in

Health Education'. Another speaker was Baroness Birk, Chairman of the Health Education Council, a Government body which has recently established a sex education advisory panel on which the FPA is represented.

A very interesting development, within the south-west and south-east London branches of the Family Planning Association, has been the establishment of a comprehensive community education project, administered by a full-time salaried education officer, who works with a joint sub-committee from the local branches of the FPA, to the brief that an education programme should be set up to spread knowledge of family planning, and elicit motivation towards its use. Since then a programme has been planned which is designed to inform and provide training courses for doctors and other medical personnel, social workers, local authority officials, FPA officials and others who are, or should be, involved or concerned with family planning. The project will progress using local FPA officials, who have already attended a course, to spread relevant information to teachers, parents, students, young couples, and members of youth groups. Finally, it is envisaged that relevant aspects of this information will be included in secondary school courses, and passed on to other specific groups of the general public, by teachers and others who have previously been involved in the first and second parts of the programme. The information given to each group at the different stages in the programme is oriented to the contribution that the group can make to the local community.

V. Young people's attitudes to sex education

Michael Schofield's survey into the 'Sexual Behaviour of Young People' (see page 50) also investigates young people's attitudes to sex education. The survey findings showed that a quarter of the boys and a third of the girls interviewed thought that they should have been told more about sex by their parents, while it was fairly clear that more boys would prefer to receive this information from a teacher, and that about a third of the girls would also have preferred to be given more information by teachers. There were also indications that both boys and girls would appreciate guidance on sexual problems from teachers. Rather disturbing findings from the survey were that most of the young people interviewed thought that they had learnt more from their friends than they could from adults, and that nearly half of those interviewed thought they knew all that there was to know about sex. Clear indications elsewhere in the survey demonstrated that the information young people thought they possessed, included a lot of misinformation about birth control and venereal disease, and only limited information on other matters.

In a survey among a group of young patients at a venereal diseases clinic,[3] it was revealed that the majority of the group felt that more sex education should be given in schools by someone who was 'both knowledgeable and unembarrassed'. Most of this group also thought that a doctor or nurse should visit the school in the context of sex education, although, among the control group in the survey, none of the 23% who had any knowledge of venereal disease expressed views on the necessity of such visits.

In 1968 a survey to investigate young people's attitudes,[4] which was carried out by the Medical Offcer of Health in the City of Leicester, showed that 100% of the young males and females interviewed thought that children should taught the facts about contraception. Among the group interviewed 46% of the males and 40% of the females thought that parents should provide this information, 46% males and 22% females thought that teachers should have this responsibility and 22% males and 33% females thought that doctors should provide information on contraception.

VI. Comment

A final chapter in the report of the investigation 'The Sexual Behaviour of Young People' 1965 (see page 50 and above) was headed 'Questions for Public Concern'. The following statement is quoted from this chapter, 'It is an urgent short-term task to make teenage sexual activities less harmful. This may be done by increasing the amount of knowledge and enlightenment on sexual matters, by introducing more and better sex education in the widest sense, and by providing individual counselling ... above all it is vital that future programmes of advice, help, and restraint should be based more on demonstrable facts, less on substantiated impressions ...'

In Britain there is evidence of a noticeable increase in interest and activity in the field of sex education during the last decade and particularly during the last five years. The information in this report, though not comprehensive, illustrates some of the major developments during this period.

Appendix 1: Other Central Government reports of relevance

In 1956 the *Royal Commission on Marriage and Divorce* called for a carefully graded system of education for young people as they grow up, in order to fit them for marriage and family living, which would also incorporate specific provision for those about to enter marriage. The Commission recommended that public money should be given to voluntary agencies that had already demonstrated their effectiveness in this field. A plea later reiterated in the Latey Report entitled 'The Age of Majority' which was presented to the Government in 1967.

The Albermarle Report 'The Youth Service in England and Wales' published in 1960 made the following points: many factors in society are changing, and these changes necessitate reorganization of the Youth Services to suit the needs of young people today. The factors of change include: earlier age of puberty, increased physical strength, changing pattern of women's lives, increases in delinquency, better housing and schooling standards, improved welfare facilities, increasing affluence, better education, higher expectations, employment problems, together with less measurable factors such as increased social mobility, conflict of values, impact of mass media, and the development of nuclear weapons. The Youth Service must be improved to cope with these, by training more youth leaders for both full and part time work. The training given to youth leaders should provide information on the psychology of adolescence, the physical needs of adolescents, changing cultural patterns in modern society including the impact of mass media, the affect of modern means of communication, and the values of adolescents at work, at home, in sex and in religion.

The Bessey Report presented to the Government in 1962, supplemented the Albermarle Report, by suggesting that there should be common elements in all youth leaders training courses, which should include instruction on the value of group work to personal development, and should also provide an opportunity to acquire an understanding of young people's attitudes, beliefs and aspirations, and a knowledge of their physical, emotional, and social development in society.

In 1967 *the Department of Education and Science* produced a pamphlet entitled 'Health in Education'. It draws attention to the features of school life that contribute most to the physical mental and social well being of pupils and makes suggestions on the context of existing health education courses which should include the necessity to prepare children for puberty. Within the context of sex education emphasis is laid on the children's need for knowledge of the basic facts of reproduction, the importance of moral education. It suggests that information should be given on venereal diseases and family life and marriage, but that information on birth control should be left to the head teacher's discretion. It states that presentation of the facts on all aspects of intercourse does not seem appropriate. Care should be taken on choice of a suitable teacher to give sex education, but it will usually be the biology teacher.

In 1967, *the Latey Report* entitled 'The Age of Majority' was presented to the Government with the following recommendations: that the minimum age for marriage, and for participating in sexual intercourse should remain at 16 years; and that the age to consent to marriage without parental permission should be lowered to 18 years. In a section of the report entitled 'Education for Marriage' it is stated that '... it is absolutely essential that everything possible should be done to educate young people in human relationships while they are still at school', particularly because it is known that more people are marrying younger. It is also stated that boys and girls need a great deal more instruction on the technical, emotional and moral problems of modern family life, and that an extra year at school as suggested in the Crowther Report should enable such instruction to be a regular part of the curriculum, and not simply a subject for the visiting specialist. It is also recommended in the Latey Report that high priority should be given to provision of grants from the public sector to such organizations as the Marriage Guidance Council and the Catholic Marriage Advisory Council, to encourage expansion of their important work in this field.

Appendix 2: An example of topics related to sex education in the General Certificate of Education syllabus

Excerpts from the syllabus of the *University of London Examination Board* 1970 to 1971:

In the *Biology* syllabus 1971 it is noted that: 'the relevance of biology to human affairs should be borne in mind'.

The syllabus includes:

Reproduction and Development (including growth)

Table 1. *Content of courses offered by the listed Examination Boards which could be relevant to sex education*

Examination Boards	Subjects which could include information on reproductive anatomy and physiology				Other subjects which could contain relevant information	
	Biology		Human biology	General science	Religious knowledge	Sociology
	Includes reproduction in animals	Special reference to man				
University of London	x	x	x	x	x	/
University of Cambridge	x	—	x	x	—	/
Joint Matriculation	x	x	x	x	x	/
Southern University	x	x	x	x	—	/
Associated Examinations	x	—	x	x	—	x
Welsh Joint Education	x	x	/	—	—	/
Oxford and Cambridge	x	—	/	x	—	/
University of Oxford	x	—	x	x	—	/

(x) = Some relevant content.
(—) = No relevant content.
(/) = Subject not offered.

Reproduction in the mammal: sexual rhythm, mating, fertilization, gestation, functions of the placenta, birth, parental care
Man's place in nature: including biological effects of man's activities on the environment.

The *Human Biology* syllabus 1970 to 1971 includes the following:

In the Anatomy and Physiology section it is noted that anatomy should not be disassociated from any functional implications. This section of the syllabus should include information on the following: the urino-genital system, male and female reproductive organs, functions of gonads, outline of female reproductive cycle, menstruation, an outline of human development, fertilization, implantation, and a brief outline of growth of embryo and foetus, and the functions of placenta.

In the *Religious Knowledge* syllabus 1970 to 1971 the following topics are noted:

Personal and social relationships and problems, to include such topics as home and family relationships, love, marriage, sex, parents and children.

Excerpts from the *Sociology* syllabus of the *Associated Examinations Board* 1970

The object of the Sociology syllabus is to enable the student to understand better the society of which he is a member. The syllabus includes such topics as the nature, changing role, and function of the family, as well as religion, moral and social behaviour, mass media, and population size and distribution, and contraception.

NOTES

1 'The facts of life for teachers', by J. Norman Greaves, *New Society,* vol. 6, no. 157, p. 18.

2 'Teacher's attitudes to moral education', by P. R. May, *Educational,* vol. 11, p. 215.

3 'Sex attitudes of young people', by M. Holmes, C. Nicol and P. Stubbs, *Educational Research,* November 1968.

4 'Young Opinions', by Dr R. W. Kind, *Family Planning,* vol. 18, no. 1, p. 121.

5 Sex Education in Schools

ALAN HARRIS

It is very difficult to assess exactly what is happening in schools at present. There have been no large-scale research projects about the 'content' of sex education in various types of school and in different parts of the country. Such research obviously presents considerable problems. Many heads are touchy about answering questionnaires. Often, especially in large schools, they have no very clear idea of what sort of sex education their own staff is providing. Nor is it easy to define and measure the success of such sex education as does take place. There are, however, various clues. We know from Michael Schofield's research (*The Sexual Behaviour of Young People,* Pelican) something of teenagers' attitudes and factual knowledge.* In his sample 56 per cent of the boys and 13 per cent of the girls claimed that they had received no sex education of any kind at school. Over half did not know anything about the symptoms of either syphilis or gonorrhoea. Because of ignorance or indifference about contraception, 8 out of every 10 girls who had intercourse were risking pregnancy.

It is open to question whether it is literally true that over half the boys had had no sex education in school. It seems probable that many pupils received what the *teacher* regarded as being sex education, but did not recognise it as being such. Schofield writes:

Sex education, when it occurred, seemed to concentrate on biological and physiological matters, and seemed to be unrelated to human affairs except when it was wholly concerned with putting across a particular moral point of view.

Anyone who has taught in a secondary school can realise how this happens. The General Science teacher follows a 'health education'

Alan Harris, 'Sex education in schools: the battle against ignorance, superstition and moralising', *New Statesman* (28 February 1969), pp. 284–7.
* See Chapter 12 [ed.].

course as far as Conception in the Rabbit, and then either gets cold feet or sticks to the examination syllabus. The RE teacher encourages 'frank discussion' of personal relationships, but to him this means making *ex cathedra* pronouncements about the sanctity of marriage and the cheapening effect of 'casual sex'. Neither in information about how teeth need calcium to grow nor in the (largely) irrelevant authority of religion do ordinary teenagers see any possibility of finding answers to their own problems. What they *really* want to know before they leave school are the answers to questions like these: How does intercourse take place? What different ways are there? What is an orgasm? What does it feel like? Is it really wrong, always, to have sex before marriage? Can we talk about this? What is an abortion? What causes a miscarriage? Does Durex stop sex being enjoyable? Is it safe? How does the Pill work?

The answers to questions of this sort would indeed constitute what most teenagers would recognise as sex education, and it seems unlikely that more than 10 per cent of secondary schools answer them at all, let alone answer them adequately and in an appropriate educational context. This figure is a guess – no one yet has tried to find out, though various research projects give fragmentary clues. For example, members of the London Institute of Education have recently questioned young people attending a VD clinic, and they make this comment:

The findings seem to show that as far as formal science teaching was concerned, there was little difference between the clinic sample and the control group. But 63 per cent of the boys and 43 per cent of the girls in the clinic group appear to have had no sex education at all at school. What is clear from the survey is that any education about VD which is to prove useful to the group of young people most at risk should be given well before the age of 15 years.

Thanks to the work of various Local Education Authorities, rather more is known about the attitudes of teachers to sex education. I can claim no scientific accuracy for the following figures which are derived from the results of questionnaires sent to a large number of Head teachers. For one thing, they are not based on a proper sampling technique, and for another they are based only on the answers of those Heads who bothered to reply. However, over 500 schools are represented here.

INFANT SCHOOLS

Nearly 75 per cent of the Heads did not think it would be appropriate to discuss sex education with parents to get their cooperation. Sixty per cent claimed, surprisingly, that children never asked questions in school about their own origin or sex (though this may be due more to the atmosphere of those schools than to lack of curiosity in the children).

JUNIOR SCHOOLS

Over half the Heads thought that girls should not be taught in *school* about menstruation before it occurred, and only 10 per cent actually gave such information. Yet over half the Heads thought that co-operation with the parents need not actively be encouraged. Over half the schools never mentioned mating, conception or pregnancy.

SECONDARY SCHOOLS

Generally speaking, more emphasis was placed on 'education in personal relationships' in non-selective schools than in selective schools.

Nearly all the schools claimed that some form of sex education was given (one wonders how on earth it was avoided in the others!) mainly in Biology (70 per cent), RE (60 per cent) and under such headings as 'human biology', 'hygiene', 'health education', etc. Nearly all the schools entrust 'specialist' teachers with this work, but outsiders were also used – mostly school doctors and visitors from the Public Health Dept. Virtually all the schools thought that some information about VD should be given: only 15 per cent said they did not provide any; 40 per cent thought that no information about homosexuality or masturbation should be given. Only 10 per cent of schools gave direct information about methods of contraception, and the majority thought that such information should not be given at all.

This is not a very reassuring picture, especially as the figures exclude those schools whose Head teachers did not bother to reply. Like most general pictures it does not show how utterly abysmal the situation is in schools where the Heads are capable of remarks like: 'I am all against "frank discussion" of these matters!', and 'Those who are determined to behave like animals can doubtless find out the facts for themselves', and 'I am sick, sick of talk about sex. I'll have none of it in my school', and 'Everything that needs to be done in my school is done individually and in private by a missionary priest.'

Nor, of course, does it indicate the enormous progress that has taken place during the last few years in the educational world as a whole. Consider, for example, the following quotation from *Sex Education in Schools,* published by the Church Information Office, 1964:

Sex education is not a 'subject'; it cannot be 'taught', it should not appear on a school timetable nor be confined to a single embarrassed talk by mother or father ... Sex education is the totality of influences which help boys and girls to understand the part sex plays in life and to recognise its physical, spiritual and moral dimensions. It should include reliable knowledge of human reproduction and of the physical and emotional developments in each sex; it should prepare both boys and girls for marriage, family and homemaking; it should help young people with their own present personal problems; it should look outwards to the wider community which has responsibilities for, and makes demands on, individuals.

Few educationists would have any quarrel with this definition. But it is worth remembering that it is only comparatively recently that official approval has been given to the idea that school teachers have an essential role to play in sex education. A survey conducted by Tucker and Pout in 1937 revealed that 94 per cent of the teachers wanted the work to be done by outside specialists, and it was not until 1943, with the publication of the Board of Education Pamphlet 119, that sex education was officially implied to be within the province of the teaching profession: 'sex instruction should be given as part of a wider course, especially biology, so that sex and reproduction may be introduced in their proper place without undue emphasis'.

This official statement came over 20 years later than a statement from the National Birth Rate Commission (set up in 1920) that 'however difficult and delicate the task may be, [sex education] is one that cannot, with due regard to the moral safety and welfare of youth, be shirked but must be undertaken, and should be therefore considered, not as an irksome duty, but as a privilege'.

Since 1943 reports and recommendations have proliferated, and most of them have been primarily concerned with persuading us that sex education should take place in biology lessons or RE lessons or both, with a general backing provided by Eng. Lit. The general purport is always that sex education should not be isolated from the rest of the curriculum, but should arise 'naturally' from science and the study of personal relationships.

One would have expected the Newsom Report (*Half our Future*, HMSO, 1963) to make some clear and progressive recommendations on the subject, but despite all its other virtues the Report disappointed. The various references to sex education might fairly be condensed to one statement: 'It's a good idea for boys and girls to mix', though the *need* for sex education is recognised clearly enough: 'We can only say that we believe it to be wrong to leave the young to fend for themselves without guidance, and wrong to conceal from them (as if we could) the differences on this issue [pre-marital intercourse] which separate men and women of real moral sensibility.' Elsewhere a highly ambiguous, and potentially dangerous, statement occurs: 'Positive guidance to boys and girls on sexual morals is essential' – a statement which incidentally encouraged those who will permit facts about sex to be given only if they are accompanied by moral indocrination.

Since Newsom, several reports have been issued by Local Education Authorities, including Hampshire and Wiltshire, then London, Birmingham and Newcastle. There are important differences of emphasis between these reports, but they all make detailed suggestions for programmes of 'health education' in schools. The actual recommendations made in most of these reports may otherwise strike liberally-minded laymen as rather timid. They tend to stay on the safe ground of biology (but get vague about if, when and how teachers should deal with human sexual intercourse, contraception and family planning).

In the Birmingham Report, along with all the enlightened remarks on Health Education in infant, junior, and secondary schools, and on the need for special courses for teachers and school counsellors, there is the same sinister ring that I noted in the Newsom Report:

We believe that this 'wholeness' is best achieved by the enlightened promotion of 'Health Education', by which we mean not only the development of the child's and young person's unique natural gifts, but also the inculcation of sound physical and mental habits, attitudes and ethical values which develop, and find expression in, a well-adjusted personality in a happy community.

How the writer supposes that 'sound ethical values' could be *inculcated* is not explained, and such a statement reminds us again of the dangers of sex education falling entirely into the hands of amateur moralists. A similar criticism applies to this remark from *Notes on Sex Education,* prepared by the London County Council: 'Sexual intercourse should *never* [my italics] be seen as transient pleasure but as a joyful consummation of close friendship, love and understanding which in marriage have time to grow and deepen.' Never?

The Newcastle Report, published this year, is more explicit. Included in a very comprehensive programme for health education and education in personal relationships are the following topics: Puberty, Development of Sexual Feelings, Boy friends and girl friends, Falling in love. Sexual intercourse, Premarital intercourse, Contraception, Patterns of sexual behaviour, Venereal diseases, Sexual perversion, Marriage, Having a baby.

On the subject of contraception, the report says that while many teachers would, if the matter arose, wish to discourage sexual experimentation, they still have the responsibility to those who do not take their advice:

Clearly they should be made to realise that they are under a moral obligation not to bring an illegitimate child into the world. It would seem to follow that the teacher is himself under an obligation not to withhold from pupils who practise intercourse such knowledge as will enable them to avoid risk of pregnancy.

Perhaps the greatest value of these LEA reports lies not so much in the actual recommendations they make as in the communication among teachers which is a necessary part of their preparation. A member of the Department of Education and Science, who has special responsibility for Health Education in schools, writes:

My own view is that Working Parties of teachers are the best way to get progress in this field ... this is by far the most important factor in getting sex education right in schools.

We have always stressed the value of putting it in perspective by making it part of the most liberal type of health education; linking it, that is, with so many other aspects of developing maturity – the need to come to terms with oneself, with society, with work, with leisure, with personal relationships in all of these.

We stress that although teachers all have a role to play, others can also help – schools MOs, General Practitioners, Health Visitors and last, but not least, parents. A new feature of the educational scene is the coming of Counsellors. These are being trained at three centres – Keele, Reading, Exeter... Some Counsellors are finding they need to do a great deal of personal counselling, others are taken up with school programmes of group counselling in courses designed to meet all the needs I have outlined above. Others are doing educational and vocational counselling – all on the lines of those in US schools.

Valuable work is being done (notably in Berkshire and Sussex) by these counsellors, who visit schools at the invitation of head teachers and run discussion groups for the pupils. And the Marriage Guidance Council also runs training courses for teachers who are selected by their LEAs to attend three-day courses in which they discuss various approaches to the problems of sex education.

Without doubt the next 20 or 30 years will see big improvements in schools as a result of all the efforts outlined above. But there are still many reasons for disquiet. There are groups of teenagers, notably the least intelligent 14- to 15-year-olds from culturally deprived homes, who never seem likely to receive adequate sex education. They are unable to derive much benefit from formal teaching or from textbooks, and, unlike more intelligent pupils, do not absorb throughout their school years the cumulative benefits of a health education programme – even if such a thing exists. In poor schools they automatically get the least efficient teachers, and by the end of their school career are hostile to any form of educational influence. They are interested only in the present, and lack the capacity for 'deferred gratification' that is more a middle-class attribute. They tend to be unable to relate their growing sexual urges to anything they may have been taught before. Sex is something new and important, but most teachers are unapproachable because of the pupils' problems of verbalising, 'politely', the questions they might otherwise ask. (Many young teachers, only too willing to help, have been shocked into embarrassed silence by the crudity of language in which sincere questions were expressed.) Yet these are the pupils whom it is most important to help. Statistically they are more likely to marry early, more likely to produce unwanted children, more likely to contract venereal diseases and less likely to form stable relationships than any other group.

Part of the answer lies in better teacher-training, which I will come to in a moment; but there is also urgent need for more radical teaching aids in the form of films, film-strips and illustrated pamphlets (in strip cartoon form if necessary). Shocking though it might seem to the faint-hearted, there is a genuine need for the use of realistic drawings and photographs to show how intercourse takes place, how to use contraceptives, how to recognise the symptoms of VD, how babies are conceived and born. Textbooks are not a suitable form of information for barely literate teenagers, whose needs are too acute to be ignored because of the sensibilities of middle-class teachers.

Another deprived group consists of the pupils in all exam-bound grammar schools, many of which view with lofty scorn such academic irrelevancies as health education or education in personal relationships. Presumably sexual knowledge is expected to be derived mysteriously as a by-product of traditional subjects, like aspirin from coal.

Even for intelligent teenagers there is a shortage of good books that could help with problems of immediate concern. Two of the most popular for the school library are *He and She* by Kenneth Barnes, and *The Opposite Sex* by Rose Hacker; neither of which, in my opinion, is well suited to the needs of most adolescents. *He and She* has many virtues. It is explicit about the physical aspects of sex and moralises less than most books of its type. But it is too difficult in style and vocabulary for the bulk of teenagers, and even Mr Barnes makes some indefensible generalisations:

Even so you should know that men who indulge in loveless copulation or brief affairs are not by any means happy men, nor inwardly certain of themselves. They are not to be envied... You can't indulge the body separately from the spirit without weakening the personality.

There is much to criticise in the work done by university education departments and colleges of education. A recent survey indicated that two-thirds of the colleges had courses which, academically at least, would equip students to tackle sex education in schools. But it is not knowledge of *facts* that matters most — especially with regard to the problems of typical secondary modern school 'C-stream' pupils. A lot more time and imagination needs to be expended on preparing students for the whole spectrum of difficulties they will face. One possibility is that groups of school pupils, representing different social backgrounds, could during their last year at school spend some time in the colleges, staying overnight in halls of residence if possible, ostensibly to attend classes given by a health education lecturer. The students could follow up the lecture by conducting seminars, thus gaining useful experience on their own ground with small groups. This would be of great social value to the visitors, and would encourage the students to devise their own teaching materials for future use. Another possibility is that visiting psychotherapists could conduct a pilot study in which they discussed with students and practising teachers the sorts of problems encountered in schools. Not only would this be beneficial to the students and teachers, but the psychotherapists could also collect information about the personality of teachers engaged in sex education.

Another problem concerns the character of those teachers into whose hands sex education falls. As much harm can be done by the insensitive 'progressive' as by the reactionary moraliser. It is alarming to read of teachers who boast about the 'thoughtful silence' that descended on their class when they described in great detail the ultimate consequences of syphilis transmitted to innocent children through the folly of their parents; of others whose approach is so clinical that one can envisage terrified teenagers donning rubber gloves in the local park.

At the other extreme there are teachers who may befog the main issues in a cloud of pseudo-psychological jargon: 'But it is natural in the sexual life, to seek towards fulfilment in a continuing and responsible relationship, whose greatest satisfactions are in procreativity and continuity. The least able a girl in a secondary school will be found to be making this great creative psychic journey,' writes David Holbrook, described in *Where?* as 'poet and teacher'.

Perhaps the greatest problem is in the moral aspect. Practically all the literature on the subject stresses the need for sex education (or some parts of it) to be given 'in the light of the Christian ethic', 'firmly in a religious context', or 'with positive moral guidance'. But the relevance of Christianity is not so obvious as it may seem. The church has a singularly poor record in the consequences of its specific pronouncements about sexual morality, and many thinking Christians now feel quite free to form autonomous judgments when sex presents moral problems. The generalised ethic derived from the Christian ideal of Love offers no specific guidance on sexual behaviour, and it could not be claimed that such a precept as 'do by others as you would be done by' is peculiar to Christianity or indeed to *any* religion.

The practical objection to the role of RE in sex education, however, is that the bulk of teenagers see no relevance to their own lives in religion, and are hostile or indifferent to any moral teaching which takes place in a religious context. The proper task of teachers is to help their pupils towards creating their own personal moral standards, and if this task, with regard to certain groups, is hindered by a religious setting then, for them, RE should be scrapped.

The whole problem of moral education is being investigated by the Farmington Trust Research Unit, Oxford. Anyone at all interested in the matter should read *An Introduction to Moral Education* by John Wilson, Norman Williams and Barry Sugarman (Penguin), in which the philosophical, psychological and sociological aspects are explored in depth. The work of the Trust is of considerable importance to educationists, though it is likely to be many years before the effects are felt in schools.

Meanwhile it is to teachers of English that the bulk of the responsibility falls for enriching the moral lives of their pupils – through literature, obviously, and through discussion and the development of creative writing. One of the best lessons on moral education currently in print is Jack Becket's *The Keen Edge* (Blackie), an anthology of children's poetry with an introduction describing his teaching methods.

The folly of *inculcating* moral standards lies in the fact that it is by no means certain that current sexual mores will be appropriate in 30 years' time. As the age of puberty gets earlier, and the age of financial independence gets later, sexual problems grow more acute. Should we *really* expect young people to remain virgins between the ages of 15 and 25 on account of mores which were formed under quite different social conditions and before contraception became readily available? Or should we openly recognise the need for young people to experiment sexually – at least in the context of relationships involving mutual affection – so that they can mature emotionally and prepare for a stable marriage? We cannot possibly do this sort of thinking *for* young people. But we must certainly help them to think for themselves, abide by their decisions with good grace, and help them to face up to the consequences of their decisions. Certainly their moral attitudes are changing. A recent survey conducted among 400 18-year-olds in south-east Leicestershire indicated that changes over the last five years have been dramatic.

Only 3 per cent of the men and 34 per cent of the women disapproved of premarital intercourse on principle, as compared

74

with 11 per cent of the men and 42 per cent of the women five years earlier. But this liberality is combined with a degree of irresponsibility beyond belief. Asked if they would take the risk of sexual intercourse without contraception, they replied as follows: among the middle-class members of the group, 33 per cent of the men and 68 per cent of the girls said that they would. (This reversed the situation five years earlier when the figures were 67 per cent and 43 per cent respectively.) Among the working-class members of the sample 77 per cent of the men and 66 per cent of the girls thought the risk worth taking. Since the bulk of the girls regard contraception as being the man's responsibility, it seems to follow that working-class girls are the most likely to become pregnant, but middle-class girls are becoming more reckless.

It is obviously a matter of priority for *all* pupils in *all* schools to be given clear information about how contraceptives work and how they can be obtained. Furthermore there seems to be a good case for making contraceptives more easily available to young women. Too many unwanted children are conceived because of the reluctance of working-class girls to consult their GPs − who often make things embarrassing and difficult by asking detailed questions about the relationship in which the girl intends to engage. Is it time for the government to establish 'anonymous' advice centres in all parts of the country?

Readily available contraception is not, of course, anything like a full answer to the problem. It would not magically foster greater responsibility in sexual relations; indeed, without adequate sex education in schools it might even promote pointless promiscuity among a small minority of teenagers. But promiscuity in itself is harmless compared with the devastation wreaked on the lives of children deprived of a stable and loving home. We can at least reduce the number of such children by teaching about contraception in schools.

Perhaps when the grosser deficiencies of current sex instruction have been removed we may perhaps even be able to take the concept of sex *education* seriously: 'We might be able,' wrote John Wilson in *Logic and Sexual Morality*, 'to create something now sadly lacking; some sense of *style* in sexual relationships, as opposed to the present furtiveness, sordidity and tongue-tied love-making. The total lack of any adequate or attractive ritual or convention in these relationships itself bears witness to our failure to include them in our education;

75

as in so many contexts, teenagers learn no conventions of behaviour from adults so that their own are naturally primitive and inarticulate.'

Finally, there is the need for more research. At present we know very little about the effectiveness of various methods of teaching, or even about the consequences of teaching certain *facts*. Is it true, as some people suppose, that teenagers informed about contraception are more likely to become promiscuous than those kept in ignorance? The available evidence is inconsistent with this hypothesis, but nobody *knows*. Is it true that psychological damage may be caused by presenting certain facts about sex before pupils have reached a certain stage of emotional development? Some psychologists think so; others disagree. These are only two out of a mass of woolly superstitions which may inhibit teachers and parents concerned with sex education. Until we have learned a lot more about problems of this sort we can only be guided in our work as teachers at the best by intelligent guess-work and worst by our prejudices.

6 Sex Education in Colleges and Departments of Education

J. NORMAN GREAVES

The first formal attempts at sex education arose out of the great expansion of the public schools during the growth of the middle classes in the nineteenth century. This development was introduced by schoolmasters such as Dr Arnold who became headmaster of Rugby in 1828, and several of his assistants who went off to found or reform other public schools. Arnold was convinced of the 'natural imperfectness' of the schoolboy, and revitalised the chapel sermon as an admonitory agency of change. The basis of their source material appears to have been a literal acceptance of certain passages in the Bible, notably from the Epistles of Paul to the Galatians, the Ephesians, and the Corinthians, written incidentally against the context of the sexual licence of later-Roman civilisation at a time when the writer was convinced that the end of the world was imminent. One further biblical derivation was to be of great importance, the term onanism as an alternative for masturbation – 'the solitary and secret vice' which came to obsess the early sex educators. The story, from Chapter 38 of Genesis clearly refers to the method of birth-control known as coitus interruptus, and it is difficult to understand why this episode should have been taken to refer to masturbation. However, the wrath of God, and the penalty 'wherefore he slew him also' has been re-directed upon the practitioners of masturbation, adding to the guilt of innumerable schoolboys, as various biographers have testified.

Nineteenth-century books of sex education were hardly ideal by modern standards. Adolescent masturbation is stated to produce 'sallow face, glassy eye, drooping form, without energy, force or purpose, a laggard at school', and various other horrors including reduced reproductive capacity and baldness. Under the prudish influence of the period, mammalian fertilisation takes place 'as a

J. Norman Greaves, 'Sex education in Colleges and Departments of Education', *Health Education Journal*, 24, no. 4 (1965), pp. 171–7.

result of proper contact with the male', while informative diagrams of reproductive systems omit the male genitalia so that tubes 5 and 14 lead to blank spaces labelled 4 and 6. However, there were good intentions. In the introduction to *Confidential Talks with Young Men,* published in 1894, the author, Dr L. B. Sperry, states that ignorance of sexual matters leads to morbid and degrading thoughts and lamentable practices. 'It is cruelty and culpably wrong to allow children to grope about, picking up half truths and distorted facts and gathering venomous ideas from corrupt playmates, vile literature, obscene pictures, vulgar stories, and unfortunate personal experiences.' How progressive such a justification of sex education was can be gathered from the following quotation, taken from the parish magazine of the Venerable T. D. Harrison, M.A., formerly Archdeacon of Chesterfield, in June 1960: 'But it is open to question whether it is not better to hear the broad details from a companion, which at least leaves a sense of shame, rather than have minute details brazenly put before them, which throws such matters open to shameless discussion, and sometimes experiment.'

Parents' attitude to sex education

In 1923, the report *Youth and Race* produced by the National Birth Rate Committee 1920-23 considered, among other things, the moral education of the adolescent. The Commission urged the Board of Education to provide facilities in the teacher-training colleges so that teachers should be adequately trained to impart sexual and moral education, but was unable to decide upon a suitable content for courses for children. The views of a strong group of religious witnesses were greatly at variance with those of several psychologists, and in particular, with the views of J. H. Badley of Bedales School. Some sex education was being given in a few schools at this time, mainly the efforts of the independent 'progressive' schools, but the first major attempt at sex education in state schools seems to have been an experiment lasting for some eight years during the nineteen thirties. This involved pupils in the elementary schools of seven Welsh Local Education Authorities, in conjunction with the Alliance of Honour. Of 15,866 parents, only 7% withdrew their children from the courses. The account of the experiment, published by Tucker and Pout in 1937, contains a survey of the attitudes of parents and teachers which indicates the fathers believe that sex education should be the mothers' province, while the mothers thought that the teachers should do it. The vast majority of the teachers (94%) wanted this work to be done by outside specialists, and this is of course one of the standard patterns arising from a study of the history of sex education, namely that it is necessary, and someone else should do it. The diffidence of teachers, at this time is understandable. The Board of Education Pamphlet 119 of 1943, *Sex Education in Schools and Youth Organisations* stated that training college students enter the colleges ill-informed on all aspects of sex, 'But the general position in the colleges on the whole matter of sex is, understandably enough, marked by vagueness, hesitation and uncertainty.' The publication of Pamphlet 119 marks the first 'official' recognition that sex education is within the province of the teaching profession. In 1956 the Ministry of Education produced Pamphlet 31, *Health Education* which repeats and enlarges upon the earlier pamphlet, again mentioning the need for personal education for training college students. This period of official acceptance marks a growing emphasis on the role of the schoolteacher in the sphere of sex education and education for family life. Several further studies and reports have emphasised the need of young people for guidance of one form or another and which can be called sex education. Again and again the parent is named as the ideal sex educator, and there can be little dispute over this. However, equally often it is admitted that parents largely fail in this responsibility, preferring that teachers or other agencies outside the family should accept the parental role in this respect, as indeed they have in so many other aspects of child welfare, health, nutrition, holidays and leisure activities, all of which are recognised as Education in the formal sense.

Lack of factual knowledge

So far, consideration has been restricted to attitudes and the wide field of recommendation. It is more difficult to discover what is actually taking place. Nearly every publication on the subject gives examples of syllabuses and lecture series which have been used somewhere or other, and this information has been available for years. On the other hand there is considerable evidence that in grammar schools at least, this aspect of education is neglected. A study published by Daines in 1962 notes that about 27% of a group of training college students felt that discussion of sex was taboo in lessons in the sixth forms they had recently left, while 64% wished to have discussions or lectures on the subject while at college. Similarly, a survey carried out for *New Society* in 1964 showed that of over 15,000 schools with sixth forms, only about 41% devoted any teaching time to 'sex, marriage and family'. Arising out of the present survey of work in Colleges and Departments of Education, the great majority of respondents affirm that their students are lacking in factual knowledge of sexual matters, including 'mature' students, who are specifically mentioned on several occasions. Four respondents supplied details of the results of their own questionnaires. They report surprise at the gaps in knowledge among ex-grammar school pupils, factual comprehension which is inadequate, murky and inaccurate, and figures of from 80 to 88% of students aware that they need instruction even in basic biological facts. Most students had received no help with sex education at their schools.

One important point which seems to have had insufficient attention is the age for sex education. The recent booklet *Sex Education in Schools* published by the Church of England Board of Education notes that many schemes are designed for the third and fourth years of secondary schools and comments that this is far too late, for a variety of reasons. This is supported by the critics' review extracts from Schofield's recent *The Sexual Behaviour of Young People* which report the findings that most boys and girls obtain their first, or even their only sex education from friends at school, and that this is often inaccurate, so that in general, sex education is required, in suitable form, far earlier than the present practice. The Church of England booklet considers the ages of nine and ten as the most suitable for the effective communication of essential information, and this is particularly true considering the steady reduction of the age of onset of menstruation which has been observed during the course of the present century.

Acceptance by the teaching profession of the responsibility for sex education must clearly depend upon appropriately educated teachers. This aspect of teacher training is little documented, and to clarify the situation, a questionnaire was sent to all the Colleges and Departments of Education, in England, during the autumn of 1964. Replies from 111 establishments represented a 66% response. Details of course work were supplied by 48% of respondents, although only 38% organised formal courses under the specific title of sex education. In general, respondents preferred not to 'highlight in an unfortunate way' the topic of sex, and stated that the subject was dealt with as part of other courses, notably *Principles of Education* and *Health Education*. Of the courses, 26 were initiated before 1958, 13 between 1958 and 1962, and 6 since 1963. The students have themselves requested the provision of a course in 7 instances. There is considerable variation in the length of courses, from a minimum of 90 minutes to a maximum of 21 hours, with the majority being of less than 6 hours. 22% of University Departments of Education were in favour of organising specific courses for their students but were prevented by shortage of time. Six out of eight Art Colleges also do not provide courses dealing with sex education. One Principal states that he trains specialist art teachers and that sex education forms no part of the course, 'nor would it be their concern as art teachers'.

As has already been mentioned, many respondents refer to their students' ignorance concerning sex, and 71% of respondents intend their courses to be primarily for the personal benefit of their students in forming their own set of values etc. Equally, the response from the students is stated to be good, with some 10% of respondents mentioning rejection by a few students. In two establishments the majority of students were critical, and it is possible that this is connected with a central problem, to be mentioned later, namely that of the right person to conduct the course. Altogether, 90% of respondents recommend that sex education should appear in the teacher-training curriculum, but there is clear indication that this may not in fact happen in 25% of replies. While many of the questionnaires had apparently been filled in by the staff most actively concerned, a number were completed by Principals and departmental heads using phrases such as 'as the need arises', and 'most tutors co-operate'. In nine establishments the courses are voluntary, and clearly not every student receives a course even when it is official college policy that they should.

Only 32% of establishments make any attempt to prepare their students to teach sex education in the schools. Half of these stress that this must wait until the students are older and more experienced. 'I do not believe in giving students the idea that they can or should teach sex education in schools. They must decide for themselves later', and, more strongly, 'To aim at turning out the amateur "teacher" of sex appears undesirable and dangerous.' 6% are doubtful of the value of courses in sex education, and one respondent actively disapproves.

Social and moral aspects

One section of the survey dealt with the style and content of courses, and 60 respondents supplied detailed information. The courses usually deal with the moral and social aspects of sexuality, with emphasis on family life, personal commitment, illegitimacy, etc. A few mention that their students complain that premarital attitudes to sex are neglected, but most try to deal with this topic. Forty-four courses give basic biological information, several of the others assuming that such facts are known. This assumption is of course against the general run of replies. Only twenty-nine respondents mention sexual psychology, this seems a rather low figure. 'Health' is widely covered, and presumably that includes information on venereal diseases, which are specifically mentioned by thirteen respondents. The students themselves often raise the subject of VD, and it seems clear that even nowadays young people are ill-informed on this subject. In only nine instances are courses stated to include information on contraception. Most courses consist of lectures followed by discussion, eleven are of discussions only, and nine of lectures only. Twenty-one are supplemented by films, including 'Birth of a Baby', 'To Janet a Son', 'Human Physiology' series, 'Learning to Live', 'Growing Girls', 'A Brother for Susan', while one college has produced its own film of a natural childbirth as part of a special study by two students, and this is on loan to other colleges and schools.

Many respondents refer to the problem of the 'right person' to run their courses. Twenty-one establishments use a combination of college staff and 'outside experts', while nineteen use college staff only, and eleven use outsiders only. Opinions expressed are evenly divided as to whether the course should be taken by persons known to the students or not, but of recent changes in courses, one now makes greater use of outsiders, and a second now depends solely on outsiders. Of the 63% of establishments making partial or exclusive use of outside agencies, over half use the facilities of the National Marriage Guidance Council, the next major group being local medical practitioners. Others include Health Visitors, Headmasters, Youth Officers, a Consultant Psychiatrist, a Social Worker, a Sociologist and a Clergyman. Only 10% of all respondents mention readily available facilities for individual student counselling.

Most teacher-training establishments are providing some form of sex education for their students, and about a third attempt to prepare them to undertake similar work themselves. Most of the women students will spend little time in the schools before marriage and family commitments cause their retirement, probably before they feel that they have enough experience to undertake sex education. If they can be persuaded to return to teaching afterwards they could well be useful in the sphere of sex education. However there are still signs of diffidence among teachers. The last Ministry of Education short course for teachers which was to have dealt with sex education had to be cancelled for lack of support in 1963. It is proposed to run a regular one-year full-time course each year, beginning this year, at the City of Birmingham College of Education, and this year the course begins 'with a small number of students' possibly the result of inadequate advertising. The Principal has written that there have been a very large number of enquiries from Local Education Authorities concerning the 1966 course, and it is expected that recruitment in the future will be at the rate of 10 to 12 experienced teachers each year.

REFERENCES

Church of England Board of Education, *Sex Education in Schools* (Church Information Office, 1964).

Daines, J. W. *An Enquiry into the methods and effects of Religious Education in Sixth Forms* (University of Nottingham Institute of Education, 1962).

Harrison, T. D. 'The venture', *Chesterfield Parish Magazine,* vol. 26, no. 6, June 1960.

New Society, 'School social studies', vol. 4, no. 101, 3 September 1964.

Sperry, L. B. *Confidential Talks with Young Men* (Oliphant, Anderson and Ferrier, 1894).

Tucker and Pout, *Sex Education in Schools, An Experiment in Elementary Instruction* (Howe, 1937).

7 Sex Education: Press and Parental Perceptions

D. G. GILL, G. D. B. REID and D. M. SMITH

Since 1968, considerable attention has been directed towards the possibility that sex education programmes might be provided in the schools, perhaps arising from a growth in public awareness of the problems associated with the increase in teenage sexual activity. Certainly the problems posed by human sexuality in general have received increased attention in the past decade, ranging from investigations of the moral and religious aspects of sexual behaviour (the *Quaker View of Sex*, 1965, and *Sex and Morality*, S.C.M. Working Party Report, 1966) through a relaxation of the obscenity laws as applied to literature and the cinema, to detailed examinations of physiological and biological responses during intercourse in laboratory situations (Masters and Johnson, 1966, 1970).

Further confirmation that sex has become a topic open to public debate is provided by the frank discussion of such matters in the mass media and the rapid increase in '... the appearance of and great demand for "marriage manuals"—a euphemism for texts providing instruction in sexual techniques and the psychology of sexual adjustment' (Illsley and Gill, 1968).

While attitudes to sexuality have undoubtedly become less restrictive, responses in the press to discussions of sexual matters often include statements of a dogmatic nature. Do such views represent the attitudes of a sample of mothers with children aged 14 years? Before examining either press or parental attitudes towards the provision of sex education courses, it was decided to attempt some predictions of what would be important in this area. Clearly the first question had to be: 'Is it necessary to provide children with information about sex?' Given a positive response then three other questions seemed to be equally relevant: 'Who should provide this information, at what age, and what should be included?'[1]

D. G. Gill, G. D. B. Reid and D. M. Smith. 'Sex education: press and parental perceptions', *Health Education Journal* (March 1971), pp. 1–8.

A preliminary examination of leading articles, editorial comment, reports of education committee meetings where sex education courses were discussed, and readers' letters, tended to confirm that the above four questions were central areas of concern. We examine in this paper the difference between opinions expressed in the press towards sex education and those held by the mothers of a sample of Aberdeen school-children, as well as considering the implications of these views for the provision of such courses.

In order to assess press reaction to the question of sex education, we scrutinized a file of press-cuttings compiled by a professional agency for Grampian Television Ltd., covering the company's TV series 'Living and Growing'.[2] While this source drew on a wide range of relevant publications, both national and provincial, and might be said to be representative of press comment in general, it was not intended to conduct a detailed analysis with a view to stating where the balance of opinion lay. Indeed, if a balance of opinion derived from press sources could be constructed, it would simply reflect editorial policy and the news-gathering process rather than public opinion.

The four questions will now be discussed in turn, illustrated by selected quotations from the press files:

(1) *That sex education should be given.* Several references to this view mentioned the anticipated 'payoff' in terms of reduction of perceived social problems. Thus 'sex education should be included in primary and secondary curricula ... as a means of trying to reduce the illegitimacy rate', or '... teenagers, for good or ill, are increasingly exposed to situations where a knowledge of the facts of life is desirable ... one only has to look at the 10 per cent illegitimacy rate in Glasgow to appreciate that many of these births were unwanted and that some at least could have been averted. ...' Other examples stressed more basic educational reasons – 'How can honesty in this or any other subject harm a child? How can the truth corrupt?'

Others were equally outspoken in their condemnation, and there were frequent references to the 'erosion of moral values'. It was claimed, for example, that sex education 'encourages the abuse of the marriage act', that it puts out 'a barrage of filth to the children', encourages 'these so-called humanists to de-Christianize society', and is additional evidence, along with 'gambling, drinking, drugs, hooliganism, murder and layabouts' of the 'fact' that Britain, 'once famous for dignity and decorum ... was now noted for degradation and unqualified obscenity'.

Even a universal acceptance of the principle of sex education in some form would not, however, end the debate.

(2) *What it the appropriate agent of sex socialization – home, school or both?* 'This is a subject for the home—for mother and daughter, for father and son', is one view. 'Let the parents do the bringing up of their families' another similar view. Others agreed it was the parents' duty, but 'it was not happening'. Parents were accused of 'escapism' by some, asking teachers to hold 'a hot potato because they have not faced up to their responsibilities'. It was suggested, too, that parents 'were not always equipped ... to accept the responsibility'. Some parents, who had accepted that sex instruction was a part of their duty, now considered they had fallen 'very far short'. The claim was also made that it was 'no better handing this education to the teachers, for they are not prepared'.

Individual teachers were notably absent from the public debate, though one headmaster voiced the hope that the television programmes would 'inspire the children to ask questions in homes, where, up to now, the subject has never been mentioned'.

This may now in fact be happening—'I have discussed these things at home, but I did not discuss this at home before we got the programmes'.

(3) *At what age should sex instruction begin?* Press comment covers a very wide age-range indeed. Thus the Catholic Marriage Advisory Council suggests 2–3 years. Dr J. Dennis, the gynaecologist largely responsible for the Grampian Television 'Living and Growing' series, suggests that although the 5–9 age range is a relatively latent period as far as sexual interest is concerned, it is best to start then, 'before the embarrassments at the onset of puberty begin'.

This sort of view does not however pass unchallenged: 'I just don't think it's healthy to fill a young child's head with this sort of thing at such a young age ... there's plenty of time for them to find out about it later', or 'children at 8 years of age are just babies ... they would not understand the teaching of sex'. On the other hand, if no instruction is given until secondary school, by then 'the children will have read the lavatory walls. You will be preaching to the converted – and a perverted converted'. As for the question of childish innocence – '... eight-year-olds do need to know ... you should have heard some of the jokes my daughter brought home at that age. Luckily for her, this was not her introduction to the subject'.

(4) *How broad should the content be – should physiological and biological aspects only be taught or should these be placed in a wider social and moral/religious context?* Some correspondents held the view that: 'there can hardly be much wrong with simply getting the facts straight', while others found it 'objectionable' that sex education should be treated 'in isolation from love, marriage, the family, morality and religion', taking the view that 'we have got to try and teach the whole responsibilities and joys of parental

growth and not simply the biological facts'. If a moral content is to be included in a standardized course, however, it raises the difficulty that one set of normative assumptions may not be generally acceptable – 'I have my own beliefs about what are "correct" moral attitudes but it would be arrogant and stupid of me to try to force other people to accept these beliefs.'

In addition, as another writer pointed out, there may in any case be a danger in linking 'basic facts about reproduction' with 'moral and religious teaching', especially in secondary schools, 'for once a teenager throws over the authoritative teaching of the Church he may throw out, at the same time, the same attitude to sex which such teaching gives. And the young people most at risk here are those who are least likely to hold onto orthodox religious beliefs'.

From this analysis of press reports and readers' letters it is apparent that considerable differences of opinion exist concerning the four themes. A crude count of letters and articles, for and against, would not provide any assessment of the balance of opinion since no estimate can be made of the representativeness of such views. Moreover both protagonists and antagonists often claim that their particular views represent majority opinion. What views *are* held by our respondents? As part of a longitudinal study of child and adolescent socialization and of the use of mass media, questions designed to test mothers' attitudes towards sex education were included in an interview schedule/questionnaire which formed part of the larger study.

Before analyzing the responses to the questionnaire, it is necessary to consider what advantages or disadvantages ensue from an investigation of attitudes towards sex education in a particular locality. The choice of Aberdeen as an area of study produces the possibility of a particular bias in the population under review. Aberdeen was the first area of Britain in which a television series for schools on sex education was produced. As early as 1966, the Grampian Television Schools' Advisory Committee proposed that a series should be produced and the programmes were first televised in January-March 1968. When our population of mothers was interviewed, in the autumn of 1969, both they and their children had had an opportunity to see these programmes. Now it could be argued that exposure to these programmes would result in a tendency for viewers to adopt a more 'liberal' attitude towards sex education for school-children. On the other hand, such exposure might serve to confirm existing prejudices against an attempt to provide sex instruction within the school curriculum.

Whatever the direction of this bias, its extent could best be estimated by interviewing a control sample of mothers matched for social class, age, family composition, etc., drawn from an area which had not received the programmes; unfortunately, lack of time and resources precluded this approach. However, the respondents were asked to state whether or not they had seen any of the programmes and 43 per cent answered in the negative. The responses of mothers who had not seen the programmes could then be compared with those of the women who said they had seen the programmes, and any variation noted. In the case of informational and educational programmes, of which sex education may be regarded as an example, numerous studies have shown that exposure is closely related to the recipient's social class.[3] Moreover attitudes towards sexuality (Reiss, 1967) and patterns of sexual behaviour (Kinsey *et al.*, 1948, Rainwater, 1960) differ by social class, and variations in the responses of this sample of mothers may stem from the above rather than the influence of the television programmes. By analyzing the responses by social class *and* exposure category it is possible to gain some indication of the relative importance of these two factors.[4]

THE NEED FOR SEX EDUCATION

Table 1 shows that the majority of mothers in all social class and exposure categories felt that 'it is necessary to provide children with information about sex' rather than '... children have enough opportunity to acquire information about sex for themselves'.[5] When the social class groups are combined there is a statistically significant tendency for the mothers who had not seen the programmes to provide less support for the former statement. This difference does not stem from variations between any two equivalent social class groups when comparisons are made by exposure category.

Nevertheless the strongest numerical contribution from the overall chi-square is produced by variation between exposure categories within social classes 4 and 5. There is, therefore, some suggestion that mothers from social classes 4 and 5, when exposed to the programmes, show a higher proportion in favour of sex education than those who had not seen the programmes, but this conclusion needs to be treated with extreme caution. This study

Table 1. *The need for sex education*

Grampian TV series on sex education	Social class category	% in each social class	Needed	Not needed	Total
Seen	Non-manual (1, 2 and 3a)	56·2	86·5	13·5	100 (155)†
	Skilled manual (3b)	26·8	81·1	18·9	100 (74)
	Semi- and unskilled (4 and 5) manual	17·0	85·1	14·9	100 (47)
Totals	Social class combined	100·0	84·8	15·2	100 (276)*
Not seen	Non-manual (1, 2 and 3a)	38·7	80·0	20·0	100 (80)†
	Skilled manual (3b)	33·8	74·3	25·7	100 (70)
	Semi- and unskilled Manual (4 and 5)	27·5	75·4	24·6	100 (57)
Totals	Social class combined	100·0	76·8	23·2	100 (207)*

NOTES

Needed/Not Needed by exposure, $X^2 = 4·96$; $d.f.$ 1, $p < 0·05$.

Needed/Not Needed by social class within exposure categories respectively, $X^2 = 1·25$, $d.f.$ 2, N.S.: $X^2 = 0·52$, $d.f.$ 2, N.S.

Social class composition of those who had seen the programmes differed significantly from those who had not seen the programmes $X^2 = 15·36$, $d.f.$ 2, $p < 0·001$.

* The total number of respondents was 541. Of these 47 were excluded from the analysis because of anomalies in family circumstances, i.e. single parent households, guardians, etc. A further 11 were excluded since occupational data was insufficient or lacking, thus precluding any satisfactory analysis in terms of social class.

The responses of the 47 women who represented incomplete family units would have been of considerable interest since they are the mothers whose daughters are at high risk in terms of illegitimacy (see for example Thompson (1956)). However, while comparison by social class between these women and the 'normal' mothers in the sample is possible further complexities arise because of the diversity of their marital position and often as a consequence of changed or changing socio-economic circumstances. For these reasons the families without a male head were excluded from the analysis.

† The sample on which this research is based is an area sample devised for the purposes of a longitudinal study of children's values and mass-media usage. Its composition is not representative of Aberdeen as a whole. As Table 1 shows the social class composition is nearly equally divided, with 49 per cent non-manual (professional, technical and routine clerical occupations) compared with 31 per cent for the city of Aberdeen according to the 1961 census data. The corresponding figures for the manual groups (skilled, semi-skilled and unskilled manual work) are 51 per cent in the sample and 69 per cent for the city as a whole.

provides no information on other intervening variables which may influence the attitudes of mothers to what would appear to be, from the press reports, a highly contentious issue. Nevertheless, the two exposure categories differ significantly in terms of social class composition, with those who stated they had seen the programmes containing a higher proportion of mothers whose husbands were in the higher socio-economic groups. Given that educational programmes are more likely to attract audiences drawn predominantly from the upper social classes (as this sample once again confirms) and who might be expected to favour sex education, it is even more noteworthy that the vast majority of respondents in both exposure categories provide strong support for such a course.

Table 2. *Preferred agent of sex education*

Grampian TV series on sex education	Social class	Parents only	School only	Parents and school together	Other responses including 'Don't know'	Total
Seen	1, 2 and 3a	35·1	12·0	44·0	8·9	100 (134)
	3b	40·0	16·7	43·3	0·0	100 (60)
	4 and 5	37·5	22·5	32·5	7·5	100 (40)
Totals	Social class combined	36·8	15·0	41·9	6·3	100 (234)
Not seen	1, 2 and 3a	53·1	14·1	26·6	6·9	100 (64)
	3b	25·0	26·9	36·5	11·6	100 (52)
	4 and 5	37·2	37·2	18·6	7·0	100 (43)
Totals	Social class combined	39·6	24·5	27·7	8·7	100 (159)

NOTES

The difference between exposure categories (social class combined) by tendency to select parents and school against parents only plus school only is significant $\chi^2 = 9·70$, *d.f.* 1, $p < 0·01$. The other chi-square calculations listed below are calculated for working class occupations against middle class occupations (3b, 4 and 5—1, 2 and 3a), because of small cell sizes.

(1) M.C. mothers who had seen the programmes were more likely to select parents and school together than M.C. mothers who had not seen the programmes $\chi^2 = 6·63$, *d.f.* 1, $p < 0·01$; therefore, by inspection M.C. mothers who had not seen the programmes were more likely to select parents only.

(2) W.C. mothers who had not seen the programmes were more likely to select school only than W.C. mothers who had seen the programmes $\chi^2 = 4·64$, *d.f.* 1. $p < 0·05$.

PREFERRED AGENT OF SEX EDUCATION

The respondents were asked an open-ended question about who they felt should be responsible for providing children with information about sex. As Table 2 indicates, the vast majority in all social class and exposure categories favoured either parents, the school or shared responsibility between the two. Less than 10 per cent of the sample did not choose one of the above categories, and of those who did not, half mentioned either parents or school or both, in addition to some other agent. Other responses were diverse, including health visitor, doctor, family relative, minister of religion, and the numbers were too small for meaningful classification.

Significant differences were apparent overall between the two exposure categories, with those who had not seen the programmes tending to select parents and school less frequently and the school somewhat more frequently. When the relationships within and between social class and exposure categories are examined the variations are much more complex. Mothers from social classes 1, 2 and 3a, who had not seen the programmes, were less likely to favour shared responsibility and more likely to emphasize the role of parents than those who reported seeing the TV series. Mothers from social classes 3b, 4 and 5 who had not seen the programmes were the most likely to emphasize the role of the school in sex education. The differences between these two broad social class groupings were statistically significant.

Moreover, when the selections of those who had seen the programmes are examined, it is apparent that no differences exist between the social classes in preferred agent of sex education. It appears that exposure to the programmes tends to eradicate differences between social classes in preferred agent of sex education. The TV series was at pains to advocate a shared role between parents and school in this area but it would be dangerous to infer from this data, alone, that these differences in preferred agent of sex education stemmed from exposure or non-exposure to the programmes.

MINIMUM AGE FOR THE PROVISION OF SEX INFORMATION

The respondents were presented with eight age-bands at which children might first be told anything about sex, plus the opportunity to select 'it depends'. If this last selection were made the respondents were then asked: 'On what does it depend?' Their responses fell into either: 'When they ask' or 'It depends on the child'.

Again, differences exist between the two exposure categories with more of the mothers who had seen the programmes, as opposed to those who had not, suggesting that information should be given 'when the children ask'. For the mothers from social classes 1, 2 and 3a there are no significant differences by exposure categories. Thus the overall difference between the exposure categories stems from the variation in response in social classes 3b, 4 and 5. In these social class categories the mothers tend to specify a given age at which sex information should first be provided.

For those who had not seen the programmes there was a tendency to specify an even later age for the provision of such information. Consequently these mothers (i.e. working class—3b, 4 and 5) were less likely to accept that children should be provided with information 'when they ask'. In this theme it appears that the pattern of mothers' responses is determined more by social class than exposure on non-exposure to the programmes.

TOPICS SELECTED FOR INCLUSION IN A COURSE ON SEX EDUCATION

The respondents were presented with a list of topics which might be included in a course of sex education for children and they were also invited to specify any other topics for inclusion. As is evident from Table 4, very few respondents chose to add to the list of topics. Six individuals felt that venereal disease should be included and other subjects mentioned were homosexuality (male and female) and sexual perversion. These answers were given by too few respondents for meaningful comparisons, and the subsequent analysis is concentrated upon the eight items in the original list.

Cicourel (1964) has pointed to the danger which may accrue through the use of fixed-choiced questionnaire items unless they are 'constructed in such a way that the structure of everyday life experience and conduct is reflected in them' (p. 120). Experience with parent-teacher associations, adult education groups and health education personnel, teachers, tutors, lecturers and health visitors, suggested the relevance of the eight items included. Clearly items such as 'sex and religion', 'sex and love', and 'sexual morality', are open to a wide range of interpretation by the respondents. However, this paper is more concerned with a search for variations in patterns of response by social class and exposure categories, rather than an attempt to assign the cultural meaning of such items for these respondents.

Although there appears to be a tendency for those who had not seen the programmes, compared with those who had, to make fewer selections, this difference is not statistically significant. There is very little difference in the rank ordering of items for inclusion in a course on sex education between the exposure categories when the social Class groups are combined. However, when Table 4A is examined it is apparent that 'biological and physiological aspects of sex' is more

Table 3. *Minimum age for the provision of sex information*

Grampian TV series on sex education	Social class	Under 11	11–12	13+	When they ask	Depends on the child	Other and no answer	Total
Seen	1, 2 and 3a	11·9	21·6	6·7	54·6	2·2	3·0	100 (134)
	3b	11·7	33·3	10·0	38·3	6·7	0·0	100 (60)
	4 and 5	15·0	40·0	17·5	22·5	2·5	2·5	100 (40)
Totals	Social classes combined	12·4	27·8	9·4	44·9	3·4	2·1	100 (234)
Not seen	1, 2 and 3a	10·9	21·9	10·9	46·9	4·7	4·7	100 (64)
	3b	9·6	38·5	21·2	25·0	1·9	3·8	100 (52)
	4 and 5	2·3	48·7	25·6	14·0	4·7	4·7	100 (43)
Totals	Social classes combined	8·2	34·6	18·2	30·8	3·8	4·4	100 (159)

NOTES

There is a significant difference by exposure category between those mothers who select 'when they ask' and those who specify a minimum age $\chi^2 = 7·02$, $d.f.$ 1, $p < 0·01$. The other chi-square calculations listed below are calculated for working class occupations against middle class occupations (i.e. 3b, 4 and 5— 1, 2 and 3a) because of small cell sizes.

(1) W.C. mothers who had not seen the programmes were more likely to select a minimum age for sex information to be provided than M.C. mothers in the same exposure category, $\chi^2 = 14·24$, $d.f.$ 1, $p < 0·001$.

(2) W.C. mothers who had seen the programmes were more likely to select a minimum age for sex information to be provided than M.C. mothers in the same exposure category $\chi^2 = 11·90$, $d.f.$ 1, $p < 0·001$.

(3) There is no significant difference between M.C. mothers in the two exposure categories by tendency to select 'when they ask' or specify a minimum age. $\chi^2 = 0·53$, $d.f.$ 1, N.S.

(4) There is no significant difference between W.C. mothers in the two exposure categories by tendency to select 'when they ask' or specify a minimum age. $\chi^2 = 3·49$, $d.f.$ 1, N.S.

Table 4. Topics selected to be included in a course on sex education by percentages of individuals choosing each item and rank order

Grampian TV series on education	Social class	(1) Sex and religion	(2) Courtship	(3) Pregnancy before marriage	(4) Marriage and the family	(5) Biological and physiological aspects of sex	(6) Sex and love	(7) Sexual morality	(8) Birth control and family planning	Venereal disease	No answer	Total*
Seen	1, 2 and 3a	57·5 (4)	47·0 (8)	53·7 (5)	73·9 (1)	68·7 (2=)	47·8 (7)	68·7 (2=)	52·2 (6)	3·7	5·2	134
	3b	53·3 (4)	40·0 (7)	41·7 (6)	75·0 (1)	55·0 (3)	31·7 (8)	56·7 (2)	50·0 (5)	0·0	1·7	60
	4 and 5	62·5 (3=)	60·0 (6)	67·5 (2)	62·5 (3=)	70·0 (1)	45·0 (8)	52·5 (7)	62·5 (3=)	0·0	5·0	40
Totals	Social class combined	57·3 (4)	47·4 (7)	53·0 (6)	72·2 (1)	65·4 (2)	43·2 (8)	62·8 (3)	53·4 (5)	2·1	4·3	234
Not seen	1, 2 and 3a	53·1 (4)	42·2 (6=)	42·6 (6=)	70·3 (1)	62·5 (2)	40·6 (8)	54·7 (3)	46·9 (5)	0·0	9·4	64
	3b	40·4 (6)	36·5 (8)	51·9 (4=)	61·5 (1=)	51·9 (4=)	38·5 (7)	61·5 (1=)	55·8 (3)	1·9	7·7	52
	4 and 5	55·8 (3)	46·5 (4)	44·2 (5)	62·8 (1)	41·9 (6=)	32·6 (8)	41·9 (6=)	58·1 (2)	2·3	2·3	43
Toals	Social class combined	49·7 (5)	41·6 (7)	45·9 (6)	65·4 (1)	53·5 (2=)	37·7 (8)	53·5 (2=)	52·8 (4)	1·3	6·3	159

There is no overall difference between the exposure categories by selection or non-selection of items. $X^2 = 1·58$, $d.f.$ 1, N.S.

* Totals do not sum to 100% since respondents could select 0, 1–8 or more items. Figures in parentheses indicate the rank order of each item in the relevant social class and exposure categories.

Table 4A. *Percentage difference between choices of items for inclusion in a course on sex education by exposure and social class categories*

Differences between categories	(1) Sex and religion	(2) Courtship	(3) Pregnancy before marriage	(4) Marriage and the family	(5) Biological and physiological aspects of sex	(6) Sex and love	(7) Sexual morality	(8) Birth control and family planning
Seen by social class *(1)*								
1, 2 and 3a— 3b	4·2	7·2	7·0	-1·1	13·7	16·1+	12·0	2·2
1, 2 and 3a— 4 and 5	-5·0	-13·0	-13·0	11·4	-1·3	2·8	16·2	-10·3
3b—4 and 5	-9·2	-20·0+	-25·8+	12·5	-15·0	-13·3	4·2	-12·5
Not seen by social class *(2)*								
1, 2 and 3a— 3b	12·7	5·7	-9·7	8·8	10·6	2·1	-6·8	-8·9
1, 2 and 3a— 4 and 5	-2·7	-4·3	-2·0	7·5	20·6+	8·0	12·8	-9·2
3b—4 and 5	15·4	-10·0	7·7	-1·3	10·0	5·9	19·6	2·3
Exposure categories within social classes *(3)* *Seen* *Not seen*								
1, 2 and 3a—1, 2 and 3a	4·4	4·8	11·5	3·6	6·2	7·2	14·0	5·3
3b —3b	12·9	3·5	-10·2	13·5	3·1	-6·8	-4·8	-5·8
4 and 5 —4 and 5	6·7	13·5	23·3	-0·3	28·1++	12·4	10·6	4·4
Social classes combined *(4)* *Seen* *Not seen* All social classes								
All social classes	7·6	5·8	7·1	6·8	11·9+	5·5	9·3	0·6

N.B. Negative values indicate that the item is chosen more frequently by the second category in the paired comparisons. +, ++ = the differences are significant at the 0·05 and 0·01 levels respectively.

popular with women who had seen the programmes. This table summarizes the popularity of the eight items for inclusion in a course on sex education, both within and between social class and exposure categories.

The whole concern of the TV series was to demonstrate the relevance of a knowledge of the biology and physiology of sex to the educative process and it may be that the programmes, screened especially for the benefit of parents a week before they were shown in the schools, persuaded those parents who watched the series (particularly in social classes 4 and 5) of the appropriateness of this point of view. The TV series also stressed the ethical and moral aspects of sexual behaviour, yet 'sexual morality' was just as popular with those who had not seen the programmes, at any rate when the social classes were combined. Presumably most mothers of 14-year-olds are concerned that their children should receive information on the 'rules and regulations' which govern sexual behaviour.

When differences between the same social class groups by exposure category are examined (row 3 of Table 4A) there is again very little variation with the exception of social class 4 and 5. In this social class category, the tendency for mothers who had not seen the programmes to select fewer items was statistically significant ($\chi^2 = 10 \cdot 2$, *d.f.* 1, $p < 0 \cdot 01$), with 'pregnancy before marriage' and 'biological and physiological aspects of sex' selected less frequently by these women. That exposure to the programmes in this social class might help to clarify, for these women, the issues associated with sex education and enable them to respond more completely to the questionnaire is a possibility, but more information would be required before this very tentative explanation could attract firm support.

Mothers from social classes 1, 2 and 3a also tend to make slightly fewer selections than their counterparts who have seen the programmes ($\chi^2 = 4 \cdot 80$, *d.f.* 1, $p < 0 \cdot 05$) but this is not manifest at a statistically significant level between the exposure categories for any of the eight items. Mothers from social class 3b show no significant differences in either their propensity to select items, or in the relative emphasis placed on items by exposure category.

When exposure category is held constant and attention directed towards the variations between social classes, it is evident that for those mothers who had not seen the programmes very little difference in responses is apparent, except for item 5 – 'biological and physiological aspects of sex' – already discussed. But for those who had seen the programmes, a very different pattern of responses emerges. Social classes 1, 2 and 3a and 3b show very similar rank orders. Indeed, the only significant difference between these two groups stems from the tendency of mothers from social class 3b to place less emphasis upon 'sex and love'. Social classes 4 and 5, however, as well as producing a very different rank order from the other two class categories, are more likely to stress 'courtship' and 'pregnancy before marriage'. In social classes 4 and 5 'pregnancy before marriage' and 'illegitimacy' are relatively common phenomena.

Among fish workers in Aberdeen (a numerically important category of semi- and unskilled workers) illegitimacy and pre-nuptial conception account for more than 50 per cent of all first births (Gill, 1970). In this occupational group, it is statistically deviant to marry first and conceive later. In these circumstances it is perhaps not surprising that those women should be more concerned with 'courtship' and 'pregnancy before marriage' and to allocate higher priority (although not at a statistically significant level) to 'biological and physiological aspects of sex' and to 'birth control and family planning' than is the case for the other two social class groups who had seen the programmes. Moreover there is some indication that mothers from social classes 4 and 5, who had not seen the programmes, also share some of the same concern in that they place 'birth control and family planning' high in their rank order.

Thus far the analysis has been concerned largely with the differences between exposure categories and social classes, but certain similarities in choice of items to be included in a course on sex education are characteristic of this sample of mothers. Almost all categories of mothers place 'marriage and the family' at the head of the rank orders. At the other end of the scale 'sex and love' attracts the least support, with only two groups placing it other than last. Clearly sex education for the mothers of these children is closely associated with marriage and the family, the context within which sexual behaviour is construed as normative in British society. Conversely 'sex and love' is accorded a lower priority. This may be because these mothers view the combination 'sex and love' as a possible threat to the stability of the family and marriage, but again much more information would be required before this interpretation could be accepted or rejected.

DISCUSSION AND CONCLUSIONS

The overall conclusion must be that this sample of mothers favoured very strongly a course on sex education. Indeed the questions presented to the respondents were phrased in such a way that it required them to opt 'into' rather than 'out of' supporting such a course. Four-fifths of the respondents felt that '. . . it is necessary to provide children with information about sex'. Thus, 77 per cent of those who had not seen any of the Grampian TV series 'Living and Growing' supported such a course, and the percentage in favour increased to 85 for those mothers who had seen the programmes.

In the other three themes (preferred agent of sex education, minimum age for the provision of sex education, and topics selected to be included in a course on sex education) differences between exposure categories were apparent but tended to be small. There may be a slight tendency for mothers who had not seen the programmes, in both lower social class groups, to emphasize the school as the responsible agent for sex education and this, along with their propensity to select a later age at which sex information should be provided, may indicate that these mothers find it difficult to communicate this information to their children.

To investigate this possibility further, it would be necessary to question the respondents in much greater detail than was possible in this preliminary analysis of parental attitudes towards sex education. Nevertheless, Bernstein's (1961) studies of language codes among middle and working class groups suggest that the latter face considerable difficulty when it is necessary to discuss subjects requiring conceptualization and abstraction. Discussion of sexual behaviour and human sexuality, in general, is fraught with difficulty at most cultural levels and it is perhaps not surprising that those mothers whose verbal skills are less well-developed may be particularly inclined to shed this responsibility. Clearly the data presented in this paper are insufficient to evaluate this hypothesis but it might prove fruitful to investigate this suggestion in future studies.

Our examination of the press reports suggested a tendency towards a polarization of opinion on sex education, with press coverage often presenting extreme points of view (both for and against) particularly where apparently contentious issues such as 'birth control and family planning' and 'pregnancy before marriage' were concerned. It was, therefore, all the more interesting to note that such issues were relatively heavily selected by this sample of mothers. High priority was given to themes such as 'marriage and the family', 'sexual morality' and 'sex and religion', but a course on sex education would clearly be incomplete for these mothers without consideration being given to 'biological and physiological aspects of sex' and the 'problem areas' mentioned above.

Given the style and format of press coverage on this issue, it is easy to sympathize with the cautious approach adopted by the professional communicators when they present material on human sexuality. The Grampian TV series, for example, was exceedingly brief on the 'mechanics' of sexual intercourse and made no reference to birth control and family planning. When an issue, formerly 'taboo', is aired publicly, it tends to generate a strong counter-movement as Gusfield (1963) points out. Adapting his terminology, it may be that the objections made in the press were not so much aimed at sex education *per se* but, instead, at the alleged trend towards a 'permissive' or 'degenerate' climate of opinion of which sex education is seen as a symbolic manifestation. Our respondents did not see the issue of sex education in this context. But does this 'liberal' conclusion arise from the fact that 57 per cent of this sample of mothers reported that they had seen the programmes? Apparently not. Differences between exposure categories in the four themes tended to be small and, as was shown from Table 1, exposure to the programmes increased only slightly the tendency for mothers to stress the need for a course on sex education.

Professional communicators, directors of education, school teachers, medical officers of health, indeed all connected with the development and implementation of sex education courses for school children, might widen the scope and content of future courses and/or programmes on this subject. It would be naive, however, to argue that unanimity would be possible, or even desirable, in certain of the content areas which were given high priority by our respondents. 'Sexual morality', 'sex and religion' and 'birth control and family planning', would have different connotations in the various socio-cultural groups which make up British society.

The position of the Roman Catholic community is an obvious example of a group likely to adopt very different attitudes from the majority. Those responsible for the development of programmes and/or courses on sex education would clearly wish to adjust their content in accordance with local biasses and prejudices. Given the population pressure in even the 'over-developed' Western countries, it would seem indefensible, if educationists, communicators and politicians were to seize on those peripheral problems as an excuse for inaction.

ACKNOWLEDGEMENTS

We wish to acknowledge with gratitude the assistance provided by Mrs E. Garrett, Education Officer of Grampian Television Ltd by making available to us her file of press cuttings. Grateful thanks are also due to Mr W. R. Bytheway, Statistician in the Medical Sociology Unit of the Medical Research Council, for valuable assistance and advice in the analysis of the material. Colleagues both in the Unit and the Department of Sociology gave, unstintingly, advice and encouragement, especially Mr G. W. Horobin and Dr Barbara Thompson.

Appendix A

THE 'LIVING AND GROWING' SERIES

This eight programme series, intended for 10–13 year-olds, covered the following themes: the idea of the human life cycle, placed in the context of the family unit; the uniqueness of every human being and inheritance; a basic vocabulary of the sex organs; sex differences at childhood and puberty; the menstrual cycle and fertilization; the development of the foetus and the preparation for birth; labour, birth and post-natal care; a spontaneous discussion programme in which the presenter is questioned by a group of children; and finally a summary programme in which the process of 'Living and Growing' is shown as a cycle, re-emphasizing the central role of the family.

The series, which was awarded the Japan Prize for educational television in Tokyo in 1968, sought as its aim to establish a basis for home or classroom discussion rather than to replace parent or teacher as the agent of sex socialization.

Appendix B

QUESTIONNAIRE

Here are a number of topics which might be included in a course of sex education for children. Please indicate which ones you would want to be included by putting ticks in the boxes provided.

1. Sex and religion ☐
2. Courtship ☐
3. Pregnancy before marriage ☐
4. Marriage and the family ☐
5. Biological and physical aspects of sex ☐
6. Sex and love ☐
7. Sexual morality ☐
8. Birth control and family planning ☐
9. Any other. Please specify ☐

Did any of your children see the Grampian Television series on sex education called 'Living and Growing' when it was shown in schools in early 1968?

    (1) Yes   (2) No

Did you see any of these programmes when they were repeated in the evenings?

    (1) Yes   (2) No

Do you think

        (1)   that children have enough opportunity to acquire information about sex for themselves?

or   (2)   do you think it is necessary to provide children with information about sex?

                        (Probe)

If answer (2) provide children with information, ask

    (a)   Who do you think should be responsible for providing information about sex?

    (b)   When do you think children should first be told anything about sex?

        1. 3–4 year old.
        2. 5–6 year old.
        3. 7–8 year old.
        4. 9–10 year old.
        5. 11–12 year old.
        6. 13–14 year old.
        7. 15–16 year old.
        8. 17 and over.
        9. It depends.

If say 'it depends', ask

    On what does it depend?

NOTES
1 M. Schofield's *The Sexual Behaviour of Young People* closes with a plea for more realistic sex education for teenagers within the school context. The four questions developed above are drawn at least in part from Schofield's analysis of sexual knowledge or lack of such knowledge among teenagers.

2 See Appendix A for a brief description of the series.

3 For a critical review of studies relating to selective exposure and perception see David O. Sears and Jonathan L. Freedman, 'Selective exposure to information', *Public Opinion Quarterly* (31), 1967, Summer, pp. 194–213.

4 We acknowledge the possible relevance of other background variables such as family size, social and sexual composition of the family, ordinal position and sex of the index child. However, to control for such factors would both complicate the study in a way not warranted by the sample size and deflect it from its major focus, namely the overall desirability of sex education courses as perceived by a sample of mothers.

5 The respondents were presented with two choices in an attempt to create a situation where they had to make a positive response in favour of sex education rather than express merely indifference or the absence of strong negative feelings. (See Appendix B for the questionnaire.)

REFERENCES

Bernstein, B. (1961). 'Social class and linguistic development: a theory of social learning.' In Halsey, A. H., Floud, J. and Anderson, C. A. *Education Economy and Society* (Glencoe, The Free Press, New York).

The British Council of Churches (1966). *Sex and Morality* (S.C.M. Press, London).

Cicourel, A. V. (1964). *Method and Measurement in Sociology* (The Free Press, New York).

Gill, D. G. (1970). 'Changing trends in illegitimacy and changing modes of explanation', *Journal Royal Society of Health*, 90/3, 154.

Gusfield, J. R. (1963). *Symbolic Crusade: Status Politics and the American Temperance Movement* (University of Illinois Press, Urbana).

Illsley, R. and Gill, D. G. (1968). 'Changing trends in Illegitimacy', *Social Science and Medicine*, vol. 2, p. 415.

Herson, A. (1963). *Towards a Quaker View of Sex* (Friends House, London).

Kinsey, A. C., Pomercy, W. B., *et al.* (1948). *Sexual Behaviour in the Human Male* (W. B. Saunders Co., Philadelphia).

Masters, W. H. and Johnson, J. E. (1966). *Human Sexual Response* (Little Brown and Co. Boston).

Masters, W. H. and Johnson, J. E. (1970). *Human Sexual Inadequacy* (Churchill, London).

Rainwater, Lee (1960). *And the Poor Get Children* (Quadrangle Books, Chicago).

Reiss, I. L. (1967). *The Social Context of Premarital Sexual Permissiveness* (Holt, Rinehart and Winston, New York).

Schofield, M. (1965). *The Sexual Behaviour of Young People* (Longmans, London).

Sears, D. O. and Freedman, J. L. (1967). 'Selective exposure to information', *Public Opinion Quarterly* (31), Summer, pp. 194–213.
Thompson, B. (1956). 'Social study of illegitimate maternities', *British Journal of Social and Preventive Medicine* (10), pp. 75–87.

8 Counseling with Sexually Incompatible Marriage Partners

WILLIAM H. MASTERS and
VIRGINIA E. JOHNSON

At least one result of the cultural relaxation of sexual taboos has been of major consequence. Today, more – many more – marital partners are seeking professional assistance when sexual incompatibility threatens their marriage. Anyone exposed professionally to the emotional anguish and disrupted marriages caused by such clinical problems as impotence and frigidity will look upon this help-seeking trend with considerable satisfaction.

Most of the sexually distressed people are bringing their problems to their family physicians. Although the individual or combined efforts of psychiatrists, psychologists, marriage counselors, social workers, and/or clergymen may be needed in addition to those of the chosen physician to solve some problems of sexual inadequacy, it is the family physician, taking advantage of initial rapport and established confidence, who ordinarily overcomes any patient reluctance or embarrassment and builds motivation for further treatment.

Unfortunately, until recently the physician has been hampered in treatment by three major stumbling blocks:

First, there has been a long-standing and widespread medical misconception that a patient will not reveal sex history background with sufficient accuracy and in adequate detail for effective therapy.

Second, in the past the physician has been provided with very little basic information in sexual physiology upon which to develop any effective treatment of sexual inadequacy.

Third, many physicians have been convinced that since most sexual problems are psychogenic in origin, only a specialized psychopathologist can treat them effectively.

Increasingly large numbers of physicians are demonstrating

William H. Masters and Virginia E. Johnson, 'Counseling with sexually incompatible marriage partners', in Richard H. Klemer (ed.) *Counseling in Marital and Sexual Problems* (Williams and Wilkins Co., 1965). Reproduced by permission.

clinically that none of these obstacles now has much substance in fact.

Almost ten years of investigation in the broad areas of human sexual response has brought conviction to the writers that if the interviewing physician can project sincere interest in the patient's problem and, even more important, exhibit no personal embarrassment in an open sexual discussion, almost any individual's sexual history will be reported with sufficient accuracy and in adequate detail for treatment purposes. Others, such as Eisenbud,[1] who have worked with human sexual problems, also believe that patients are usually very ready to talk freely about their disturbed sexual behaviour patterns once they have gathered their courage to a degree sufficient to seek professional guidance.

While it is true that the amount of research in sexual physiology has in the past been meager indeed, this situation is rapidly being corrected.[2-6] Some of this recent material is synthesized in the latter part of this chapter and quite possibly may provide a minimal baseline for the more adequate clinical treatment of frigidity or impotence.

With regard to the third stumbling block – that of requisite referral to the psychopathologist of problems of sexual incompatibility – two things should be noted. First, there is ample clinical evidence for the observation that sexual imbalance or inadequacy is not confined to individuals who have been identified with major psychoses or even severe neuroses. Secondly, long-maintained individually oriented psychotherapy for sexual inadequacy frequently places irreversible strains on the marital state. While the psychopathologist is working with one marriage partner or the other toward the resolution of his or her individual sexual inadequacy, the marriage itself may be deteriorating. One or two years of therapy directed specifically toward the impotent male or frigid female frequently leaves the unsupported marital partner in a state of severe frustration. Not only are unresolved sexual tensions of the non-treated spouse of major moment, but frequently no significant attempt is made by the therapist to keep the supposedly adequate partner apprised of his or her mate's fundamental problems and/or the specifics of therapeutic progress. Such situations of spouse neglect not only are sure to increase the performance pressures on the sexually inadequate partner, but obviously may lead to many other areas of marital strife and, for that matter, stimulate extramarital interests.

105

As the result of these observations, the conviction has grown that the most effective treatment of sexual incompatibility involves the technique of working with both members of the family unit. The major factor in effective diagnosis and subsequent productive counseling in sexual problems lies in gaining access to and rapport with both members of the family unit. This approach not only provides direct therapy for the sexually inadequate partner, but provides something more. An indirect therapeutic gain results from enlisting the complete cooperation and active participation of the adequate spouse (the husband of the frigid woman or the wife of the impotent male). It is virtually impossible for the mate of the sexually distressed partner to remain isolated from or uninvolved in his or her partner's concern for adequate sexual performance. Therefore, most of these individuals can and will be most cooperative in absorbing the necessary material of both physiologic and psychologic background necessary to convert them into active members of the therapy team.

As in so many other areas of medical practice, treating sexual incompatibility involves, first, recognizing the nature of the patient's problem; second, determining the type and degree of the incompatibility and third, developing and activating the therapeutic approaches applicable to the particular clinical involvement.

Recognizing the sexual problem

The patient with sexual distress defines the problem directly with increasing frequency during this era of marked change in our cultural attitudes toward sexual material. However, many women initially may discuss such symptoms as fatigue, 'nerves,' pelvic pain, headaches, or any other complaint for which specific pathology cannot be established. The physician-interviewer must anticipate conscious vocal misdirection when Victorian concepts of sexual taboos still exist, or where there is a personal demand to fix blame on the marital partner.

If, for example, the female is the partner experiencing major dissatisfaction with her marriage, for any one of a number of reasons, she purposely may obscure her basic personal antipathies by describing gross sexual irregularities on the part of her marital partner. Sometimes when it is the husband who wishes to end the marriage, he often employs the pressure of partial sexual with-drawal, or even complete sexual refusal. At this point, medical consultation is sought solely to justify condemnation of what is termed the mate's unfair, inadequate, or perverted sexual behaviour.

Actually, the marital incompatibility that brings the couple to the physician usually is not primarily of sexual origin. Sexual incompatibility may well be the secondary result of marital disagreement over such problems as money, relatives, or child care. Such areas of dispute easily may undermine any poorly established pattern of sexual adjustment. Frequently, withholding of sexual privileges is used as punishment in retaliation for true or fancied misdeeds in other areas. If the preliminary history reveals such a situation of secondary sexual incompatibility, the physician must decide whether he wishes to carry the full, time-consuming burden of total marriage counseling or if referral is in order. In the latter case, he still may wish to retain an active clinical role in the psychosexual aspects of the problems involved.

However, once the problem is established as primarily sexual in nature and as the cause and not the effect of the marital incompatibility, the complaint should be attacked directly and with the same sense of medical urgency with which clinical complaints of either a medical or surgical background are investigated. Otherwise, permanent impairment of the marital relationship may be inevitable.

The sexual history

The need to acquire accurate and detailed sexual histories is basic to determining the type and the degree of the incompatibility of the members of the distressed family unit.

Sex histories must reflect accurately details of early sexual training and experience, family attitudes toward sex, the degree of the family's demonstrated affection, personal attitude toward sex and its significance within the marriage, and the degree of personal regard for the marital partner. While the actual nature of the existing sex difficulty may be revealed during an early stage of history-taking, the total history, as it discloses causation and subsequent effect, provides the basis for the most effective means of therapy.

The first step in the team approach to diagnosis and treatment has been to see the husband and wife together as a complaining unit during the initial interview.[7-9] Procedures and philosophies are explained to them. If the couple desires to continue after the investigative concepts have been outlined, they are separated for individual interrogation but only after each partner is assured that similar background material will be covered simultaneously by the two interviewers.

The knowledge that both unit members are undergoing similar interrogative procedures, that essentially the same background material will be investigated, and that all areas of professed concern will be probed in depth, produces an atmosphere that encourages honest reporting and an unusual amount of patient attention to detail.

Finite details of past and present sexual behaviour may be obtained during the initial interview with the facility and integrity anticipated for the recording of a detailed medical history. Encouraged by a receptive climate, controlled, brief questioning, and a non-judgmental attitude, the patient is just as free to discuss the multiple facets of, for example, a homosexual background, as he might be to present the specific details of a chronic illness in a medical history.

It should be noted particularly that in the process of acquiring a detailed sexual history, the usual basic physical and social histories of medical and behavioral significance also are recorded.

For the rapid diagnosis and treatment of sexual incompatibility, a male-female therapy team approach has been developed as reported elsewhere.[9] This approach involves the male marriage partner being interviewed first by the male member of the therapy team. Simultaneously, material from the female partner of the involved marital unit is acquired by the female member of the therapy team. Prior to the second investigative session, members of the therapy team exchange pertinent details of the marital unit's reported sexual distress. During the second session the female partner of the complaining couple is reinterviewed by the male member of the therapy team. Meanwhile, the husband is evaluated by the female therapist. At the third interview, the therapy team and the marital couple meet to review the positive features of the earlier interrogative sessions and to discuss in detail the active degree of the sexual incompatibility.

While the male-female therapy approach has been found to be eminently satisfactory, obviously this technique usually is not possible in the typical physician's practice. However, the broad general steps toward diagnosis and evaluation that are outlined here can be adopted by the individual physician. For instance, the advantage of honest reporting obtained by simultaneous interviews of members of the marital unit can be retained by interrogating them consecutively.

The therapeutic process

Once the background of the individual couple's sexual imbalance has been defined, and the clinical picture explained to their satisfaction and understanding, a discussion of therapeutic procedure takes place.

In general terms, the psychotherapeutic concepts and physiologic techniques employed to attack the problems of frigidity and impotence are explained without reservation. Specific plans are outlined for the therapeutic immediacies and a pattern for long-range support is described. With this specific information available, a decision must be reached as to whether the couple has sufficient need or interest for active participation in the therapeutic program. The decision obviously is based not only on a joint evaluation of the quality of the marriage and the severity of the sexual distress, but also on a review of the individual abilities to cooperate fully with the program. If doubt exists, on the part of either member of the investigative team or either partner of the sexually incompatible marital unit, as to real interest in remedial techniques or ability to cooperate fully as a unit, the couple is directed toward other sources of clinical support.

Since the two major sexual incompatibilities are frigidity and impotence, treatment for these problems will be discussed in detail.

Impotence

Three major types of impotence ordinarily are encountered in the human male. They are:

(1) *Failed erection*. Penile erection cannot be achieved.

(2) *Inadequate erection*. Full penile erection either cannot be achieved or, if accomplished, is maintained fleetingly and lost, usually without ejaculation.

(3) *Nonemissive erection*. Full penile erection is achieved, but ejaculation cannot be accomplished with the penis contained within the vagina.

Note. Premature ejaculation – ejaculation before, during, or immediately after mounting is accomplished – while not considered a form of impotence, is discussed in this chapter due to the similarity of therapeutic approach.

Impotence is rarely, if ever, the result of lesions of the posterior urethra. Once the possibility of spinal cord disease or certain endocrinopathies, such as hypogonadism or diabetes insipidus, has been eliminated, the total history should be scrutinized for the omnipresent signs of psychogenic origin for the specific type of male impotence reported.

In the case of the male with failed or inadequate erection, history-taking should stress the timetable of symptom onset. Has there always been difficulty, or is loss of erective power of recent origin? If recent in origin, what specific events inside or outside the marriage have been associated with onset of symptoms? Are there any masturbatory difficulties? Is there a homosexual background of significance?

Further questioning should define the male's attitude toward his sexual partner. Is there rejection not only of the marriage partner, but also of other women? Are the female partner's sexual demands in excess of his levels of sexual interest or ability to comply? Is there a sexual disinterest that may have resulted from the partner's physical or personal traits, such as excessive body odor or chronic alcoholism?

In the case of a patient with premature ejaculation, questions should be concentrated in a different area. Does this rapid ejaculatory pattern date from the beginning of his sexual activity? Has he been exposed to prostitute demand for rapid performance during his teen-age years? Does he come from a level of society where the female sexual role is considered to be purely one of service to male demand?

When working with the male with a non-emissive erection still other questions are more appropriate. Has the male always been unable to ejaculate during intercourse or has this difficulty been confined to exposure to his marital partner? Are nocturnal emissions frequent, especially after heterosexual encounters? Is there an active homosexual history?

Actually, the fundamental therapeutic approach to all problems of impotence is one of creating and sustaining self-confidence in the patient. This factor emphasizes the great advantage in training the wife to be an active member of the therapeutic team. All pertinent details of the anatomy, physiology, and psychology of male impotence should be explained to her satisfaction. The rationale of treatment, together with an explanation of the specific stimulative techniques most effective in dealing with the specific type of impotence distressing her husband must be made clear to her.

In the early stages of treating failed or non-erective impotence, it is wise to avoid emphasizing the demand that intercourse be the end of all sexual play. Frequently, the male's inability to meet just such a repetitive female demand is already one of the primary factors in his impotence. Some males find release from fear of performance when they are given to understand that sexual play need not necessarily terminate in intercourse. They are then able to relax, enjoy, and participate freely in the sexually stimulative situations created by their clinically oriented wives to a point where erection does occur. After several such occasions of demand-free spontaneous erections, the males may even initiate the mounting procedure and complete the sexual act. This casual mating may well be the beginning of release from their chronic or acute failed or non-erective impotence.

In most cases, manual penile manipulation varying in degree of intensity and duration probably will be necessary. This controlled penile stimulation must be provided by his previously trained female partner. The male with inadequate erection syndrome should be exposed to long and regularly recurrent periods of manual stimulation in a sensitive, sexually restrained, but firmly demanding fashion.

In the opposite vein, the male with the difficult problem of premature ejaculation should be manually stimulated for short, controlled periods with stimulation withheld at his own direction as he feels ejaculation is imminent. The shaft of the penis should be well lubricated to reduce cutaneous sensation. This technique will fail frequently and ejaculation will occur. However, the couple should be encouraged to return to the technique repetitively until the male's obviously improved control leads to the next therapeutic step. This will be a female superior mounting, which can later be converted to a non-demanding lateral resting position. These progressive control techniques emphasize the unit approach to the problem of sexual inadequacy and from here on psychogenic support and the cooperation of the wife certainly will reclaim many of those males who were formerly inadequate sexually.

The problem of the male with non-emissive erection is somewhat different. His is largely an infertility problem rather than one of sexual incompatibility. In these cases, reassuring both husband and wife that the problem is of little clinical consequence provides the basic therapy. Sometimes the infertility concern connected with this variant can be overcome by artificially inseminating the wife with her husband's seminal fluid obtained by manipulation. Since psychotherapy has produced so few positive results with this type of impotence, providing clinical reassurance and conceptive information may have to suffice in these cases.

Frigidity

There is a great deal of misunderstanding over the connotation of the word 'frigidity'. It is often used in a context that presumes an irrevocable lack of sexuality on the part of a female sexual partner. Misconceptions are likely to occur when this word is used too freely as a diagnostic term.

From a therapeutic point of view, the maximal meaning of the word should indicate no more than a prevailing inability or subconscious refusal to respond sexually to effective stimulation. A woman is not necessarily lacking in sexual responsiveness when she does not experience an orgasm. Therefore, the achievement of orgasmic response should not be considered the end-all of sexual gratification for the responding female. Unhappily, many women, unable to achieve an orgasmic level of sexual response in the past, have been labeled frigid not only by their marital partner but also by the physician they may have consulted.

The free use of this term frequently does great psychologic damage. Frigidity is a term that should rarely be employed in the presence of the sexually inadequate female for it may well add shame, and/or fear of inadequate performance to whatever other psychologic problems she may have.

It is true that there are a number of women who experience a persistently high degree of sexual tension, but, for unidentified reasons, are not able to achieve a satisfactory means of tension release. In evaluating this problem, initial exploration should be concentrated in two areas of psychosexual withdrawal. The first is to determine the presence or absence of psychologic inability to respond to effective sexual stimulation. The second is to define the possible existence of sexual incompatibility caused by misunderstandings resulting from a difference in the sex tension demands of the marital partners.

As described elsewhere,[7] three positive indications of female psychosexual inadequacy can be developed by careful history-taking:

(1) Attitude toward sex and its significance within the marriage.
(2) Degree of personal regard for the marital partner.
(3) Fear of pregnancy.

In investigating the attitude toward sex, existing negative concepts should be pursued by careful interrogation. Questioning should explore early sexual training and experience, exposure to lack of demonstrated parental affection, history of homosexual experience, if any, and/or any traumatic sex-oriented incidents that might have affected natural sexual responsiveness.

When exploring the area of personal regard for the marital partner, the female partner's disinterest or lack of cooperation with the consulting physician may be an interesting clinical symptom of itself. When essential indifference toward a marital partner has been exposed, the existence of a basically unwanted marriage or marriage undertaken without intelligent preparation or emotional maturity is a real possibility. Perhaps, in these cases, referral to a marriage counselor or undertaking marriage counseling in the more general frame of reference is in order, rather than concentrating on the sexual aspects of the problem.

When there is any indication of fear of pregnancy the therapeutic approach is obvious to the counseling physician. Actually, satisfactory results are ordinarily more easily achieved in pregnancy-phobia situations than in either of the other two areas of psychosexual withdrawal.

After the background of the female's sexual unresponsiveness has been established, and the marital unit has accepted the conclusions presented during the diagnostic sessions, therapy may begin. Female sexual responsiveness may well depend upon the successful orientation to the following framework of therapeutic approach:

(1) The possibility of anatomic or physiologic abnormalities that can contribute to varying shades of discomfort during intercourse should be eliminated. Orientation to male and female sexual anatomy, directly if necessary, should be accomplished.

(2) Affirmation that sexual expression represents an integral basis for sharing within the marriage should be emphasized.

(3) A mutually stimulative sexual pattern should be developed and adapted to the individual psychosocial backgrounds of the marriage partners.

(4) Gentleness, sensitivity, and technical effectiveness in the male partner's approach to sexual encounter should be encouraged.

(5) Emphasis should be placed on the fact that female orgasm is not necessarily the end-all of every sexual encounter.

With regard to pelvic abnormalities, it might be noted that a history indicating actual pain or any other physical displeasure during sex play or coition certainly suggests the need for an adequate physical examination. If physiologic variants, such as pelvic endometriosis, causing severe, recurrent discomfort during intercourse with deep penile penetration are revealed, subsequent medical and/or surgical adjustments may be indicated. However, it should be noted that sometimes the simple clinical expedient of teaching the couple proper positioning for coital activity may remove the female partner's distress despite existing pelvic pathology.

A high percentage of psychologically based problems of inadequate female response begin as the result of rejection of, or ignorance of effective sex techniques by either or both marital partners. The physician may also be called upon to provide reassurance as to the propriety of variants of stimulative sexual behavior. Although the number of patients who are sexually incompatible as the result of the wife's or husband's total lack of sexual experience before marriage may well be declining, patients with this type of problem are seen occasionally. Moreover, many women have been taught that only certain specifics of sexual stimulation or certain coital positions are acceptable. These women do not readily accept any deviation from what they consider 'right and proper', regardless of the interests of their marital partners. Victorianism, although vanishing from the American social scene, left a residual influence that may well require attention for at least another fifty years.

Teaching the sexually inadequate woman and her partner the basic rudiments of sexual anatomy may be extremely important. Many males, however experienced in coition, are unaware of the importance of adequate techniques for clitoral area stimulation. Few are aware that it is the gentle friction of the mons area or of the clitoral shaft rather than the clitoral glans that provides the most effective stimulation for the female partner. Moreover, many females as well as males are not aware of the basic physiology of sexual response and of the fact that physiologic orgasm takes place within the vagina and in the clitoris, regardless of where sensation is perceived by the female or initiated by the male.

In the development of mutually stimulative sexual pattern it is important that the marital unit's move toward maximal female sexual responsiveness should be accompanied by the female's vocalizing such things as: specific sexual preferences, desired zones of erogenous stimulation, choice of coital positioning and, particularly, the fact of her approaching orgasm. The couple must be taught to consider moments of individual preference for sexual encounter. Experimentation with varieties of time, place, and sexual techniques should be made in order to achieve the necessary mood conducive to the female's successful sexual response. It is well to bear in mind that the two basic deterrents to female sexual responsiveness are *fatigue* and *preoccupation*.

The item in the therapeutic framework emphasizing gentleness and sensitivity needs little elaboration. But it should be noted that the male's approach – his ability to project both security and affection to the female – may be an absolute essential to any improvement in the female's sexual responsiveness. A re-evaluation of the male's attitudes toward sex and toward women may be as important to the progress of therapy as the attention paid to his education in specific sexual techniques.

The second major area to be explored with the couple is the possible difference in the degree of basic sexual tension demonstrated by the wife as opposed to that indicated by the husband. In analyzing this area, it should be emphasized that an impression of low-level female sexual demand should only be established in relative comparison to a higher-tension partner. A lower level of demand does not necessarily connote either inability to respond adequately to effective heterosexual stimulation or homosexual tendency. Yet, when such a divergence in sexual interest is encountered, there are inevitable misunderstandings between the marital partners. In some cases there may be a conscious sexual withdrawing by the lower-response partner, developing from a sense of personal inadequacy or from a wish to punish what is considered as excessive demand. Conscious sexual withdrawal also may develop from a deep resentment or a sense of rejection felt by the partner wishing a higher degree of sexual participation.

The marital unit's understanding and acceptance of a difference in sexual tension demand is far more important than its causation and the determination of a specific spouse role-playing. A higher level of demand may well belong to either partner. This is evident in marriages between younger partners as well as in many marriages between older individuals. Feelings of sexual inadequacy, distrust, or withdrawal may be corrected by education of each mate to the other partner's individual, highly personal, sexual requirements. Thereafter, the problem becomes one of adjusting acknowledged differences in sexual tension to a mutually accepted plan for effective release of the higher level of demand. It has been noted frequently that the relief of inhibitions of the lower-tension partners (once the marital unit problem is understood) may be marked by a more receptive, or even increased willingness to participate in sexual activity, even though there is no permanent elevation of the lower-level partner's own sexual tension.[9]

As emphasized many times previously, the individual or combined interests of psychiatrists, psychologists, medical specialists, marriage counselors, social workers, and clergymen may be needed to solve severe problems of sexual incompatibility. However, the advice of the initially consulted family physician frequently will be the most important step in relief of marital sexual maladjustments. The physician's forthright guidance and initial reassurance, whether be refers his patients to other professionals or treats them himself, provide the best foundation for the solution of problems of sexually incompatible marriages.

NOTES

1 Eisenbud, J. 'A psychiatrist looks at the report', in *Problems of Social Behavior,* (New York: Social Hygiene Association, 1948), pp. 20–7.

2 Masters, W. H. 'The sexual response cycle of the human female: I. Gross anatomic considerations'. *West. J. Surg.* 68: 57–72, 1960.

3 Masters, W. H., 'The sexual response cycle of the human female: II. Vaginal lubrication'. *Ann. New York Acad. Sc.* 83: 301–17, 1959.

4 Masters, W. H. and Johnson, V. E., 'The physiology of vaginal reproductive function'. *West J. Surg.* 69: 105–20, 1961.

5 Masters, W. H. and Johnson, V. E. 'The sexual response cycle of the human female: III. The clitoris: anatomic and clinical considerations'. *West. J. Surg.* 70: 248–57, 1962.

6 Masters, W. H. and Johnson, V. E. 'The sexual response cycle of the human male: I. Gross anatomic considerations'. *West J. Surg.* 71 : 85–95, 1963.

7 Johnson, V. E. and Masters, W. H. 'Treatment of the sexually incompatible family unit'. *Minnesota Med.* 44: 44: 466–71, 1961.

8 Johnson, V. E. and Masters, W. H. 'Sexual incompatibility: diagnosis and treatment', in Charles W. Lloyd, ed., *Human Reproduction and Sexual Behavior* (Philadelphia: Lea & Febiger, 1964), pp. 474–89.

9 Johnson, V. E. and Masters, W. H. 'A team approach to the rapid diagnosis and treatment of sexual incompatibility'. *Pac. Med. & Surg.* (formerly *West. J. Surg.*), 72: 371–75, 1964.

SECTION B
Psycho-Sexual Development

Overview

A generally acceptable definition of sex education would perhaps be a deliberate decision on the part of society to compliment learning which occurs incidentally through the child's own observations of reality (both directly and vicariously through the eyes of the mass media) with information provided in a deliberate, structured educational situation. Such educational decisions do not arise accidentally but rather are the result of the recognition of a state of need, either on the part of the child or of society at large. In this second section, we examine the kinds of evidence about psychosexual development that are the basis of the movement towards formalized sex education.

The selection of this group of readings has been made with a view to bringing together the kinds of knowledge about sexual development that seem directly relevant to the sex educator's justification of his decision to supplement the 'normal' flow of information about sexuality reaching the child. The emphasis, therefore, is not on hypotheses about sexual development (e.g. that of the Freudians) but on the types of empirical findings that bear directly on the sex educator's case. In particular, they are centred on:

(1) The extent to which the child explores sexuality both intellectually (that is, seeking knowledge) and behaviourally (in other words, 'experimenting').

(2) The nature of the environment in which the child explores. For example, the role of peers, family and school.

(3) The adequacy of the knowledge he acquires.

(4) The attitudes of children and parents to sex education.

Section B, then, is devoted to an empirical examination of the need for education. To begin I have chosen a paper by Hans and Shulamith Kreitler. This is a valuable starting point not only because it looks at the very young child[1] but also through its discussion and examination of two major theoretical accounts of psycho-sexual development, those of Piaget and Freud. The paper, therefore, offers a perspective from which later material may be examined.

Three major points stand out from this research:

(1) It illustrates the way in which the determined researcher can overcome the communication problems associated with the limited language and conceptual development of the pre-school child.

(2) Its questioning, in terms of empirical findings, of two major theories of child development.

(3) The suggestion that the child faced with a knowledge gap will 'work' on the deficiency, filling it with an internally generated fantasy theory.

This last point is one to which I attach particular attention, as the process resembles the later role of 'old wive's tales' and may be of significance in the subsequent development of sexual attitudes. Once we see learning as an active process, lack of adequate knowledge reaching the the child can lead not just to a knowledge gap but to inaccurate knowledge that may take considerable effort to unlearn.

The paper by Elias and Gebhard (Chapter 10) takes up the story very much where the previous paper leaves off, and covers the years 4-14. Apart from providing a valuable set of references (modern and historical), this paper gives the first available account of data collected by Kinsey not of childhood sexual behaviour *as recalled by adults* but of the behaviour reported by children themselves. The questionable reliability of behaviour recalled after a period of many years may have reduced the acceptance of the widespread sexuality of childhood shown by Kinsey's original surveys. In the face of this additional data, however, which strikingly resembles that from adult recall, no room for doubt remains. Although the actual data may have limited applicability over time and across cultures, the authors' discussion of levels of sexual knowledge, sources of information, social class differences and educational implications has a more substantive relevance.

In the study by Ripley *et al.* (Chapter 11), we learn of the sexual knowledge of youngsters and the attitudes of both children and parents in a small urban community in the UK. This data is recent (1971) and although not necessarily completely typical of the country as a whole, does tell us a good deal about the current situation in Britain. The study makes it clear that an inadequate grasp of basic sexual knowledge is still the norm for children entering adolescence and by no means totally eliminated by 14-15 years. One reason for this can be found in the data quoted about origins of sexual information, where peers (particularly for the boys) were a major source. It is perhaps not surprising, therefore, that sexual anxieties were rated high on a list of worries by both boys and girls. Two further aspects of the study that should be highlighted are: First, the high acceptability of formalised sex education to the parents (a point also revealed in the editor's research (see Chapter 18)), and, second, the observation that high sexual knowledge score in the first year of secondary schooling was associated with attending a primary school where sex education was given. This latter point is a valuable argument in favour of the long-term effectiveness of pre-adolescent instruction.

No examination of this area would be complete without some consideration of the work of Schofield. The first extract I have chosen (Chapter 12) covers the major conclusions of his 1965 study of the sexual behaviour of British teenagers. It discusses, in addition to sex education itself, findings of premarital sexual intercourse, illegitimacy, venereal disease and also considers the social implications of the data. The picture that emerges from this data provides the educator with considerable justification for sexual instruction. Neither home nor school were reaching many children with sexual information, resulting in learning from equally ignorant peers. Further, many children wanted sex education or, in the case of the instructed, wanted something better than the education they had received. Finally, one particularly disturbing consequence of the lack of adequate knowledge (which, as would be expected, extended to contraception) was that, when sexual activity did start, less than half were taking adequate 'precautions'.[2]

More than half a decade later, Schofield conducted follow-up interviews with subjects from his original study. The result is a pool of data reflecting the attitudes and experiences of young adults in the 1970s. In Chapter 13, I have selected a passage where responses to questions concerning sex education are discussed. As will be seen, school-based and parent-based sex education were the preferred methods of the respondents although they were not the learning routes that most had *actually* experienced. Both sources (school and home) were seen as being capable of giving very much more than

123

they did. It is particularly interesting to speculate on the findings that despite the fact that nearly all the interviewees felt capable of helping their children learn about sexuality, considerable numbers of them nevertheless felt that their own sexual knowledge was still inadequate.

NOTES

1 The children studied were Israeli-born of 'Western' or 'Oriental' parentage. The data from the former are likely to offer the closer 'match' to the results we might expect from children in the UK or USA.

2 Of course, sex education and the provision of contraceptive information do not have to be seen as inevitably linked. Indeed, in the case of the acceptability of sexual instruction to Catholic schools the association could prove a very negative one. However, the general point can be made that the acceptance and efficient use of birth control (including 'rhythm') is likely to depend not only on 'psychological' factors but also on an adequate knowledge of the physiology of sex.

9 Children's Concepts of Sexuality and Birth

HANS and SHULAMITH KREITLER

The present article deals with the information and views of children about sexual differences and the creation of babies. The method consisted in interviewing by aid of a questionnaire 185 children in the age range of 4–5½ years, boys and girls, from European and American as well as from North-African and Asian ancestry. It was found that the level of information about sexual differences and the readiness to talk about sexuality are much higher than usually assumed. Concerning the creation of babies, the views center about three theories: the baby is created in the mother's belly from the food she eats, the baby has always existed in the mother's belly, the baby should be swallowed by the mother.

Further results refer to the role of the father and to the status of the embryo and the manner in which it leaves the belly.

The conclusions relate to Freud's and Piaget's theories in this domain, to cultural differences, and to the assumed impact of the children's views upon later personality development and behavior.

The views held by children about the creation and birth of babies are considered of great importance in psychopathology and in developmental psychology. Nevertheless, no systematic empirical material about this subject has existed until now. Freud (1959), who refers to infantile concepts of sexuality in most of his works, has indeed devoted a special study to children's concepts of sexuality, but his material is based only in small part on direct observations of children. Although he considers the direct reports given by children as 'the most unequivocal and fertile source' (Freud, 1959, p. 209) of information, the factual basis of his own postulations and hypotheses is provided mainly by the memories of adult patients concerning their childhood. The same is true of his followers, with

Hans and Shulamith Kreitler, 'Children's concepts of sexuality and birth', *Child Development*, vol. 37 (1966), pp. 363-78.

the difference that what to Freud was a hypothesis became for them a dogma. Thus Rank (1922) compared children's theories of sexuality, as reported by Freud, with various primitive myths, and by means of speculative analysis, found many correspondences. Yet he by no means investigated whether the given concepts of sexuality actually correspond to what children think and believe.

Piaget (1960, pp. 360–369), who pioneered in the empirical study of children's concepts, also made various postulations about infantile concepts of sexuality without basing himself on any systematic collection of material. He justifies this procedure, which is contrary to his usual method, by claiming that a systematic questioning of children in this domain is contraindicated by moral and pedagogic considerations. Since Freud also attributed our lack of information about infantile sexual theories to the moral outlook of adults, there exists, at least on this point, a certain agreement between these two scientists; but as far as children's concepts of sexuality are concerned, the conclusions of Freud and Piaget are entirely different.

Since we are of the opinion that, in the long run, less harm is done by the careful questioning of children than by scientific hypotheses devoid of empirical basis, we decided to collect systematic information about infantile concepts of sexuality. External conditions were particularly favorable for such a study. In view of the fact that the parents of Israeli kindergarten children are the natives of about 50 different countries and are mostly new immigrants, from the very outset we could attribute to our results general, and not merely local, validity. The attitude of the parents was also encouraging. In the beginning, when we asked them somewhat clumsily for permission to interview their children about sexual problems, we met mainly with refusal; but when we hit ultimately upon the idea of showing them the actual questionnaire, permission was accorded without exception.

The aim of our study was to learn as much as possible about infantile concepts of sexuality by questioning a representative group of children. Since the theories and speculations of Freud and Piaget play a great role in psychopathology and in social and developmental psychology, we used them as working hypotheses and formulated some of our questions in a manner which allows for confirmation or refutation of Freud's and Piaget's postulations in this domain.

According to Freud (1959), boys up to the age of 6 believe in the universality of the penis, namely, they attribute the possession of a penis to women, too. This infantile conviction is assumed to be so powerful that boys either ignore their contrary observations concerning mothers and sisters or assume that in the case of the small girl the penis has not yet grown, and in the case of the grown-up woman that it has been lost, cut off as a punishment, etc. Elsewhere in his writings, Freud hints that small girls as well, after having seen a penis, consider themselves – and later other women too – as having been castrated, which means that they too believe in the universality of the penis. As a result of this concept and of the infantile assumption that the sexual act is nothing but sadistic aggression, children supposedly cannot construct a realistic theory of birth on the basis of what they do know about pregnancy. The concepts they build correspond, rather, to the libidinal phases and fixations. The commonest concept about birth is based on anal experiences and is simply that babies are born through the anus. Since the relation between stool and eating is already known to them, children assume that the mother must eat something definite in order to become pregnant. Nevertheless, Freud stresses that this theory of birth is entirely anal and not oral because its starting point is birth through the anus, while the eating of something definite is merely a logical complementary conclusion.

According to Piaget, whose starting point is intellectual and not libidinal development, children are at first not interested in knowing how a baby is made. They tend, rather, to consider the baby as having existed fully alive before it came into relation with the parents. Piaget calls this concept 'pre-artificialist'. The concept which is formed in the subsequent developmental phase represents a combination of artificialism and animism. Children believe that babies are produced limb by limb, but that in spite of this artificial mode of creation they are alive. Somewhat later, but often even at the same time, children come to grasp that babies are created in their parents' bodies and out of the material of their parents' bodies (e.g., flesh, blood), which means that children attain rather early a quite realistic understanding of the process.

These and several other postulations made by Freud and by Piaget and not mentioned above have provided us with a great number of problems and partial questions, which we have strived to solve by means of our investigation. Yet, in the present article, we have had to limit ourselves to results concerning the following aspects:

(1) How much do children know about sexual differences, and how ready are they to talk about them freely?

(2) Where do children think the baby was prior to its birth?

(3) What, according to children, should the mother do in order to get a baby, and how is it born?

(4) What do children think the father's role is in the creation of the baby?

(5) Does the process of creation formulated by the child apply to all parents, his own included?

(6) What, according to children, happens to the baby in the mother's belly?

Method

Our subjects were 185 children: 95 boys and 90 girls, in the age range of 4–5½ years. All the children were born in Israel, but their parents were born in the following countries: Israel, Yemen, Iraq, Syria, Persia, Libya, Morocco, Russia, Poland, Lithuania, Hungary, Rumania, Germany, Holland, Denmark, England, and the United States. The educational level of the families from the Arab countries and from Persia was generally very low (more than 50% of the parents were illiterate), and the atmosphere at home corresponded largely to the patriarchal habits of the Orient. The parents from Europe and the United States had had at least 6 years of schooling and, in many cases, had reached university level. The parents of 40 children lived in collective agricultural settlements (kibbutzim); all the others lived in larger or smaller towns located in most parts of the country. All but five children had elder or younger siblings.[1]

The interviewers were 25 kindergarten workers attending a postgraduate course of studies at the Psychological and Pedagogical Department of the Tel-Aviv University. They had been specially trained for the interviewing and were continuously supervised.

The interviews took place mainly in kindergartens and sometimes took the form of a question-and-answer game, but were always conducted in such a way that each child was interviewed separately and not in the presence or within hearing of the other children.

The questionnaire included 22 questions, some of them alternative questions. If a child mentioned that the baby was in the mother's belly before his birth, he could then be asked how the baby entered the belly or came out of it. But if none of his answers included any hint of pregnancy, the succeeding questions had to be skipped. The procedure of questioning enabled the child to talk freely, sometimes to digress from the theme, and even to express his fantasies, or 'to romance' in the sense given to this term by Piaget (1960, pp. 10ff.).

As a consequence, the children often offered material relevant for questions which had not yet been posed. Nevertheless, these questions were asked at the appropriate point. The formulation of each question was fixed, and no interviewer ever changed it. Apart from several alternative questions, the serial order was also fixed and allowed for no changes. In the case of 17 children who from the very beginning did not cooperate or manifested clear signs of anxiety, the questioning was interrupted early. These children are not included in our group of 185 subjects. All the answers and talk of the children during the interview were recorded in their entirety and used in the evaluation of the results.

Analysis of the results has shown that significant differences existed only between the answers of children from Western families and those of children from Oriental families but not between the answers of children classified according to the particular countries from which their parents came. Also, the results for children from collective settlements and from towns were fairly homogeneous. Accordingly, the only classifications preserved in the presentation of the material are those of sex and of Oriental or Western origin of the parents. Our group included 60 Western boys, 60 Western girls, 35 Oriental boys, and 30 Oriental girls.

Results and discussion

DIFFERENCES IN SEX

The question whose purpose was to provide information about the amount of knowledge children have about sexual differences and about their preparedness to talk of what they know was as follows: 'Where does the pipi come out?' And thereafter: 'How is it [for boys] with girls, [for girls] with boys?' (To Israeli children, 'pipi' means urine, as well as the sexual organs, and was used here in the sense of urine). We chose this somewhat indirect way of asking, since it is much more usual for children to talk about urinating than to discuss differences in sexual organs.

As can be seen from Table 1, Western children are better

Table 1. *Answers to the question: 'Where does the "pipi" come out?'*

Type of answers	Boys' replies (%)		Girls' replies (%)	
	Oriental	Western	Oriental	Western
From 'here' (points to place)	15	32	20	6
From the hole in the 'pipi'	55	45	40	41
From the behind	10	15	35	27
From the belly	—	6	5	16
Evasive answers	20	2	—	10

Table 2. *Answers to the question: 'How is it [for boys] with girls, [for girls] with boys?'*

Type of answers	Boys' replies (%)		Girls' replies (%)	
	Oriental	Western	Oriental	Western
Detailed description of sex organs of the other sex	40	77	45	80
From the behind	30	16	10	—
'It is different'	—	4	15	17
'There is no difference' (accompanied by description)	10	2	—	2
'I don't want to say'	10	—	5	—
'From the trousers when he stands'	—	—	15	—

informed about the location and function of their sexual organs than are Oriental children; and the boys in each group are better informed in this respect than are the girls in the respective groups. The latter result may stem from the fact that for a boy it is relatively easy to differentiate between the penis and the anus, while for a girl the similarity and nearness of vulva and anus may favor the formation of one unitary concept.

The results summarized in Table 2 are similar in that the information boys have about the sexual organs of girls is more exact than that which girls have about the sexual organs of boys. Here again, Western children seem to be better informed or more ready to communicate their knowledge frankly than are Oriental children. But the most important result in this domain is that the overwhelming majority of Western children, and more than half of the Oriental children, are able to give such exact information about the sexual organs of the other sex. This result clearly contradicts Freud's claim that boys of this age believe unconditionally in the universality of the penis and distort or ignore any observations which testify to the contrary. Only 2 per cent of Western boys and 10 per cent of Oriental boys knew of no differences between boys and girls, and only 1 per cent and 10 per cent respectively, abstained from answering at all.[2] Still more important is the fact that not even one boy hinted in any way, through any additional remark, that he considered the girl to be a castrated boy. Also, the answers and additional remarks of the girls do not justify any assumption in this direction.

Accordingly, we regard these results as a direct refutation of the Freudian thesis about the infantile belief in the universality of the penis. Whether Freud's claim was at least valid in regard to the children of his own time, or whether he was altogether mistaken because he had no empirical observations upon which he could rely, can no longer be decided unequivocally. We lean more to the second possibility. Though in Western families a remarkable liberalization has taken place in regard to sexual taboos in children's life – and this is in great part thanks to psychoanalysis – Oriental families (also those in Israel) have remained almost untouched by this development. Nevertheless, 40 per cent of the Oriental boys gave exact descriptions about girls, and not a single one of their answers hinted at the possibility that girls have lost their penises.

In addition to their theoretical importance, the results summarized in Tables 1 and 2 are methodologically important for the research as a whole in that they provide a kind of criterion for the sexual ingenuousness of the children. Since overall differences in sex are in general discussed more rarely and with greater inhibition than are pregnancy and birth, we may assume that the children will divulge their concepts concerning the origin of babies as readily as they did their knowledge about the differences in sexual organs.

CONCEPTS ABOUT THE CREATION AND BIRTH OF BABIES

In order to avoid the possibility of the interviewed children getting hints or information through questions which mention pregnancy directly, two introductory questions were used with the aim of finding out which of the children grasped the relation between the enlarged belly of the mother and the subsequent birth of the baby. The two questions were: 'How does a baby come into the world?' and – in case the answer related only to the hospital, doctor, etc. – 'Where was the baby before?' In their answers, 95 per cent of Western boys, 94 per cent of Western girls, 87 per cent of the Oriental boys, and 92 per cent of Oriental girls mentioned the enlarged belly of the mother. Accordingly, the subsequent questions which related directly to the mother's belly were posed only to 166 children (later mentioned as 'reduced experimental group').

The two questions, the answers to which were intended to provide information about infantile theories on the creation of babies, were as follows: 'What must the mother do in order to get a baby?' 'How is it that the baby is in the mother's belly?' The results are given in Tables 3 and 4. A summary of the children's answers, based upon the results of Tables 3 and 4, reveals the existence of several concepts about the origin of babies, among which three are particularly frequent, while the others find so little support that we shall not dwell upon them now. The commonest theory is that the baby is created in the mother's belly from the food which she eats. The fatness of the mother and the creation of the baby are grasped as identical. Accordingly, in order to get a baby, the mother must eat a lot, with the quantity of food counting much more than the quality.

With a somewhat lesser frequency appears the theory that the baby need not be created because it has always existed in the mother's belly and was already there when the mother was still a small girl. Some children add hereto that the baby was previously in the grandmother's belly, and one subject went so far as to claim that the baby was originally 'in the belly of our Mother Eva, that old one in Paradise. Then it was in the belly of her daughter, and then in the belly of her daughter's daughter', and so on 'until it came to the belly of its own mother'. The food which the mother eats also seems important to the supporters of this theory, not however because the baby is created out of it, but because it becomes bigger and grows through it. Accordingly, not the quantity but the quality of the food is stressed. Many children enumerate 'the good things' which mother must eat for the baby, for example, meat, milk, cream, eggs, much butter, etc.

In the third degree of frequency appears the theory that the mother must first swallow the baby in order to be able to bear it later. The supporters of this theory also stress that the mother must eat well in order to make the baby grow, but they mention neither special kinds of food nor big quantities in particular.

A comparison of these results with Piaget's claim reveals that precisely the artificialistic concept, to which Piaget attributes central importance in the domain of birth theories, does not appear here at

Table 3. *Answers to the question: 'What must the mother do in order to get a baby?'*

Type of answers	Boys' replies (%)		Girls's replies (%)	
	Oriental	Western	Oriental	Western
Eat much (stress put on fatness of the mother and a swollen belly)	—	72	50	15
Eat in order to feed the baby in her belly (stress put on kinds of food)	35	10	22	30
Swallow the baby through the mouth	40	5	5	—
Go to the hospital in order to give birth to the baby	15	2	23	17
Perform intercourse with the father	—	2	—	—
Various details of caring for the baby after birth	—	8	—	15
Various details of caring for herself during pregnancy	—	—	—	10
'Fantastic' theories	5	1	—	—
No answer	5	—	—	13

all. Neither do we find even the remotest hint at the belief that the parents construct the baby artificially. Also, what Piaget calls the 'pre-artificialistic' concept finds no direct expression but seems to form the conceptual basis of the third birth theory, for the baby must first exist independently of the parents in order to be swallowed by the mother later. Again, the answers which have been summed up by us to form the second theory (the baby has always been in the belly) are suggestive of the concept of immanence, although in a sense different from that of Piaget, for here the emphasis is upon a direct and bodily relation between mother and baby. Our results also lend indirect confirmation to Piaget's observation that the concept of immanence, which clearly precedes causal thought, belongs to a rather early developmental stage. While the first birth theory, which is based upon causal thinking, was advanced mostly by children of Western origin, the second and third theories were formulated most frequently by children of Oriental origin, who, as shown earlier, possess less sexual information than children of the former group.

Table 4. *Answers to the question: 'How is it that the baby is in the mother's belly?' (Answers of 'reduced experimental group')*

Type of answers	Boys' replies (%)		Girls' replies (%)	
	Oriental	Western	Oriental	Western
He is formed from the food mother eats	5	73	50	17
He was swallowed through the mouth	48	5	10	—
He entered through the sexual organ	—	5	—	2
He has always been in the belly	45	8	25	38
'Fantastic' theories	2	2	15	10
The belly was cut open and the baby put inside	—	7	—	10
No answer	—	—	—	23

Also, our findings lend only partial confirmation to the findings of Freud about infantile theories of the creation and birth of babies. But since, according to Freud, the children's starting point is not the creation but the birth of the baby through the anus, from which fact they conclude that it must have been created through the mouth, a comparison of our results with Freud's claims can only follow the presentation of the children's answers to questions which deal with the actual birth of the baby. The question posed to the subjects of the 'reduced experimental group' was: 'How does the baby come out of the mother's belly?' After the children answered this question, a series of further specific questions was posed to them with the aim of ascertaining whether the child thought it possible that the baby came out through the anus, the mouth, the navel, the sexual organ, or whether its exit necessitated the opening of the mother's belly. The children had to answer each of these questions with a 'yes' or a 'no' (see Tables 5 and 6). If the child mentioned, in the previous, spontaneously formulated, answer a possibility not enumerated here, this possibility was also offered him in order to examine the reliability of the answer.

The far-reaching correspondence between the results of these two tables is very surprising, but still more so is the content of the answers. The commonest answer is the one referring to the opening of the belly, which was given spontaneously by 52 per cent and was accepted as possible by 63 per cent. On the other hand, birth through the anus was mentioned spontaneously by only 2 per cent of the Western boys, that is, by 0.5 per cent of the whole experimental group, and was accepted as possible by only 5 per cent of the children, while 95 per cent declared such a form of birth to be impossible. This concept ranks last among the spontaneously offered solutions and is the last but one in rank among the forms of birth accepted as possible.

In view of these results, Freud's claim that the anal theory of birth is the commonest one is no longer tenable. His apparently very logical interpretation – that children conclude from the anal theory of birth that the creation of the baby is through the mouth, since the relation between food and stool is already known to them – is similarly refuted. However, the oral theory of creation, which Freud postulated but did not consider as important, is supported by our results, and even appears more frequently than any other theory (see Tables 3 and 4). In regard to both Freud's and Piaget's claims about infantile theories of the creation and birth of babies, our results lend support precisely to those points which did not seem important to these researchers, since they did not play a central role in the formation of their theories. But those claims which form the basis of the theory of Piaget and of the contradictory one of Freud in this problem have been refuted by our results.

THE TASK OF THE FATHER

From an anthropological viewpoint, the children's answers to the question: 'What should the father do in order to make a baby appear?' are of particular importance (see Table 7).

The predominant feature characterizing the results is that it seems

Table 5. *Answers to the question: 'How does the baby come out of the mother's belly?' (Answers of 'reduced experimental group')*

	Boys' replies (%)		Girls' replies (%)	
Type of answer	Oriental	Western	Oriental	Western
Through the belly which should be cut open	68	50	50	58
Through the sexual organ	—	2	—	12
Through the navel	8	6	5	8
Through the mouth	—	2	5	—
Through the anus	—	2	—	—
By its own will	4	10	15	5
He has to be born	18	18	10	10
'Fantastic' theories	—	—	10	5
No answer	—	—	5	7

Table 6. *Answers of reduced experimental group to a series of specific questions*

	Boys' replies (%)		Girls' replies (%)	
	Oriental	Western	Oriental	Western
Can the baby come out through the:				
Anus?				
Yes	4	3	5	8
No	96	97	95	92
Navel?				
Yes	24	6	35	21
No	76	94	65	79
Mouth?				
Yes	4	6	—	6
No	96	94	100	94
'Pipi'?				
Yes	4	8	—	33
No	96	92	100	67
Cut-open belly?				
Yes	75	50	85	47
No	25	50	15	51

difficult for the children to grasp any causal relation between the father, on the one hand, and the pregnancy and birth, on the other hand. Since in almost all the concepts we found that the nourishment of the mother plays an important role concerning the origin of babies, the most direct relation between the father and pregnancy follows from those answers which refer to food and eating. Summing up the answers of boys and girls from both cultural groups, we find that only 22 per cent of all the children believe that the father must

Table 7. *Answers to the question: 'What should the father do in order to make a baby appear?'*

Type of answer	Boys' replies (%)		Girls' replies (%)	
	Oriental	Western	Oriental	Western
Prepare food for the mother, to feed the mother	16	20	25	14
Take the baby out of the mother's belly in the hospital	—	1	—	—
Give the mother his semen	—	2	—	—
Eat himself in order to have a baby	1	—	10	2
Pray to God	—	—	5	—
Nothing	14	20	—	7
Earn money and help the mother after the baby has appeared (e.g., do all the household chores)	25	47	60	75
Behave nicely to the mother while she is in hospital	—	10	—	—
Persuade the mother to have a baby	—	—	—	2
Mentioning of various routine activities of the father which have nothing to do with the baby or the mother	44	—	—	—

give the mother something to eat, or even himself eat, in order to make a baby appear. However, the overwhelming majority of the answers refer to the father's task in the period after the birth of the baby: 75 per cent of the Western girls and 60 per cent of the Oriental girls, though only 47 per cent of the Western boys and as few as 25 per cent of the Oriental boys, consider the father's participation to consist in helping the mother after birth, for instance, in earning money for her, or in preventing the other children from making too much noise or from harassing her too much. There are more girls than boys, and there are more Western than Oriental children, who gave answers belonging to this category. Apparently, masculine help at home already finds more favor with small girls than with small boys. However, the reason for the fact that only 25 per cent of the Oriental boys mention direct help by the father after the birth of the baby becomes clear from another group of answers. Of the Oriental boys, 44 per cent, a percentage higher than that found in any other category of answers in this group, mention as the task of the father in the creation of babies activities which have nothing to do with the mother or with the household but which correspond to the usual habits and occupations of men in their environment, such as reading the newspaper, going for a walk, or beating the mother. The superior rank and the priority of men in the Orient are reflected most clearly in these answers. The fact that not even one Western boy gave an answer which belongs to this category allows us to assume that the birth of a baby probably influences the father's mode of life more markedly in a Western than in an Oriental milieu. But the fact, also, that no Oriental girl gave an answer which belongs to this category suggests the conclusion that infantile concept formation is conditioned not only by the family milieu but by one's own wishes too, which are also shaped by the sex to which one belongs, and that perhaps the germ of the future emancipation of the Oriental woman already exists in the concepts of the small girl.

GENERALIZATION AND SPECIFICATION

Since the questions mentioned until now about the role of the parents in the creation of the baby do not yet allow us to conclude whether the children referred in their answers to their own parents, to all parents, or to specific parents, we posed two further questions in this domain: 'Is it so with all parents?' and 'Have your parents also done the same thing(s)?' The first question was meant to yield information about the extent of generalization of the concept, while the second question referred to Freud's claim that the creation and birth theories of the children are not valid in most cases for their own parents. Since the answers of the children showed no significant differences between the sexes and between the cultural groups, the presentation of the results in the form of a table can be foregone in the interests of brevity. The answers to both questions reveal that 72 per cent of all the children hold their concept to be of all-inclusive general validity, that 20 per cent said that almost all parents did it in the specified manner, and that 8 per cent confessed they did not know. While 60 per cent declared their concept to be valid also for their own parents, 18 per cent said their own parents did it in a different manner (although they did not specify it), and 8 per cent gave answers suggestive of a sexual act. Another 14 per cent said they could not remember, they were not told, etc. Our results warrant the conclusion that the overwhelming majority of the

Table 8. *Answers to the question: 'What happens to the baby while it is in the belly of the mother?'*

Type of answer	Boys' replies (%)		Girls' replies (%)	
	Oriental	Western	Oriental	Western
He grows and develops	20	48	20	—
He eats (the food which the mother eats)	40	27	25	2
Description of various 'active' activities (e.g., he jumps, plays, kicks, punches)	—	25	—	4
He sleeps	25	—	25	10
Description of feelings and the miserable state of the baby (e.g., cries, trembles, is lonely, is afraid of the dark)	—	—	30	75
Nothing happens to him, and he does not do anything	10	—	—	9
Causes pains to the mother	5	—	—	—

children generalize their concept to include all pairs of parents, with more than 70 per cent of the children believing that their own parents did it like the other parents. Freud's claim, then, is adequate to describe only the beliefs of a small minority of children.

ACTIVITIES AND CONDITION OF THE FETUS

In order to learn more about the ideas of the child in regard to the fetus, we asked the subjects of our 'reduced experimental group': 'What happens to the baby while it is in the belly of the mother?'

This question allows almost unrestricted free play to the child's fantasy. Nevertheless, as can be seen from Table 8, the Western and

Oriental boys as well as the Oriental girls prefer most clearly those categories of answers which refer to the growth and nourishment of the baby. It seems warranted to conclude that the children who gave such answers have grasped a logically correct causal relation between their theories about the origin of the baby and its fetal fate. An interesting exception is provided, however, by the Western girls. Of this group, 75 per cent claimed that the baby in the belly suffers, and they gave very detailed and impressive descriptions of the fetal suffering. In the group of Oriental girls this category appears only in the second rank of frequency (30%), and the descriptions are by no means so drastic. Since not even one boy gave an answer which hinted in any way at a similar representation, it seems we have encountered here a specifically womanly concept, which is related more to the Western than to the Oriental cultural atmosphere. Since most children are well aware of the fact that they themselves were once in the mother's belly, it may well be that the idea that life begins with a period of suffering is apt basically to influence the character and formation of the neurosis of the European woman.

Of anthropological interest is the fact that 25 per cent of the Oriental boys and girls, but only 10 per cent of the Western girls, and not a single one of the Western boys consider the baby as spending a great part of the time in sleep. This fact lends increased significance to the results we obtained in the framework of a yet unpublished research on the self concept of children and which revealed that Western children also describe themselves in much more active and dynamic terms than do Oriental children.

Discussion

A survey of our results shows that the sexual concepts of the children deviate in essential points from the concepts ascribed to them by Freud and Piaget. Freud's theory about the infantile belief in the universality of the penis was refuted directly by our results. The argument frequently mentioned in discussions about psychoanalytic theses – that the methods of the questionnaire or the interview are unfit for the examination of such theses, since they do not reveal repressed material – cannot be raised here. For, according to Freud, children express directly the belief that women also have a penis and are fully aware of it, while they tend to repress or to distort eventually perceived sexual differences. Since our young subjects were well informed about sexual differences and talked about them freely but gave no direct or indirect hint about the Freudian 'pan-penisism', this psychoanalytic hypothesis no longer can be upheld. Accordingly, another theoretical basis would have to be found for the castration complex, which is very often explained precisely through this hypothesis.

Furthermore, our results yield no support for the Freudian claim that children uphold the theory of birth through the anus and only very meager support to the claim that children hold that their own parents have created babies in a manner different from that of other parents. However, we have found confirmation for Freud's theory about the creation of babies in an oral manner.

In regard to Piaget, it is noteworthy that his theory about the artificialistic concept, to which he ascribes great importance, was in no way confirmed, while his claim that children believe in the independent pre-existence of babies and that this belief is more primary and primitive corresponds in general with our results.

Summing up, our results – regardless of Freud and Piaget – reveal that children between 4 and 6 years of age are well informed about sexual differences and speak freely about what they know. They explain the creation of babies by the eating of particular types of food, through the swallowing of a ready-made baby, or through the immanent existence of the baby in the mother's belly. The function of the father consists, according to them, mainly in helping the mother. The fetus is envisaged as sleeping, playing, or suffering; birth is explained mostly through the concept of opening the belly.

The conclusions and implications of these results are far too rich to allow for their comprehensive clarification within the framework of this article. We will, therefore, restrict ourselves to some brief remarks. Of great importance to psychopathology is the question of how far children in the age range of 4–6 years are able to form adequate sexual concepts. As a conclusion from our results, it can no longer be claimed that insufficient causal thinking (Piaget) or infantile libidinal development (Freud) hinder the adequate sexual enlightenment of the children. Therefore, there is no reason to encourage children in forming 'infantile' sexual concepts through offering them false or defective information. The pathogenetic danger concommitant upon some of these concepts becomes evident when we remember that the infantile concepts are generally not corrected through knowledge acquired later but are merely covered up by it. For instance, the infantile concept of birth through the opening of the belly may possibly lie at the core of the neurotic anxiety of pregnancy, or the concept of creating the baby through the mouth may underlie complaints about indigestion, etc.

Also of social-psychological importance are our results about the infantile ideas concerning the role of the father in the creation of babies. Through the almost exclusive stress on the role of the mother in all the concepts of creation and birth, the conceptual foundations for an intensive relation between mother and baby are already established a priori. The participation of the father, however, is mostly seen only in the form of social help. It should not surprise us, therefore, that it takes adult men and women so long to understand that the role of the father is far from being fulfilled by the earning of money. Accordingly, we may assume that a modification of the infantile father concept should prove contributive to the later problem of coming to terms with the real father role.

Although we have not examined the modifiability of infantile sexual concepts directly, our results also yield some hints about this problem. From the fact that we not only found differences in concepts between Western and Oriental children but have also observed time and time again how, for instance, the typical life habits of the Oriental families are reflected in the concepts of the Oriental children, we may conclude with a high degree of probability that infantile concepts may be changed, at least up to a certain degree, through changes in the milieu of the home in which the child lives. Therefore, it does not seem to us over-optimistic to hope that psychic and social adjustment may be facilitated through planned influence intended to shape the concept formation of children.

NOTES

1 From here on, children of European and American ancestry will be referred to as 'Western children' and those of North-African and Asian ancestry as 'Oriental children'.

2 All percentages in the text and tables are rounded off.

REFERENCES

Freud, S., 'On the sexual theories of children' (1908), in J. Strachey (ed.), *The standard edition of the complete works of Sigmund Freud,* vol. 9 (London: Hogarth, 1959), pp. 205–27.

Piaget, J., *The child's conception of the world* (Paterson, N. J.: Littlefield, 1960).

Rank, O. 'Voelkerpsychologische Parallelen zu den infantilen Sexualtheorien' (1912), in *Psychoanalytische Beitraege zur Mythenforschung aus den Jahren 1912 bis 1914* (Leipzig: Internationaler Psychoanalytischer Verlag, 1922), pp. 43–81.

10 Sexuality and Sexual Learning in Childhood

JAMES ELIAS and PAUL GEBHARD

The turn of the century saw an awakening interest in sexuality and sexual learning among children. The most significant work of this period was Freud's theory of infantile sexuality, which directed the attention of the world to sexuality in early childhood and its importance for the future adult role. A somewhat neglected work, by Moll (1909), was overshadowed by the Freudian wave; but Moll's observations on the sexual life of the child were the first comprehensive writings done in this field. In an earlier study, Bell (1902) examined childhood sexuality through the study of the activities of children.

RESEARCH SINCE 1917

Numerous studies resulted from this increased interest in childhood sexuality. Among them were Blanton (1917), looking at the behavior of the human infant during the first 30 days of life; Hattendorf (1932), dealing with the questions most frequently asked by pre-school children; Isaacs (1933), studying the social development of young children; Dudycha (1933), examining recall of pre-school experiences; and Campbell (1939), writing on the social-sexual development of children. Conn (1940*a*, 1940*b*, 1947, 1948) has done a series of studies dealing with various phases of sexual awareness and sexual curiosity in children. Other important studies were made by Halverson (1940), on penile erection in male infants; Conn and Kanner (1947), on children's awareness of physical sex differences; Katcher (1955), on the discrimination of sex differences by young children; and Ramsey (1950), on pre-adolescent and adolescent boys. Sears, Maccoby, and Levin (1957) present a discussion of labeling and parental sanctioning of sex behavior, and

James Elias and Paul Gebhard, 'Sexuality and sexual learning in childhood', *Phi Delta Kappan*, vol. L, no. 7 (March 1969), pp. 401–5.

James Elias and Paul Gebhard

Bandura and Walters (1959) examine parental response to sex information questions.[1]

Current research has tended to move away from direct studies of infant and childhood sexual behavior. Sexuality has its roots in man's biological make-up, and the development of gender role or sex differences has become one of the main focuses of present research.[2] Since the molding forces, or socializing agents, are the family and the peer group (among others), sexuality is being pursued as a form of social development. Receiving special emphasis are the development of the male and female role – for example, the part aggression plays in developing an aggressive adult male sexual role and the concomitant emphasis on non-aggressiveness in the development of an adequate female role. Other areas of current research are found in the work of John Money and Joan and John Hampson, on the ontogeny of human sexual behavior.[3]

THE KINSEY DATA

The discussion utilizes previously unpublished data from the Institute for Sex Research, taken from case histories of pre-pubescents interviewed by Alfred Kinsey and his co-workers. These histories are somewhat outdated (before 1955), but the information contained in them provides one of the few sources of actual interview information on pre-pubescent children. Questions were asked regarding sources of sexual knowledge, extent of knowledge, homosexual and heterosexual pre-pubertal play, and masturbatory activity, all of crucial importance for any educator, counselor, doctor, or other professional who deals with children. Some of the critical problems encountered in preschool counseling find their source in the sexual area. Educators recognize that differences between males and females, ethnic groups, and socioeconomic status groups is essential for an understanding of the attitudinal and behavioral patterns that children exhibit. Adequate sexual adjustment in early childhood is a prime factor in later adult sexual adjustment, as healthy attitudes toward self and sexuality are the foundations of adult adjustment.

Partly through necessity, many school systems are presently moving into education programs with a maximum of speed and often a minimum of preparation regarding the specific needs of the population the particular program is to serve. Sex research can offer some aid to the educational community by providing information

144

about critical factors in the lives of children and how these factors affect later adjustment.

THE SAMPLE

The sample consists of 432 pre-pubescent white boys and girls ranging in age from four to 14.[4] There are 305 boys and 127 girls in the study, and they are grouped by occupational class (social class) and age.[5] The occupational classifications originally used in the work at the Institute for Sex Research have been combined in order to increase the number of cases and to provide social-class categories. The occupational classifications consist of: (1) unskilled workers who are labeled as lower blue-collar, (2) semi-skilled and skilled workers who comprise the upper blue-collar, (3) lower white-collar workers, and (4) business and professional men, here termed upper white-collar. A mean age is given for the children in each social class to make explicit the unequal age distribution.

The sexual behavior of younger children often lacks the erotic intent attributed to similar adult activities, raising the question, in some cases, of the validity of labeling some childhood activities as sexual. This research does not label childhood behavior as sexual unless it includes one of the following: the self-manipulation of genitalia, the exhibition of genitalia, or the manual or oral exploration of the genitalia of or by other children. Of course, many of these activities could be motivated by mere curiosity concerning a playmate's anatomy.

The term 'sex play' as used here includes those heterosexual and homosexual activities involving more than one person which occur before the onset of puberty. Among the males, 52 per cent report homosexual pre-pubertal activity and 34 per cent report heterosexual pre-pubertal activity. These percentages seem accurate when we compare them with the self-reports of adults in the earlier Kinsey volumes. Adult males recalled homosexual experience in their pre-adolescent period in 48 per cent of the cases, just four per cent less than is reported by these children in their pre-adolescence.[6] The adult males also indicated that heterosexual pre-adolescent activity occurred in approximately 40 per cent of the cases, but the reports of the children indicate only about 34 per cent of pre-pubescent males engage in heterosexual experiences. However, many of the children in this study have not reached the average age at which these experiences first occur. The average age among males for homosexual play is 9·2 years and for heterosexual play, 8·8 years.

Among female children, 35 per cent report homosexual pre-pubertal sexual activity and 37 per cent report heterosexual pre-pubertal experiences. The incidence of homosexual activity in the females is much less than that reported by males, but is very close to the percentage recalled by adult females in the 1953 Kinsey volume (33 per cent). The adult females recalled heterosexual pre-adolescent activities in 30 per cent of the cases, and the reports of the children show 37 per cent with such experience.

One of the noteworthy findings coming from this analysis of the case histories of pre-adolescents is the surprising agreement between pre-pubertal report and adult recall. Another important finding is the lack of any consistent correlation between socio-sexual activity and parental occupational class. The percentages do vary, but in no meaningful way.

MASTURBATION

Masturbation is most often described as self-stimulation leading to sexual arousal and usually to climax or orgasm, accompanied (after puberty) by ejaculation on the part of the male. Some writers prefer to believe that pre-pubertal children do not masturbate but simply fondle their genitals. These present data concerning pre-pubertal masturbation are not derived from reported 'fondling of the genitals' but rather from deliberate activity done for pleasure and often accompanied by pelvic thrusts against an object (e.g., a bed) or manual manipulation. Sometimes a state of relaxation or satisfaction comparable to the post-orgasmic state is achieved; in other instances indisputable orgasm occurs.

More males than females masturbate in childhood, as is the case later in adolescence and adulthood. Among pre-pubescent males, 56 per cent report masturbatory activity, while only 30 per cent of the females do so. In comparison, information received from adults in self-reports indicates pre-adolescent masturbation in 57 per cent of the cases. These actual childhood reports are within one percentage point of the recall data from adults as reported in the earlier works.

Looking at age groupings and social class, one finds that the blue-collar classes contain the highest percentages of boys who have masturbated – 60–70 per cent. The majority of those in the blue-collar and lower white-collar classes who masturbate are in the 8-10-

year age group. The upper white-collar class has the lowest percentage of those who have masturbated (38 per cent), with more beginning in the 3-7-year age group than at any subsequent time. The mean age for first masturbation is as follows: Lower blue-collar, 8·6; upper blue-collar, 8·8; lower white-collar, 7·8; and upper white-collar, 6·0. The probable explanation for the lower mean age, lower percentage of those who have masturbated, and lower average age at first masturbation for upper white-collar boys is the fact that their average age of interview is 7·2 years, while the average ages for the boys of other social classes are two to four years older.

Fewer girls tend to masturbate than boys, and only 30 per cent of the girls report that they have masturbated. The highest percentage is among the lower blue-collar females (48 per cent); the other three classes have lower and quite similar figures (between 25 and 29 per cent). The average age of masturbation for girls is lower than that of the boys. By class, it is: lower blue-collar, 7·5; upper blue-collar, 7·4; lower white-collar, 5·7; and upper white-collar, 6·7.

Masturbation has been designated in the past as the prime cause of mental illness, low morals, stunted growth, among other things. These stigmas are the most part behind us, but tradition dies slowly and many children are still being told 'old wives' tales' concerning the alleged effects of masturbation. This is unfortunate for in early childhood masturbation might influence the child to accept his body as pleasureful rather than reject it as a source of anxiety. Society has progressed to a point where few parents punish their offspring for masturbating, but it is noteworthy that fewer still encourage it.

SEXUAL KNOWLEDGE

In this study, additional measures are taken of current knowledge while controlling for child's age and occupation of father. The occupational level is dichotomized into lower (blue-collar) and upper (white-collar) classes for purposes of analysis. Presence or absence of knowledge about the following topics is examined: intercourse, pregnancy, fertilization, menstruation, venereal disease, abortion, condoms, and female prostitution. In general, the white-collar class surpasses the blue-collar class in all sex knowledge categories. Of special interest to the educator are some of the differences in learning which occur on the part of the children in these two groups. For example, while 96 per cent of the blue-collar boys have an understanding of sexual intercourse by ages 13-14,

147

only four per cent have any knowledge concerning the 'coming together of the sperm and the egg' – fertilization. Twenty-seven per cent of the upper white-collar group in the same age range understand the concept of fertilization, and this nearly seven-fold difference is indicative of the language level and sources (hence quality) of information for the two groups. Blue-collar boys learn about intercourse, abortion, condoms, and prostitution earlier than do other males, especially by age 8-10. These words and activities become a part of the sex education of lower-class boys much earlier than of the boys whose fathers are employed in higher-status occupations, as a result of most sex information being provided by peers on the street.

This earlier and more extensive knowledge of coitus is reflected in pre-pubescent heterosexual activity, wherein nearly three times as many blue-collar boys have, or attempt, coitus than do white-collar boys. Interestingly enough, more blue-collar males know of intercourse than know of pregnancy (except in the 4-7-year-old group) and just the reverse is true for the white-collar males. The white-collar male surpasses the blue-collar male in sexual knowledge in later age groupings, perhaps indicating that many of the more formal aspects of his sex education come from his mother, with peers 'filling in the gaps' concerning some of the more sensitive areas, such as methods of birth-control and prostitution.

The pattern for girls stands in marked contrast to that for boys. Pre-pubescent girls, unlike boys, are not inclined to discuss or joke about sexual matters. Also, the girl eavesdropping on conversation by adult females is less apt to hear of such matters than is the boy listening to adult males. Lastly, there is reason to believe that the lower-class mother is more inhibited about, and less capable of, imparting sex education to her daughter. Consequently, the lower-class girl generally lags behind her upper-class counterpart in sexual information.

Thus, for example, in age group 8-10, not quite half of the lower-class girls know of coitus, whereas close to three-quarters of the upper-class females have this knowledge. This gap is found even with regard to menstruation, a thing sufficiently removed from overt sexual behavior that one would expect it to escape from taboo. On the contrary, at lower social levels, menstruation is often regarded as dirty and somehow shameful. The result is that among the 8-10-year-olds roughly a quarter of the lower-class and nearly three-quarters of the upper-class girls possess this inevitable knowledge.

On more technical matters the lower-class girls are equally or even more disadvantaged. For example, none of them grasp the concept of fertilization: the idea that pregnancy is the result of the fusion of an egg and a sperm.

Among upper-class girls from age group 8-10 on, the knowledge of pregnancy is universal, whereas many of their lower-class counterparts are unaware of where babies come from. Indeed, in age groups 8-10 and 11-12, more lower-class girls know of coitus than of pregnancy. This situation, so incongruous to an upper-class reader, is explicable. Thanks to their contact, both physical and verbal, with lower-class boys (a substantial number of whom have attempted coitus), more lower-class girls hear of or experience coitus than hear of pregnancy. Note that while a boy may attempt to persuade a girl to have coitus, it is most improbable that he will defeat his aim by informing her of the consequence.

Lastly, the differences in knowledge between upper- and lower-class girls hinge to some considerable extent on literacy and on communication with parents. The upper-class girl, more prone to reading, and in a milieu where books and magazines with sexual content are available in the home, will educate herself or ask her parents to explain what she has read. The upper-class parent, having been told by innumerable magazine articles and books on child-rearing of the desirability of sex education, is far more likely to impart information than is the less knowledgeable and more inhibited lower-class parent. This statement will be substantiated in the following section on sources of sexual knowledge.

SOURCES OF SEXUAL KNOWLEDGE

By looking at the sources of sexual learning for children, one can see the origin of sexual 'slang' terms and sexual misinformation frequently unacceptable to the middle-class teacher. Though a large portion of this mislabeled and often incorrect information is the product of children's 'pooled ignorance', the problem is only confounded by adult non-communication.

The main source of sex education for most boys is the peer group – friends and classmates. Nevertheless there are important differences, depending on the child's social class (measured here as father's occupation). The peer group is overwhelmingly important as a source of information for all the boys from blue-collar homes:

From 75 per cent to 88 per cent of them report other boys as their major source. The boys of lower white-collar homes seem a transitional group, with 70 per cent so reporting, while the boys whose fathers are lower white-collar men find their mothers as important as their peers with respect to information. The boys from upper white-collar homes derive little from their peers, most from their mothers, and a relatively large amount from combined educational efforts by both parents. These figures are in striking contrast to those of the blue-collar boys: only eight per cent cite peers as the main source, 48 per cent report the mother, and 24 per cent both parents. This inverse relationship between parental occupation and the importance of peers as an informational source is one of the major, though anticipated, findings of this study. As the occupational level of the home increases, the child's mother plays a growing role in the sex education of her son, rising to nearly half of the cases for males whose fathers are upper white-collar men. For all occupational levels, the father seems to play a marginal role as a source of sex information for boys, and when he does play a role in his boy's sex education, it is mainly when both parents act as a team. While we can only speculate on the basis of our data, the mother is probably the 'prime mover' of the parental educating team. Other sources as major channels of information (e.g., siblings, other relatives, simple observation, etc.) are statistically unimportant, never exceeding four per cent.

Some children report that their sources of information are so evenly balanced that they cannot name one as the major source. Boys reporting this situation are more common (20 per cent) in homes of lower blue-collar fathers. The percentages tend to decrease progressively as parental occupational status increases, but this trend is unexpectedly reversed by the boys from upper white-collar homes. This reversal is probably not the result of small sample vagary, since the same phenomenon is to be seen among girls. No explanation is presently known.

TEACHER UNIMPORTANT AS SOURCE

It is interesting to note that the teacher is not mentioned by any of the children as the main source of sex education. In fact, throughout the study the contribution of the teacher and the school system to the child's information about sex is too low to be statistically significant. However, with the current proliferation of formal sex education programs in some of our nation's school systems, the role of the teacher and the school has no doubt increased in importance since the time these interviews were conducted, before 1955.

When looking at the main source of sex knowledge for girls, we see similar trends. Peers provide the main source of sex information for 35 per cent of the girls whose fathers are lower blue-collar men and for 25 per cent of the girls whose fathers are upper blue-collar workers. By contrast, only nine per cent and four per cent, respectively, of the girls whose fathers are white-collar men report the peer group as their main source of sex education. The mother's importance as a source of sex education increases with increased occupational status, being the major source for 10 per cent of the daughters of lower blue-collar workers and up to 75 per cent of those whose fathers are upper white-collar men.

For girls, fathers provide very little sex education, and then only as a member of a father-mother combination. It is interesting to observe that significantly more girls than boys report no main source of sex education, especially those girls from homes in which the father has a lower-status occupation. For example, 45 per cent of the daughters of lower blue-collar workers report no main source of sex education, as compared to 20 per cent of the boys whose fathers are at this occupational level. Other possible informational sources, such as siblings and printed material, are inconsequential.

NUDITY

The general level of permissiveness regarding nudity in the home, a sex-related phenomenon, also varies in relation to the occupational level of the family. As a rule, boys are allowed more nudity than girls, except in homes where nudity is a common practice – in which case the girls report a higher incidence of nudity. Differences between occupational groups are great, with 87 per cent of the lower blue-collar workers never allowing nudity among their sons, as compared to only 28 per cent of upper white-collar men. Again for boys, 40 per cent who come from upper white-collar families report nudity as very common, compared to only three per cent whose fathers are lower blue-collar workers. Among girls, we find the same patterns emerging, with 44 per cent of the girls from upper white-collar families reporting nudity as very common, and none of the girls from lower blue-collar families reporting nudity as usual in the home. Thus nudity in the lower-class home is more the exception than the rule for both girls and boys; in the upper-class home almost the reverse is true. This upper-class permissiveness regarding a sex-related behavior, nudity, fits nicely with our finding that upper-class parents communicate more freely on sexual matters with their offspring.

IMPLICATIONS FOR EDUCATION

The main implication of the reported data for those in the field of education is the need for educators to be aware of the differences in information and experience which exist between boys and girls, between different occupational and socioeconomic groups (and though not treated in this article) the differences which may occur between ethnic groups. An apparent problem regarding these differences, still evident in much of our educational system today, is an often inflexible adherence to the 'middle-class yardstick'.

The sexual experiences and the sexual vocabulary of the heterogeneous student population, especially the pupil who has not come from the same socioeconomic, occupational, or ethnic background as his teacher, create definite problems in expectations, understanding, and communication between teacher and pupil. An adequate knowledge of the sources of sex education, types of experiences, and the vocabulary and attitudes of these students will enable the teacher to gain a wider understanding of some of the problems of pupils regarding sexual matters and to modify his or her teaching accordingly.

Counseling the child in the school system raises some of the same problems encountered by the classroom teacher in an even more intense, personal situation. The counselor should have some idea of differences in pre-adolescent sexual activities and knowledge, enabling him to aid the child and his parents more intelligently as they deal with questions and problems of sexuality. If the average age for pre-adolescent homosexual experiences, for instance, is around nine years, this activity should be recognized as possibly a part of normal sexual development rather than as a sexual aberration. There is great danger of confusing activities accompanying normal sexual development with pathological behavior.

It is also apparent from the data presented here that many lower-class children will probably experience problems in learning and adjustment because of the lack of accurate information from informed sources. Neither the teacher nor the parent will completely replace peer-group influence in the process of providing sexual information, especially in the lower class, but the educator has the opportunity to provide programs to meet the needs of children otherwise inadequately prepared to cope with sexuality because of restraints imposed by social-class position. Therefore education should continue to initiate programs which will help fill this void created either by peer misinformation or by similar misunderstanding and reluctance on the part of parents.

NOTES

1 Sigmund Freud, 'Three essays on sexuality', *Standard Edition of the Complete Psychological Works*, pp. 135–245 (London: Hogarth, 1953); Albert Moll, *The Sexual Life of the Child* (New York: Macmillan, 1923) (originally published in German in 1909); S. Bell, 'A preliminary study of the emotion of love between the sexes', *American Journal of Psychology* (1902), pp. 325-54; M. G. Blanton, 'The behavior of the human infant during the first thirty days of life', *Psychological Review* (1917), pp. 956-83; K. W. Hattendorf, 'A study of the questions of young children concerning sex: a phase of an experimental approach to parent education', *Journal of Social Psychology* (1932), pp. 37-65; S. Isaacs, *Social Development of Young Children: A Study of Beginnings* (London: George Routledge and Sons, 1933); G. J. and M. M. Dudycha, 'Adolescent memories of preschool experiences', *Pedagogical Seminar and Journal of Genetic Psychology* (1933), pp. 463-80; E. H. Campbell, 'The social-sex development of children', *Genetic Psychology Monographs* (1939), p. 4; J. H. Conn, 'Children's awareness of the origin of babies', *Journal of Child Psychiatry* (1948), pp. 140-76. 'Children's reactions to the discovery of genital differences', *American Journal of Orthopsychiatry* (1940a), pp. 747-54; 'Sexual curiosity of children', *American Journal of Diseases of Children* (1940b), pp. 1110-19; J. H. Conn and Leo Kanner, 'Children's awareness of sex differences', *Journal of Child Psychiatry* (1947), pp. 3-57; H. M. Halverson, 'Genital and Spincter behaviour of the male infant', *Journal of Genetic Psychology* (1940), pp. 95-136; A. Katcher 'The discrimination of sex differences by young children', *Journal of Genetic Psychology* (1955), pp. 131-43; C. V. Ramsey, *Factors in the Sex Life of 291 Boys* (Madison, N.J.: Published by the author, 1950); R. Sears, E. Maccoby, and H. Levin, *Patterns of Child Rearing* (Evanston, Ill.: Row, Peterson, 1957); A. Bandura and R. Walters, *Adolescent Aggression* (New York: Ronald Press, 1959).

2 R. Sears, 'Development of gender role', in Beach (ed.), *Sex and Behavior* (New York: John Wiley and Son, 1965); E. Maccoby (ed.), *The Development of Sex Differences* (Stanford, Calif.: Stanford University Press, 1966).

3 J. Money, J. Hampson, and J. L. Hampson, 'Hermaphroditism: recommendations concerning assignment of sex, change of sex, and psychologic management', *Bulletin of Johns Hopkins Hospital* (1955a), pp. 284-300; 'An examination of some basic sexual concepts: the evidence of human hermaphroditism', *Bulletin of Johns Hopkins Hospital* (1955b) pp. 301-19.

James Elias and Paul Gebhard

4 The following table presents the number of boys or girls in each category (N) and the mean age of that category:

		Males		Females	
		N	Mean age	N	Mean age
Blue-collar	Lower	59	11·2	21	9·5
	Upper	79	11·5	17	10·1
White-collar	Lower	115	9·9	53	6·9
	Upper	37	7·2	35	6·6

5 The blue-collar—white-collar distinction provides an excellent indication of social level *vis-à-vis* the occupational level. The association between occupation and education (used in the original Kinsey publications) is very close. See p. 328, *Sexual Behavior in the Human Male* (Philadelphia, Pa.: Sanders, 1948).

6 A. Kinsey, W. Pomeroy, and C. Martin, *Sexual Behavior in the Human Male* (Philadelphia, Pa.: Sanders, 1948), p. 168.

11 A Survey of Sexual Knowledge and Attitudes in Borehamwood

G. D. RIPLEY, C. BURNS and V. A. DICKINSON

This survey set out to ascertain parental attitudes towards the provision of sex education for their children at school, comparing this with the sexual knowledge shown by the children. Information was also sought as to the attitudes shown to the anxieties to be faced at adolescence by the children and by their parents concerning their children. An attempt was made to relate the children's knowledge ratings with parental attitudes and such factors as type of school and social class. Additionally, the attitudes of their teachers were inquired into.

THE SAMPLE

The survey was carried out in Borehamwood, Hertfordshire: a town of some thirty-five thousand persons twenty miles (32 km) from Central London, with a predominantly working-class and artisan population (socio-economic groups III and IV). Borehamwood has five secondary schools, of which, at the time of the Survey, one was a grammar school. Parents of all the first- and fourth-year pupils at these schools were asked if they would object to their children taking part in a survey of sexual knowledge, and the children of non-objectors were included in the survey.

METHOD

Children's questionnaire. Multiple-choice questions were used with the exception of an open-ended question regarding the children's anxieties. A basic questionnaire was used for the first year of secondary school (aged 11 to 12), with three additional questions for fourth-year pupils (aged 14 to 15). The questionnaire had been tested on a group of 60 children in another district.

G. D. Ripley, C. Burns and V. A. Dickinson, 'A survey of sexual knowledge and attitudes in Borehamwood', *The Practitioner*, vol. 207 (September 1971), pp. 351–60.

Parental questionnaire. This consisted of three multiple-choice questions and two open-ended questions designed to elicit the extent of agreement between the two parents and parental anxieties, respectively. The distribution of the parental questionnaire was delayed until any home discussion of the children's questionnaire was likely to have died down.

Confidentiality. No names appeared on the children's papers and both children and parents were informed that the answers would be treated in complete confidence but, by means of appropriate index marks, it was possible to match children with the parental replies.

RESPONSE

Parental permission. Of a total 881 parental permissions requested, only 20 (2·3 per cent) refused permission for their children to be questioned.

Children's questionnaires. Ninety-five children were absent from school on the day of the paper (there had been no prior notice as to the date), leaving 838 children who completed the questionnaire.

Parental questionnaires. 779 were sent out initially and 325 (41·7 per cent) were returned. Reminders were sent out to the non-returners after three weeks and a further 172 (22·1 per cent) were returned, with a further 82 (10·5 per cent) on the second reminder a month later. Over-all, 579 (74·3 per cent) were returned, four of these being blank.

Teachers' questionnaires. Returns from teachers were insufficient in number to be significant – except by their absence!

RESULTS FOR CHILDREN'S QUESTIONNAIRE

The age/sex distribution of children is given in Table 1.

The multiple-choice questions were answered as shown in Table 2, from which it is noticeable that questions 1, 3, 4, 5 and 11 produced no difficulty for fourth-year pupils, so that all but a very small handful knew the basic 'facts of life' by the age of fourteen or fifteen.

Question 2: The testicles produce? Only just over a third of 11- to 12-year-olds were able to select the correct answer to this question, and almost a quarter of the older children were unable to do so. Over a third of the younger children and 10 per cent of the older ones stated that they did not understand the question. Twice as many girls as boys admitted to not understanding the question, while 17 per cent of the boys, as opposed to 10 per cent of the girls, gave wrong answers. The adolescent male is evidently less willing to admit ignorance even anonymously. It is interesting that in the younger age-group almost half the girls gave the correct answer, while slightly under one-third of the boys were able to do so.

Question 6: Venereal disease (V.D.) is caught? Like question 2 this question was better answered by the older age-groups. A high proportion (a third) of the younger children stated either that they did not know or did not understand the question, whilst only 3·5 per cent of the older ones did so. It is perhaps disturbing that just over 10 per cent of 14- to 15-year-olds were evidently ignorant of the nature of venereal disease.

Table 1. *Age-sex distribution of children*

Age-group	Boys	Girls	Total
1st year	221	187	408
4th year	214	216	430
Total	435	403	838

Question 7: Menstruation (the monthly period) is? This question discriminated strongly both between the age-groups and between the sexes, the girls being better informed than the boys. This was particularly striking in the younger age-group where two-thirds of the girls and one-third of the boys answered correctly. Even in the older group the difference was well marked, with 97 per cent of the girls as compared with only 80 per cent of the boys giving the right answer.

Question 8: Masturbation. Almost half the younger children and over a quarter of the older ones answered either that they did not know the answer or did not understand the question. As regards the two sexes, a substantially greater proportion of boys than girls answered correctly.

Question 9: (4th year only) *Birth control.* Three-quarters of the children gave the correct answer to this question. A rather surprising 25 per cent of the boys and 19 per cent of the girls believed that only women could use birth-control methods.

Question 10: (4th year only). *Is it possible for a woman to become pregnant without the man's penis fully entering her?* Only 50 per cent of the girls answered this question correctly, 12 per cent

Table 2. *Number of children responding as shown to multiple-choice questions*

Paraphrase of question	Response	1st year		4th year	
		Boys	Girls	Boys	Girls
		No. (%)	No. (%)	No. (%)	No. (%)
(1) Babies come from the mother's womb	Right	152 (68)	168 (90)	207 (97)	214 (99)
	Wrong	62 (29)	14 (7)	5 (2)	2 (1)
	Don't know	7 (3)	5 (3)	2 (1)	—(—)
(2) Testicles produce semen	Right	70 (32)	80 (43)	165 (77)	161 (75)
	Wrong	63 (29)	40 (21)	37 (17)	24 (10)
	Don't know	84 (40)	67 (36)	12 (6)	31 (14)
(3) Gestation period is nine months	Right	167 (76)	161 (86)	210 (98)	216 (100)
	Wrong	38 (17)	13 (7)	2 (1)	—(—)
	Don't know	16 (7)	13 (7)	2 (1)	—(—)
(4) Women have breasts to feed babies	Right	198 (90)	176 (94)	213 (100)	214 (99)
	Wrong	9 (4)	7 (4)	—(—)	1 (—)
	Don't know	14 (6)	4 (2)	1 (—)	1 (—)
(5) Intercourse is necessary in order to have a baby	Right	202 (91)	181 (97)	213 (100)	216 (100)
	Wrong	1 (—)	2 (1)	—(—)	—(—)
	Don't know	18 (8)	4 (2)	—(—)	—(—)
(6) V.D. caught through intercourse	Right	87 (39)	88 (47)	186 (87)	198 (92)
	Wrong	59 (27)	30 (16)	19 (9)	12 (6)
	Don't know	75 (34)	69 (37)	9 (4)	6 (3)
(7) Menstruation is the cast-off lining of the womb	Right	71 (32)	119 (64)	172 (80)	209 (97)
	Wrong	76 (34)	51 (27)	30 (14)	5 (2)
	Don't know	74 (33)	17 (9)	12 (6)	2 (1)
(8) Masturbation in most cases does no harm	Right	77 (35)	49 (26)	164 (77)	106 (49)
	Wrong	56 (25)	26 (14)	22 (10)	21 (10)
	Don't know	88 (40)	112 (60)	28 (13)	89 (41)
(9) Contraception available for both sexes	Right			151 (71)	166 (77)
	Wrong			58 (27)	45 (21)
	Don't know			5 (2)	5 (2)
(10) Pregnancy possible through incomplete intercourse	Right			133 (62)	108 (50)
	Wrong			65 (30)	81 (38)
	Don't know			16 (7)	27 (13)
(11) In intercourse penis is placed in the vagina	Right			210 (98)	210 (97)
	Wrong			1 (—)	2 (1)
	Don't know			3 (1)	4 (2)

admitting inability to understand or answer. The boys were somewhat more knowledgeable, 62 per cent answering correctly.

SOURCE OF SEXUAL KNOWLEDGE

Table 3 shows the answers to the question regarding the main source of the child's information, analysed by age-group and sex. A striking difference emerged between the sexes as regards the attention given to imparting sexual information by parents. Just under half the first-year girls and a quarter of the boys referred to parents as the

Table 3. *Main source of sexual knowledge*

Main source	1st year		4th year	
	Boys	Girls	Boys	Girls
	No. (%)	No. (%)	No. (%)	No. (%)
Teachers	32 (14·5)	36 (19·3)	55 (25·7)	65 (30·1)
Parents	56 (25·3)	84 (44·9)	32 (15·0)	73 (33·8)
Peers	122 (55·2)	58 (31·0)	118 (55·1)	70 (32·4)
Don't understand	4 (1·8)	4 (2·1)		
Not answered and other	7 (3·2)	5 (2·7)	9 (4·2)*	8 (3·7)*
Total	221 (100·0)	187 (100·0)	214 (100·0)	216 (100·0)

* A number of pupils mentioned books and magazines as main sources.

principal source of information, whilst in the older group a third of the girls and only one in seven boys did so. But, even in the sub-group where more children referred to parents as a source of information than any other, i.e. the first-year girls, less than half did so. Still fewer children referred to teachers as a source of information and, although there was an increase in this respect between the younger and the older groups, less than one-third of the senior girls and only a quarter of the senior boys admitted receiving information from teachers, whilst with the younger children the proportion fell to one-sixth. In both age-groups other children were the most frequently mentioned source by the boys, rather more than half mentioning this source at each age. About a third of the girls referred to other children as the source of their information and this too remained more or less constant between the two-age-groups.

G. D. Ripley, C. Burns and V. A. Dickinson

It is of interest to compare these figures with those obtained by Schofield in 1965.

Teachers as a source of knowledge have increased their representation from 12 per cent for boys and 18 per cent for girls to 25·9 per cent and 29·9 per cent, respectively, in the similar age-group. From 11 per cent of boys revealing parents as their main source of knowledge and 28 per cent of girls in 1965 there is little significant change to our findings of 14·8 per cent and 34·1 per cent, respectively.

Further, if we examine those children who learnt mainly from their peers, we find that 59·3 per cent of our older boys received only limited or no personal instruction in an area where no other type is satisfactory. That more than half our young men and one-third of our young women received their sexual education from peer groups or the mass media must be alarming.

RATING OF SEXUAL KNOWLEDGE

In order to make comparisons, a measure of sexual knowledge was needed and a simple score of the number of correct answers given to the multi-choice questions was used. The spread of scores is given in Tables 4 and 5, from which it can be seen that the questions provide useful discriminatory scales.

Questions 9, 10 and 11 were asked of only the fourth-year children so that the maximum score for the first-year group was 8 and for the fourth-year 11. The Tables show that at first-year level the boys scored significantly lower ($p < 0.01$) than the girls, whereas at fourth-year level the difference was not statistically significant. The difference at first-year level probably reflects a greater likelihood that girls will be given information by their mothers at about the time of the menarche.

Primary schools attended. The pupils had attended a spread of at least eighteen primary schools, but four schools dominated, taking between them about half the pupils. The scores of sexual knowledge in these four primary schools were compared with one another and with the remaining schools. One school, where the head personally provided sex education, stood out with a significantly higher score of 6·3 compared with the average for all schools of 5·0.

Present school attended. Table 6 gives the average score for each group by secondary school attended. It will be seen that in school 'B', the grammar school, first-year children scored significantly

Table 4. *No. of first-year pupils with score shown*

Score	0	1	2	3	4	5	6	7	8	Total	Average
Boys	7	8	18	33	33	45	32	28	17	221	4·63
Girls	2	6	2	10	25	49	38	31	24	187	5·47
Both	9	14	20	43	58	94	70	59	41	408	5·01

Table 5. *No. of fourth-year pupils with score shown*

Score	3	4	5	6	7	8	9	10	11	Total	Average
Boys	1	—	3	10	11	26	30	72	61	214	9·45
Girls	—	1	1	—	19	34	55	57	49	216	9·34
Both	1	1	4	10	30	60	85	129	110	430	9·40

Table 6. *Average score by school attended at time of survey*

School	1st year		4th year	
	Boys	Girls	Boys	Girls
A	4·50	*5·21	8·70	8·78
B	5·40	6·21	9·95	10·00
C	3·81	*4·62	8·71	8·91
D	3·61	5·21	10·09	9·72
E	5·61	5·92	9·55	9·28
All schools	4·63	5·47	9·46	9·34

* Less than 30 pupils.

higher than the others, which is hardly surprising for children selected for their higher intelligence. A somewhat higher score at school 'D' for the fourth-year children suggests that some sex education may have been given, and this was confirmed by the headmaster. The high average score for first-year pupils at school 'E' is due to the fact that 40 per cent of these pupils came from the primary school at which sex education was given. The difference is not sustained into the fourth year.

161

ANXIETIES OF ADOLESCENCE

Both age-groups were asked the same question: 'What are the things that worry you most about growing up?' A large variety of answers was given to this question and it was necessary to reduce these for analytical purposes to a manageable number of categories. Table 7 shows the categories of anxiety tabulated according to the number of children in each age-group and sex expressing them. The following points seem worthy of mention.

Menstruation. One-third of the first-year girls expressed worries related to menstruation. By the fourth year this had dropped to 7 per cent. Evidently this is a subject much charged with anxiety for the younger girls but the reality proves less worrying than the anticipation.

Sexual intercourse. Fears related to sexual intercourse were referred to by 8 to 10 per cent of the girls in both age-groups and by rather fewer boys—fewer still in the older group.

Premarital pregnancy. Very few of the younger girls expressed anxiety on this score but a somewhat larger – although still small – number of the older girls did so. It is interesting that a slightly larger number of older boys expressed a fear of being the cause of premarital pregnancy than did girls in this age-group of becoming pregnant.

Childbirth. Almost half of the younger girls expressed anxiety regarding childbirth whilst only one in five of the older girls did so. These figures may be taken together with those referred to regarding menstruation as indicating anxiety regarding sexual maturity in the younger girls which is lessened as maturation takes place. Of the younger boys, 4·1 per cent expressed anxiety regarding the ordeal which their future wives would face in childbirth: a chivalrous concern evidently not persisting into later adolescence since it was referred to by only one (0·5 per cent) of the older boys. Among the older girls, 32 (14·8 per cent) expressed other anxieties connected with the reproductive process, including particularly sterility and the possible production of an abnormal child.

Adult responsibility, work, money. The boys in both age-groups referred to worries under this heading far more often than the girls. It is evident that, in this group of children at any rate, the sexes see their respective roles as sharply defined along traditional lines, the boys in particular regarding themselves as future breadwinners and therefore expressing concern about the general responsibilities of adult life and more specifically about their employment prospects and future earning capacity. This type of anxiety was much less often expressed by girls, very few of whom evinced any concern regarding their employment prospects. When they did refer to

Table 7. *Anxieties expressed by children*

Anxiety	1st year		4th year	
	Boys	Girls	Boys	Girls
	No. (%)	No. (%)	No. (%)	No. (%)
No entry or written 'nothing'	88 (39·8)	54 (28·9)	98 (45·8)	82 (40·0)
Periods	—	64 (34·2)	—	16 (7·4)
Venereal disease	—	1 (0·5)	6 (2·8)	—
Sexual intercourse	12 (5·4)	19 (10·2)	6 (2·8)	18 (8·3)
Getting involved in pre-marital intercourse		3 (1·6)	7 (3·3)	5 (2·3)
Pre-marital pregnancy	—	4 (2·1)	—	15 (6·9)
Causing premarital pregnancy	1 (0·5)	—	18 (8·4)	—
Relations with opposite sex in general	5 (2·3)	11 (5·9)	9 (4·2)	12 (5·6)
Other sexual anxieties	3 (1·4)	2 (1·1)	8 (3·7)	3 (1·4)
Childbirth itself	9 (4·1)	86 (46·0)	2 (0·9)	39 (18·1)
Abnormal child	6 (2·7)	4 (2·1)	2 (0·9)	19 (8·8)
Sterility	1 (0·5)	1 (0·5)	1 (0·5)	13 (6·0)
Marriage and finding right partner	56 (25·3)	13 (7·0)	28 (13·1)	25 (11·6)
Work, finding and holding a job	63 (28·5)	5 (2·7)	52 (24·3)	8 (3·7)
Adult responsibilities	40 (18·1)	7 (3·7)	30 (14·0)	15 (6·9)
Inward-looking fears	25 (11·3)	11 (5·9)	22 (10·3)	25 (11·6)
School-work, exams	8 (3·6)	3 (1·6)	10 (4·7)	3 (1·4)
Relation with parents	—	2 (1·1)	1 (0·5)	10 (4·6)
Other anxieties	13 (5·9)	9 (4·8)	16 (7·5)	16 (7·4)

money, this was in the context of ability to handle it rather than capacity to earn it; indeed, none of the older girls referred to earning capacity at all as being among their concerns. In this area therefore, which is predominantly social class III and IV in population make-up, the adolescent girls clearly regard work as something to fill the interval between school and marriage where their role is that of the prudent manager of financial resources provided by the husband.

RESULTS OF PARENTAL QUESTIONNAIRE

There were five questions in the parental questionnaire. The first three attempted to measure parental attitudes, the fourth to discover parental anxieties, and the last to assess parental agreement. In fact,

Table 8. *Parents' Question 3: No. of parents giving replies shown*

Question and response	No.	(%)
If it were proposed to introduce sex education at your child's school, would you:—		
(1) Be pleased that you were being helped to do a difficult and embarrassing job?	223	38·8
(2) Object because you believe this to be the parents' responsibility?	17	3·0
(3) Object because you think that the child may want to try it himself?	5	0·9
(4) Feel that your own children had been—or would be—adequately informed by their parents but be interested to know how the subject was dealt with at school?	231	40·1
(5) Be afraid of the questions your children might ask you?	—	—
(1) and (4)	74	12·9
(2) and (3)	4	0·7
(2) and (4)	8	1·4
(3) and (4)	2	0·3
Not answered	11	1·9
Totals	575	(100·0)

this was almost unanimous. In most cases parents answered the questionnaire together; 20 did not answer this question, and only eight stated that they disagreed.

In response to the first two questions 80 per cent of parents stated that their children asked where babies come from, and 90 per cent said that they could discuss sex with their children.

The replies to the third question are given in Table 8. If the first and fourth responses are accepted as being favourable towards sex education, then 528 parents (91·8 per cent of the returned questionnaires) would not be against sex education in schools. Twenty-six parents (4·6 per cent) objected, 10 gave ambivalent responses and 11 did not reply. In fact, of the 63 parents who stated that they were 'embarrassed' or 'did not know the right words' when discussing sex with their children, 54 said at question 3 that they would be 'pleased to be helped to do a difficult and embarrassing

Table 9. *Anxieties expressed by parents*

Anxiety	No. of parents	% of all responding parents
Teenager-parent conflict in general	38	6·6
Combating outside pressure: e.g. corruption, violence, permissiveness as depicted on TV and in films, magazines and the like	77	13·4
Lowering of moral standards	102	17·7
Excessive sex education	6	1·0
Insufficient sex education	22	3·8
Lack of control exercised by other parents	17	3·0
Lack of discipline and lack of sense of responsibility in children	56	9·7
Drugs	217	37·7
Drinking	1	0·2
Smoking	3	0·5
Destructive behaviour (vandalism) and violence	36	6·3
Keeping bad company	60	10·4
Becoming pregnant/causing pregnancy	32	5·6
Contracting venereal disease	20	3·5
Assault of child	11	1·9
Future of the child	18	3·1
Misuse of leisure	6	1·0
Other anxieties	67	11·7

job'. It had been hoped to set up a scale for parental attitudes but the variation in parental responses precluded this.

In question 4 parents were invited to state what they regard as the chief anxieties faced by parents at the present time. Forty-two of the 575 parents did not answer this question and a further 21 wrote 'no anxieties' or a similar entry. The remaining 512 parents expressed one or more anxieties, and the total 789 anxieties are analysed in Table 9. The most striking feature is that over a third of the parents gave drugs as a source of anxiety, whereas not one child mentioned this. Only four parents, however, singled out the socially accepted forms of drug-taking – smoking and drinking – a point for health educationists to note. The other noticeable feature was that nearly a third of parents mentioned either the general lowering of moral standards or corrupting and permissive outside influences. Clearly, to parents these are important factors.

Parents were also asked to give their ages, father's occupation, religion and number of children in family.

RELATION OF PARENTS TO CHILDREN'S QUESTIONNAIRE

74·3 per cent of parents returned their questionnaires. We wondered if [children of] late or non-responding parents would be less knowledgeable than the children of responders. Table 10 shows that

Table 10. *Mean scores for sexual knowledge compared with time of parental response.*

Return of parents' questionnaire	1st year		4th year	
	Boys	Girls	Boys	Girls
1st request	4·86	5·95	9·64	9·54
2nd request	4·42	5·55	9·16	9·30
3rd request	4·11	5·32	9·26	9·25
Not at all	4·60	4·59	9·52	9·15

differences existed and that in general the later the response the lower the average sexual knowledge.

The position of children of non-responders is curious. If non-response is a measure of lack of parental interest, then boys seem to be largely unaffected, whilst girls suffer markedly. This, however, supports the findings of Table 7 where girls seem to rely more heavily on their parents for sexual knowledge. Apart from this no relationship was established between parental and children's responses.

DISCUSSION

Only 2·3 per cent of parents objected to their children being questioned on their knowledge of sexual matters, and of those

166

parents returning their own questionnaires (579 of 779) a total of 4·6 per cent objected to the prospect of the introduction of sex education in school. The lack of response from the teachers to their questionnaires was outstanding. The children showed a high level of sexual knowledge, even though 48 per cent recorded that this knowledge was principally gained from sources other than their parents or school. On the other hand, the need for the younger girls to receive more formal sexual education, and the considerable lack of factual knowledge about conception and contraception shown by the older boys and girls, indicate a need for remedial action in these areas at least.

The ratings of the ex-pupils of one primary school were much higher than those of other pupils. It was found that the headmaster of this particular school was actively interested in sex education.

It is hoped that this report will not be met with complacency because 78·4 per cent of the 11-year-old and 97·9 per cent of the 14-year-old children knew 'where babies came from' — but rather with the realization that one in every ten 14-year-old boys did not know the meaning of venereal disease, that one in every five 14-year-old girls thought that contraceptives could be used by women only, and that three out of every ten boys and almost four of every ten girls in the 14-year-old group were under the impression that inter-crural intercourse could not result in pregnancy.

The fact that not one of the 838 children questioned in 1969 appeared anxious about drugs surely demands explanation when 38 per cent of their parents exhibit obvious distress on this subject. Compared with these 217 parents, only four expressed concern regarding the possible ill effects of alcohol and tobacco. This, surely, merits investigation by all those involved in caring for the health of the community. . .

REFERENCES

Schofield, M. (1965). *The Sexual Behaviour of Young People* (Longman, London), p. 95.

12   The Sexual Behaviour of Young People

MICHAEL SCHOFIELD

Premarital sexual intercourse

Some readers, as they approach the end of this report, may be expecting a number of definite conclusions. But the object of this report has been to provide basic factual information, not to formulate an answer to the problem of teenage immorality. In any case we doubt whether there is any one easy solution to this problem. But we hope those who are looking for answers will be able to take into account the significant facts we have been able to unearth.

Our study of inceptive behaviour has shown that girls start before boys, but gradually the boys catch up with the girls until by seventeen there are more boys than girls taking part in these activities. Fifteen to nineteen are momentous years in the sex histories of boys; during this period most of them have moved from stage I* to stage III or beyond. These are also important years for the girls and over half will have moved from stage I to stage III, but there is a barrier at stage III for girls which is not apparent for boys. Once he has started, a boy will tend to move quickly from stage to stage; but the fact that a girl is at one stage does not mean that she will soon be moving on to the next.

More teenage boys than girls have experience of sexual intercourse. In our sample 11 per cent of the younger boys and 30 per cent of the older boys have had premarital intercourse; the relevant figure for the younger girls is 6 per cent and for the older girls is 16 per cent. By using the accumulative incidence concept, we

Michael Schofield, *The Sexual Behaviour of Young People* (Longman, London, 1965), Chapter 15.

* Schofield used a 5-stage division of sexual experience in this study:

I	–	Little or no contact with opposite sex
II	–	Limited experience of sexual activities
III	–	Sexual intimacies which fall short of intercourse
IV	–	Sexual intercourse with one partner
V	–	Sexual intercourse with more than one partner [Ed.].

estimated that at the age of eighteen 34 per cent of the boys and 17 per cent of the girls are sexually experienced.

Sexual intercourse before fourteen was rare and by sixteen 14 per cent of the boys and 5 per cent of the girls had started. The first experience of sexual intercourse was usually with someone who was already experienced; the first partner was often older and in the case of the girls was quite often an adult. It was usually with a friend and more often than not took place in the parental home of the beginner or the partner. The first experience was often unpremeditated and unplanned, and a majority said they did not enjoy it.

Boys start at an earlier age than girls because they wish to prove their masculinity to themselves, and to their friends. Although the boys start earlier, when incidence and frequency are taken together we find the total sexual outlet is very similar. Fewer girls have intercourse, but those who are experienced do it more often. The boys have more sexual partners; the girls prefer a more enduring relationship. Girls are slower to agree to intercourse, but once they have agreed they are more active sexually.

Some of the teenagers still hold attitudes which support the ancient double standard which basically states that premarital intercourse is forbidden for women but not for men. This double standard requires a minority of promiscuous and disrespected girls with whom boys are supposed to get their experience before marrying virgins.

There is another difference in attitudes between girls and boys. The girl is looking for a romantic relationship while the boy is seeking a sexual relationship. The girl is in search of security, but the boy is in search of adventure. Premarital intercourse is most likely to happen when either one modifies his or her attitude so that it comes closer to the other one's aspirations. Then if the boy gives the impression that he is in love with the girl, she is more likely to agree to intercourse; or if the girl is persuaded that sexual activities are an extension of romantic feelings, intercourse is likely to take place.

Our results have made it clear that premarital sexual relations are a long way from being universal among teenagers as over two-thirds of the boys and three-quarters of the girls in our sample have not engaged in sexual intercourse. On the other hand it is equally apparent that teenage premarital intercourse is not a minority problem confined to a few deviates. It is an activity common enough to be seen as one manifestation of teenage conformity.

Sex education

This research has shown that by the age of thirteen two-thirds of the boys and three-quarters of the girls know, or think they know, about the facts of life. In fact most of them have obtained this information from their friends and much of it is inaccurate and obscene. Prejudices and misunderstandings about sex would be avoided if children first heard about it from their parents. But this research has shown that this does not happen very often.

Two-thirds of the boys and a quarter of the girls had learnt nothing about sex from their parents. Even those who had discussed sex with their parents had usually first heard about it from another source. The only exception to this was middle-class mothers who were more likely to advise their daughters. Teenagers also reported that parental advice abour sex usually concentrated on moral problems, and was unspecific and vague. Furthermore we found that the young people who were most likely to have a serious sex problem were also those who were least likely to go to their parents for help.

In some countries, for example, in one state in Australia, sex education in the schools is disallowed because it is believed that the parents are the proper people to instruct the child. But our results suggest that this is unlikely to work out well. Even when special classes are instituted to help the parents to teach their children about sex, the people who attend these classes are probably the ones who would have talked to their children about sex in any case.

The best hope for those who believe that parents are the people who can do most to prepare a child for a healthy sexual life is to help the generation now at school to become the kind of parents who can speak simply and sensibly about sex to their children.

The school teacher is the second most important source of sex knowledge for boys, and the third most important source for girls. The teacher has an important role to play in sex education, especially for working-class children who are less likely to learn from their parents.

At present the adolescents who first learn about sex from teachers are those who find out later than their peers. If sex education had been given earlier, more people would have obtained correct information about sex in the first place. As the situation is at present many of those who receive sex education in schools are inattentive because they think they already know all there is to know about sex. If sex education comes too late, they will not listen because their ideas and prejudices about sex have already been formed.

Half the boys and 14 per cent of the girls did not receive any sex education at school. In all types of state schools, including grammar schools, as often as not there was no sex education for the boys. It was the working-class boys who were least likely to learn about sex from their parents and were least likely to receive sex education at school.

In view of all the discussion about sex education in recent years, it was surprising to find so many teenagers who said they were never taught about sex at school. A possible explanation is that the teachers think they are giving sex education but the adolescents do not recognize it as such. There were signs of a lack of frankness in the teaching. Sex education, when it occurred, seemed to concentrate on biological and physiological matters and seemed to be unrelated to human affairs, except when it was wholly concerned with putting across a particular moral point of view, which was often the case with the girls.

Nearly half the boys (47 per cent) and girls (43 per cent) felt they should have been told more about sex at school. The teenagers were dissatisfied with the amount of sex education they received, and with its quality. The difficulties of providing viable education about sex are immense; much of the moral code is based upon religious thinking which the teenagers do not accept and many of the arguments against premarital intercourse, when unsupported by moral exhortations, sound weak to many young people. In addition we have found a strong inclination among a large number of teenagers to reject adult advice of all kinds. But there is also plenty of evidence from this research that teenagers are anxious to be informed about sex and want sex education providing it is given with an assurance which is backed by knowledge and with a proper understanding of their particular problems.

Illegitimacy

It is often said that one of the consequences of premarital intercourse is illegitimacy. This is not strictly true. The birth of illegitimate children is caused by premarital sexual intercourse without adequate precaution against an unwanted pregnancy. In this sample 16 per cent of the boys and 18 per cent of the girls knew nothing about birth control and many of the others had only a slight knowledge of contraceptives.

Among those having sexual intercourse less than half the boys always used contraceptives and a quarter never used them. The girls having sexual intercourse usually left it to the man with the result that the majority neither used contraceptives themselves, nor insisted that their partner used them. Ponting (1963)[1] interviewed a much more promiscuous group of teenagers and she found that only 17 per cent took precautions.

Quite a large group in this sample either did not like contraceptives or could not be bothered with them. The most usual birth-control method was either the sheath or withdrawal, but some of the boys who possessed sheaths had not had intercourse and had bought them as a kind of status symbol.

About half the experienced boys said they were inhibited by the fear that their partner might become pregnant, but about 40 per cent seemed to be unconcerned. More of the girls feared pregnancy but they did very little about it. Many of the boys said they would marry a girl they had made pregnant, and this is what many of the girls hoped or expected. Others said they would want to keep the child if they became an unmarried mother. Neither adoption nor abortion were favoured by teenage girls, so it can be assumed that most pregnancies will lead to a hasty marriage or an illegitimate child.

There is still a strong feeling that the boy who made the girl pregnant has a duty to marry her, although this pressure is less severe when both of them are young. But Greenland (1958)[2] found that among the 45 teenage unmarried mothers in his group, the putative father was over nineteen in 24 (53 per cent) cases. A study of the Registrar General's figures since 1938 on rates of illegitimacy and premarital conceptions taken together show that although the illegitimacy rate has gone up, the percentage of teenage brides who were pregnant on their wedding day has gone down. Therefore the social pressures on the unmarried mother to marry have declined, and this decrease in the rate of premarital conceptions 'regularized' by marriage more than accounts for the increase in illegitimate births.

Our inquiries into the use of birth-control methods among teenagers have shown that many boys are not using contraceptives and most girls who are having intercourse are at risk. This does not seem to be because teenagers have difficulty in obtaining contraceptives, but because social disapproval means that many of their sexual adventures are unpremeditated. Premarital sexual intercourse among young people is often an impulsive act; it is not planned beforehand, except in the case of an engaged couple who are regularly sleeping together. When a person is acting on impulse, it is obvious that he or she is less likely to take precautions. It can be argued that if an unmarried teenager is prepared to think far enough ahead to get advice on birth-control, then he or she is acting more responsibly than someone who allows sexual desire to override their awareness of the possible consequences.

Illegitimacy is an important social phenomenon, but it is quite fallacious to suggest that it is entirely a teenage problem. Only about a quarter of all illegitimate births were to teenage girls, about the same proportion as to women over 32 years. The incidence of illegitimate births per 1,000 unmarried women is about 9 times as great for women aged 25–29 as it is for girls aged 15–19. The belief that illegitimacy is a teenage problem is presumably based on the fact that the proportion of illegitimate births to all births is very high for the younger age groups. But this proportion is high because the number of total births to girls under twenty is much smaller (72,000) than to women aged 25–29 (263,000).[3]

The idea that illegitimacy is only a teenage problem has diverted attention from more important social aspects. The National Council for the Unmarried Mother and her Child in their forty-sixth annual report stresses the need for a more sympathetic social climate 'so that individual citizens feel able to accept unmarried mothers and children in their midst, without censure, and without that hurtful comment which may have long term effects on the child'. According to one report,[4] the number of schoolgirls who become pregnant is small (less than one in 1,500), but one in 14 of all the children born in Britain is illegitimate. It is very important that teachers and others should not forget that in a school class of 30, there will probably be two children who will have been born out of wedlock.

Venereal disease

The problem of venereal diseases among teenagers is not so great as the problem of illegitimacy. Nevertheless there has been an increase in the number of infections in the last few years, although this increase has not been so great in this age group as the rise among other sections of the community. It has been shown by the reports of

Michael Schofield

the British Co-operative Clinical Group (1962,[5] 1963[6]) that the main increases in gonorrhoea have been among immigrants,[7] homosexuals and young adults. The Chief Medical Officer to the Ministry of Health wrote in his report for 1965:[8]

It must be clearly understood that the bulk of venereal infection is among people of 25 and over, and especially in men. Only 8·6 per cent of syphilis and 13·1 per cent of gonorrhoea occurs among people aged 19 or less. The prevalence of venereal disease is not due to promiscuous teenagers...

This does not mean that the risks should be disregarded. Most of the teenagers in our sample had heard about VD, but not many of the experienced ones were worried about the possibility of being infected. Ponting (1963)[1] found only 32 per cent who were afraid of VD and she obtained her information from a group who had visited a clinic at least once.

We found that there was still much ignorance about the venereal diseases and some of the misapprehensions and old wives' tales still persisted. About half the young people in our sample would not be able to recognize the symptoms if they were infected. Books were the best source of correct information although Dalzell-Ward (1960)[9] has shown that some of the books on sex education do not mention the venereal diseases at all. Friends were the biggest source of misinformation and there is still some doubt whether a person who suspected that he was infected would really go to a clinic.

As the venereal diseases are sexually transmitted, the spread of the infection must involve, not two, but at least three people; one or both of the partners in the sexual act must have had intercourse with someone else. Therefore the venereal diseases must be associated with promiscuity.

It is generally considered that a stable marriage is a safeguard against promiscuity and that single people are more likely to be promiscuous. Hitchens and James (1965)[10] investigated the amount of VD among unattached persons aged 15–50, and found that single males over the age of 20 were ten times more likely than teenagers to get VD, and single girls over the age of 20 were three times more likely to get this disease. They conclude that sexual promiscuity and recourse to prostitutes is much more widespread among older people.

This result agrees with those found in this research. . . .* We

* To simplify reading in the present format, references to other sections of _The Sexual Behaviour of Young People_ have here been omitted. The interested reader is referred to the original (Ed.).

174

reported on the number of partners for all the experienced boys and girls, but a better indication of promiscuity is the number of sexual partners *in the last year*. It was found that less than 12 per cent of the boys had more than one partner, while 6 per cent had only one partner; in addition 3 per cent of the boys had no experience in the last year although they had previously had sexual intercourse. Therefore slightly more than half the experienced boys can be said to be promiscuous in the strictest sense of the word.[11]

Less than a quarter of the experienced girls (about 2 per cent of the whole sample) had more than one sexual partner in the last year. . . . Elsewhere in this report we have noted that the boys have more partners than the girls, but this should not hide the fact that a larger number of boys have premarital intercourse with one girl only, often with the girl they intend to marry. . .

These results suggest that promiscuity, although it exists, is not a prominent feature of teenage sexual behaviour. Consequently the risks of venereal disease are not very great, and this conclusion is supported by the figures. Of course it is true that even the teenager who has had only one previous sexual partner may still infect another person. But the main danger of the venereal diseases is that many teenagers are ignorant about the symptoms, which are not always obvious, and may not go to a clinic if they are infected. Three-quarters of the boys who have sexual intercourse and four out of five of the girls at risk would not know if they had been infected. . . These people are unlikely to reach diagnosis and treatment. Morton (1966)[12] reports that about a quarter of all the new patients who attend VD clinics do not require treatment. If more people can be persuaded to go to a clinic for examination, tests and reassurance, this would help to control the spread of VD.

Only a few teenagers are restrained from having sexual intercourse by the fear of venereal disease. . . Those people who use the rise in the VD rate in their campaign against premarital intercourse should note that teenagers are not likely to be deterred by this threat.

On the other hand the fear of pregnancy was often given as the reason for not having sexual intercourse and indeed the risks of pregnancy are greater than the risks of infection by venereal disease. Adults who comment on teenage sexual activities often bracket illegitimacy and venereal disease together, but the risks of illegitimacy are greater and the consequences more serious.

Restraints and controls

It is not one of the objects of this research to suggest ways in which premarital sexual intercourse can be prevented. But it is hoped that those who are concerned about teenage sexual behaviour will be able to make use of some of the specific facts uncovered by this research. For example, it seems to be common practice to end a criticism of adolescent sexual behaviour by adding that we all know the bad ones are an exception and that most of the youth of this country are a grand clean-living bunch of lads. But this qualification is as wrong as the criticism is inept. For the results of this research show clearly that those who are having sexual intercourse are not a tiny minority. In round figures something over 350,000 boys and girls under the age of twenty have had experience of premarital intercourse.

But although it is not a small minority, it is not a majority, and those who are concerned about this problem might begin by asking why, in view of the great strength of the sexual drive, there are not more teenagers who are sexually experienced. Young men under the age of twenty are at their highest sexual potential and social pressures are by no means all on the side of restraint.

... We found that many of the teenagers gave moral reasons for not going farther, although few gave specific religious reasons. Many appeals to youth either assume Christian values or explicitly state Christian doctrines, but most of the young people we interviewed were not interested in Christianity. It is possible that many young people find their way of living incompatible with the moral teaching of Christianity and the Church's emphasis on sexual morality may make the experienced teenager feel that there is no room for him in the Christian Church.

Despite the social and physiological pressures towards sexual intercourse, many teenagers manage to resist these influences. This research has found several differences between those who do and those who do not have sexual intercourse. . . These differences do not reveal serious anti-social tendencies in those teenagers with experience of sexual intercourse. The experienced boys were gregarious and outgoing, even hedonistic, but they were not misfits. Sexual experience among teenage girls is closely associated with a desire for freedom and independence from the family, but they were not debauched.

Nor is there any evidence that premarital sexual intercourse leads to or encourages adulterous relations after marriage. Burgess and Wallin (1953)[13] found that 90 per cent of the women who had had premarital intercourse said that it had strengthened their marital relationship. Most of the young people in this sample disapproved of extramarital relations and this is as true of the experienced teenagers as of the others.

Those who are worried about the extent of premarital sexual intercourse among teenagers must accept that these activities cannot be eliminated altogether in the foreseeable future. Murdock (1949)[14] on the basis of evidence compiled from a world wide sample of 158 societies, found that premarital intercourse was permitted in 70 per cent of them; in the other societies restraints reinforced by disgrace and punishments were not always effective in preventing young people from engaging in premarital intercourse. The most effective way to prevent teenage sexual activities would be to decrease the opportunities by reintroducing ideas like chaperonage of girls and further segregation of the sexes. Descriptions of a Chinese school (Huang, 1964)[15] and family life in the Soviet Union (Mace, 1963)[16] make it clear that adolescent immorality can be reduced if not eliminated. But if this is what is required, we shall also have to accept a measure of Communist descipline and a reduction in personal freedom.

Many people will have noticed that this research has found an association between sex experience and lack of parental discipline. There is a danger that some people will seize upon this as if it is the most important finding in the report because it fits in with their preconceived ideas and because it appears to be easy to remedy. But it is not certain that further restrictions will be of value. Bier (1963)[17] in the report of a symposium on adolescents warns about the dangers of 'scrupulosity' – a tendency to make an individual see evil where there is no evil, serious sin where there is no sin and obligation where there is no obligation.

In face of much of the uninformed criticism about teenage sexual activities, it is tempting to spend too much time in pointing out that many of the generalizations are without factual foundation, that there are no signs of moral collapse, that more thought should be given to adult immorality, that many teenage attitudes are refreshing and stimulating, that there are many serious young people with great intellectual curiosity and high aspirations. But these assertions of good sense are not a substitute for factual information.

177

Indeed a disinterested look at the teenage cult will reveal several facets which are quite depressing and many signs that the least valuable and shabbiest aspects of adult society have been adopted with enthusiasm. The flaws in teenage society have been noted in detail by several writers, particularly Fyvel (1963)[18] and the Hechingers (1964).[19] The particular facet which concerns this research is the pressures towards conformity within the teenage cult and the formation of a teenage mythology. A typical example is teenage fashions which may seem daringly different from adult society, but in reality they are an illustration of strict conformism within the teenage subculture.

Four out of five people in Great Britain now live in urban areas, some of immense size. This urbanism has made possible the growth of teenage subcultures which are often at variance with adult standards. The improved economic position of the teenagers have given them more independence and greater mobility. But for many it has become a confused world as they revolt against an imposed middle-class morality and at the same time lose the assurance of their own working-class environment (Bals, 1962).[20]

Within these urban conditions has grown up the teenage mythology, built up by the press, the advertisers and the special teenage and pop music magazines. This has created an image of how the teenager is supposed to behave. Here is an organized system of behaviour expectations and attitudes, and the young person acts out his role, largely learnt from the teenage group to which he belongs.

The sexual behaviour of young people is influenced by this teenage subculture... We saw that there is a danger that a teenager may feel he is exceptional because he has not had sexual inter-course... We found that half the boys and two-thirds of the girls did not enjoy their first experience of sexual intercourse, but nearly all of them tried it again fairly soon. Yet at the time of the interview there were still 28 per cent of the experienced boys and 39 per cent of the experienced girls who did not always enjoy it.

... We envisaged a situation in which the boy and girl engaged in sexual intercourse although neither of them wanted to do this. ... We found that many teenagers felt their friends were having more sex than they were and ... We noted that the most enthusiastic advocates of teenage conformity were the sexually experienced boys and girls.

... We found that the sexually experienced were the ones who had the least respect for adult standards. Consequently the time that these people spend with adults is cut to a minimum and there is no interaction between the adult and teenage worlds. The young people no longer have what the Americans call 'corrective feedback' from adults, and youth becomes, not 'an ephemeral privilege' as Cocteau thought it ought to be, but 'a separate hardy race setting itself up in opposition to the decaying race of the old'.

Yet it is obvious that this teenage subculture has been created by the adult world, not by the young people themselves. For example, the sexually experienced went to the cinema more often than the others and therefore could see that sexual satisfaction is all important in most films, and premarital sex is acceptable in many. The teenagers with the most sexual experience were also those with the most money to spend and therefore the quarry for the very active salesmen of the teenage commercial market.

Even when we know that adult intervention may be resented, we have a social duty to help the adolescent to understand himself, and hurt himself and others as little as possible. But our ideas must be feasible if they are to be helpful. No matter what measures are taken to restrict or control or change or influence the activities of our young people, it is certain that in the immediate future a not inconsiderable number of teenagers will engage in premarital sexual intercourse. These sexually experienced teenagers are every bit as much our responsibility as the others. Whatever the long-term answer may be, there is an urgent short-term task, and that is to make youthful sex activities less harmful. This may be done by increasing the amount of knowledge and enlightenment on sexual matters, by introducing more and better sex education in the widest sense, and by providing individual counselling which on some occasions will mean making available methods of birth control to those who need them. Above all it is vital that future programmes of advice, help and restraint should be based, less on unsubstantiated impressions, and more on the demonstrable facts. It is hoped that this research has gone some way towards providing this necessary factual information.

NOTES

1 Ponting, L. I. 'The social aspects of venereal disease among young people in Leeds and London', *British Journal of Venereal Diseases,* 39 (1963), 273-77.

2 Greenland, Cyril, 'Putative Fathers', *The Medical Officer*, 99 (1958), 281-6.

3 The statistics in this paragraph are taken from figures published by the Registrar General for England and Wales in his Statistical Reviews and in the Annual Abstract of Statistics. They are based on an analysis of birth certificates and can claim a high degree of accuracy.

4 *The Health of the School Child; 1964–5* (H.M.S.O. 1966).

5 British Co-operative Clinical Group, *British Journal of Venereal Diseases*, 38 (1962), 1-18.

6 British Co-operative Clinical Group, *British Journal of Venereal Diseases*, 39 (1963), 1-18.

7 About half the increase in the VD rate is due to immigration. But over a third of these infected immigrants are not coloured, and VD is not a racialist problem. It is simply because many a young man who arrives in this country on his own without wife or girl friend is vulnerable to sexual temptations. This is nothing to do with being coloured; it is because he is lonely and unsettled.

8 *The Annual Report of the Chief Medical Officer of the Ministry of Health for the year 1965*, London, H.M.S.O. 1966.

9 Dalzell-Ward, A. J. 'Venereal diseases and the teenager – health education aspects', *Proceedings of the Royal Society of Health*, 67 (1960), 39-41.

10 Hitchens, R. A. N. and James, E. B. 'Premarital intercourse, venereal disease and young people: recent trends', *Public Health*, 79:5 (1965), 258–70.

11 The Oxford dictionary definition of promiscuity uses the words 'indiscriminate mixture' and therefore it is open to doubt if sexual intercourse with two or three people can be called promiscuity. For those who prefer a wider definition of promiscuity, it is noted that about a quarter of the experienced boys (6 per cent of the whole sample) had four or more partners in the last year.

12 Morton, R. S. *Venereal Disease* (London, Penguin, 1966).

13 Burgess, E. W. and Wallin, P. *Engagement and Marriage* (Philadelphia, Lippincott, 1953).

14 Murdock, George P. *Social Structure* (New York, Macmillan, 1949).

15 Huang, W. 'Adolescent problem solved', *Times Educational Supplement*, 255 (1964), 1342–3.

16 Mace, David and Mace, Vera. *The Soviet Family* (New York, Doubleday, 1963).

17 Bier, William C. (ed.) *The Adolescent: His Search for Understanding* (New York, Fordham University Press, 1963).

18 Fyvel, T. R. *The Insecure Offenders* (London, Penguin, 1963).

19 Hechinger, Grace and Hechinger, Fred. *Teenage Tyranny* (London, Duckworth, 1964).

20 Bals, Christel. *Halbstarke unter Sich* (Köln, Kiepenheuer and Witsch, 1962).

13 The Sexual Behaviour of Young Adults

MICHAEL SCHOFIELD

The best and the usual way

When the men and women were asked what is the best way to learn about sex, there were many suggestions.

'They should have TV programmes at school. Children are more interested in TV than anything else.'

'It's better to leave it to the schools.'

'Wait until they ask questions and then answer them truthfully.'

'Give them a book to read.'

'Have a chat with the doctor.'

'Experience.'

'It requires more publicity. Take a minute in the middle of *Coronation Street*. Take a full page in the *Daily Mirror*. It's mainly a problem with the working classes.'

'I think you only learn from example. I think you learn about sex after you're married. Nothing you learn at school sinks in.'

It is difficult to quantify these various ideas, but when they are asked to name the best person to learn from, it immediately becomes clear that there is a wide divergence between the kind of help they would have preferred and the kind they got.

Most of the women (66 per cent)[1] chose the mother, but there were also many others who mentioned the father (47 per cent) and the teacher (50 per cent). The number who mentioned the parent of the opposite sex reflects the idea widely held (noted in section 2·3) that girls feel that they do not know enough about boys, and vice versa.

The men were overwhelmingly in favour of the teacher (63 per cent) and quite a large number also chose the father (33 per cent) and the mother (30 per cent). Taken together it is clear that the majority would rather learn from the teacher (57 per cent) than from parents (42 per cent). So if we are to consider the views of the

Michael Schofield, *The Sexual Behaviour of Young People* (Allen Lane, 1973), part of Chapter 2.

adolescent, and we should, then sex education at school is more often preferred to learning from parents.

The only other group of any significance in Table 1 consists of those who maintain that the best way to learn about sex is from experience. As modern education puts the emphasis on the 'discovery method', that is, learning through experience and investigation, we

Table 1. *The best way to find out about sex compared with the way they actually found out**

Source of knowledge	Men		Women	
	Method preferred %	Actual method %	Method preferred %	Actual method %
Mother	30	8	66	24
Father	33	10	47	7
Teacher	63	5	50	8
Sibling	0	1	1	4
Clergyman	0	0	0	1
Experience	16	24	9	24
School friends	2	63	3	65
Workmates	1	11	1	16
Books	7	26	4	20
TV/Films	5	0	6	0
Others	5	4	8	10
DK	2	0	1	0
No. (100%)	219	219	157	157

* Informants were allowed to give more than one answer to each question so percentages add up to more than one hundred.

should not be too abashed if some pupils want to apply this method and decide to find the answer to their sexual questions from experiments. But there are two points to notice about the 16 per cent boys and 9 per cent girls who want to find out about sex in this way. First, it is not the result of sex education because nearly all (83 per cent) of those who chose this method had not had any sex education. Second, it is not a method to be recommended because the evidence shows that experience in this case is not a good teacher. Indeed it is one of the central conclusions of this study that sexual knowledge is something most people have failed to pick up from experience.

No other item is chosen with any frequency. There is a small demand for books (6 per cent), TV and films (6 per cent). Hardly anyone mentioned siblings or workmates, and only one person in the whole sample thought that a clergyman was the best person to help him learn about sex.

It is significant that only 2 per cent boys and 3 per cent girls preferred to find out from school friends. In Table 1 it can be seen that in fact 63 per cent of the boys and 65 per cent of the girls learnt this way, but this is not what they want. The younger generations emphatically reject the idea that it is best to pick it up from friends and it is reasonable to assume that they found out about sex in this way because we adults did not provide a better method before their curiosity was aroused. The preferred and actual source only coincides in one group of any size: those girls, about a quarter of the total number, who were informed by their mothers.

Neither the actual source of information nor the preferred source seems to be related to social class. But many of those who thought that the teacher was the best source of knowledge had not had any sex education and, not surprisingly, those who had found their sex education helpful named the teacher; those who had received sex education but thought it had been unhelpful were more likely to choose mother, father or experience.

Of the 215 who said the teacher was the best source, 185 (86 per cent) thought they could have been told more about sex at school. Even those who chose mother or father as the best person felt they should have been told more at school. Of the 168 who chose mother, 139 (83 per cent) wanted more information at school; and of the 146 who chose father, 121 (83 per cent) wanted more information at school; but of the 49 who chose experience, 32 (65 per cent) wanted more information at school. So even among those who feel that the best way was to find out for themselves, many wanted more help at school and nearly all those who preferred to learn from their parents felt that the school should have told them more about sex.

This section has shown that despite the increase in the amount of sex education, we are failing to provide for the needs of young people. Modern educationalists who maintain, with some justification, that young people learn best from others of their own age should accept that this is an exception to the educational tenet, and this is not difficult to understand. In this whole new world of mystery opening up before these children, they do not want to be led by the blind. They may not wish to be told what they may, or may not do, but they do want to get factual information from someone who knows his way around this new world so that they can be helped to avoid the obstacles and discover the pleasures.

Parents or teachers

There are still people who maintain that school is not the right place to give sex education. They argue that children mature at different ages and any large classroom will contain children of such wide levels of maturity that what is right for one child cannot be right for another; therefore the only satisfactory way to give sex education is

Table 2. *Do you feel you could have been told more about sex at school and by your parents?*

Need more information	At school %	By parents %
Yes	80	60
No	17	37
DK/NK	3	3
No. (100%)	376	376

for the parent to give the information when the child is ready to receive it. In this way sex education can start early and will be a continuous development carefully and lovingly carried out over many years.

This is an attractive argument and indeed it is an almost ideal programme for moral education. At present it is still an unrealistic programme, but certainly could be a legitimate aim for future generations. The people we interviewed were more practical and were not so positive that parents were the best people to give sex education. Although the earlier research had shown that 48 per cent had never at any time received any advice about sex from either their father or mother, a surprisingly high number (37 per cent) did not feel dissatisfied with the help they had received from their parents.

All the men and women were asked if they felt they could have been told more about sex at school and by their parents. Table 2 compares their replies to these two questions.

There is little difference between the replies given by men and women, so the results are given together. These show that the strong demand for information from the school is greater than the demand that parents give more help. It is still a majority, indeed nearly two out of three, who feel they could have been told more about sex by their parents, but it is clear that most people expect more from school than from the home.

For years we have been saying that parents are the best people to give their children sex education, if only they would. This may still be true for the child before puberty, but after that it is possible that there is too big a barrier in some families. It is not always easy for a teenager to ask mother or father for help with sexual problems. In some families it is impossible to discuss such things in the home. This has always been true to a certain extent, and it may be truer today than ever before because our ideas on sexual morality are changing so fast that what was disallowed in one generation is permitted in the next.

But it is false to think of it as a dichotomy — a choice between parents and school. In ideal circumstances sex education will be carried on in both the home and the school. At the first elementary stages when the child is learning how babies are born, most people would want the parents to play a major part because the information can be given simply and naturally as the child asks questions.

In fact we seem to have got the emphasis the wrong way round. At present it is the schools that are likely to be teaching the simple facts on conception, often too late. Most of the sex education books and the classes in school concentrate on the straightforward anatomical details of the male and female genitals leading up to the sex act. I suspect this is because it is the least difficult and least controversial part of sex education. But this is the part that can best be done by parents because most children will ask how babies are born long before they get to secondary school age.

The school should be concerned about teaching the more complex and more debatable aspects of sex education. Even in ideal circumstances it is probably better if the parents are not left to do the whole task on their own and the assistance of the school is almost sure to be needed at the post-puberty stages of sex education. Furthermore my earlier research shows quite clearly that circumstances are a long way from the ideal and many parents cannot help their children with their sexual problems. At the very least sex education has the function of supplying information parents have been unable to give, and preparing the children so that they can be more helpful when they become parents.

The Longford Report on Pornography (1972) contains a special section on sex education. The committee objects to much of the sex education that they imagine is going on in schools and in particular to books and broadcasts which 'describe techniques of sexual congress, especially when, as so often happens, it is accompanied by, or given through, the medium of visual presentation'. They conclude that 'sex education is primarily an affair for parents'. This chapter, and particularly this section, makes it obvious that the ideas of the Longford Committee are quite impractical. The choice is between learning about sex at school, or from dirty jokes. If we had to rely upon our parents to educate us about sex, most of us would still be waiting.

The new generation of parents

The men and women were asked if they thought they would be able to help their children to learn about sex. Nearly all of them (91 per cent) said they would; only 3 per cent said they would not and another 6 per cent were not sure. This shows a high level of confidence despite the dissatisfaction with their own sex education, or possibly because of it.

Perhaps the wording of the question was wrong. It is reasonable to assume that almost every parent will be able to provide some help, but it is doubtful if many of these men and women will be very good at providing all the help their children will need. Indeed a later question makes it clear that more than one in three felt that they did not know all they needed to know about sex. There were 152 (40 per cent) who felt their sexual knowledge was inadequate and 137 of them (i.e. 36 per cent of the whole group) still felt that they could help their children to learn about sex.

Of those who felt satisfied with the help given by their own parents, 91 per cent say they are ready to help their children; of those who were dissatisfied with the help given by their parents, 92 per cent are going to help their children. So it makes no difference whether their parents were helpful or not.

There is some slight indication, however, that helpful sex education made them more likely to say they would help their children. Only a very few (2 per cent) who had sex education which

186

they regarded as helpful, said they could not help their children; but 9 per cent who had what they regarded as unhelpful sex education said they could not help their children, and 11 per cent with no sex education said they could not help. This suggests the possibility that some of the sex education was valuable, but the figures are small because the great majority felt they could be helpful whether they had received sex education or not.

In this group 45 per cent had children and another 26 per cent were married, so within a few years most of them will have to fulfil their commitment to help their children about sex. When it gets to the point, the number who actually do so may not be quite as high as 91 per cent, but even so it is evident that this generation of parents are going to be less reserved and more outspoken than earlier generations.

But it is a limited consolation that more parents are willing to try, for there are considerable difficulties caused by ignorance and language. Indeed there is the possibility that many of these people are over-confident and may provide misleading information, or may implant fears instead of confidence.

This again raises the question of how much help we can provide for the parents. Inevitably there is the problem, common to many health education courses, that those who need the help will not take part and any scheme to help parents will be filled by those who do not really need to be helped. But this is not a strong enough reason to abandon such a scheme. Even those who are said not to require such a course would almost certainly gain something from it. Much could also be learnt from enquiring why others who need help do not come. More encouraging still, the fact that more than nine out of ten parents say they intend to help their children learn about sex indicates that the response from this generation of parents is likely to be much greater than in the past.

Inadequate knowledge

Everyone was asked: Do you feel you know all you need to know about sex? Only 56 per cent of the men and 64 per cent of the women thought they had an adequate amount of knowledge. Women are more confident than men; males may like to give the impression that they have nothing to learn, but privately 44 per cent admitted that they wished they knew more. Some women may be less inquisitive about sex then men, nevertheless 36 per cent were prepared to admit to a stranger that they did not know all they needed to know.

So in every ten young adults of twenty-five, four feel their knowledge of sex is inadequate. If these figures are representative of the whole population, no one can claim that our sex education programme is a success.

When they were asked this question seven years ago, more girls (57 per cent) than boys (51 per cent) said they needed to know more about sex. So over the years there has been an increase of 14 per cent which reflects either more knowledge, more confidence or both.

Where were the gaps? When they were asked about things they felt unsure about, many different answers were given. The main demand was for concrete factual information (11 per cent). There was not much demand for discussions about emotional or moral problems (3 per cent). Quite often sex education programmes are criticized because there is not enough emphasis put on love, but these people felt they knew enough about romantic love and wanted rather more practical down-to-earth information. The men wanted to know more about women and the women more about men. They wanted to learn how to get more out of their sexual activities.

NOTES

1 This is another question in which they were allowed to name more than one person, so the percentages add up to more than one hundred.

SECTION C
The Effects of Sex Education

Overview

In this final section, I want to examine what we know of the *effects* of sex education. This is, in many ways, *the* crucial issue, for almost everybody on whom decisions about sex education impinge is interested (naturally enough) in what such teaching achieves. An accurate picture of the impact of sex education could serve both to influence attitudes towards instruction and to increase teaching effectiveness. In terms of attitudes, knowledge about effects can help to allay public disquiet (often based on a misunderstanding of the aims and results of instruction) and assist in persuading both the individual teacher and the educational establishment to see sex education in the curriculum as *the norm*. On the more practical front, research can contribute to the development of more effective teaching aids and teaching methods, reveal the changing capacity of the child at different stages of development to absorb sexual information and provide the teacher with the tools with which to judge successful impact in the classroom situation.[1]

Interest in effect tends to fall into two broad categories; first, the immediate results of instruction (e.g. has it resulted in successful learning?) and, second, the longer-term picture (e.g. how will widespread sex education affect later behaviour?). The former is very much easier to study and can do much to establish degree of success in terms of day-to-day educational criteria (e.g. scores on knowledge tests or favourable parental feed-back). What such data cannot do, however, is to provide any hint as to how, for example, more accurate sexual knowledge will influence people's lives. I have, therefore, chosen researches of both kinds in this examination of effects. In doing so, I am explicitly recognising that, in placing sexual instruction in the curriculum, we are dealing with education in the broad sense and that there is an expectation that sex education will impinge on society as a whole (e.g. by helping to change sexual mores or by paving the way to more effective population control).

During the last decade, one of the major innovations in education has been the growth of television in schools. This form of instruction has several potential advantages over more conventional techniques:

(1) Very large resources in terms of time, money and skill are available for programme production.

(2) To the extent to which children are growing up in a television-orientated world, this a familiar mode of presentation and one to which they can easily relate.

(3) Television is able to exploit non-verbal forms of communication which may be particularly salient with younger or less able children.

The acceptance, therefore, by the broadcasting authorities of responsibility for sex education is a major step forward in this area. It makes easily available to almost every school in the country material that is thoroughly professional in presentation and forms part of an on-going educational experience (schools broadcasting in general). This picture contrasts markedly with the situation ten years ago, when available aids consisted of a rag-bag of films of very dubious merit which involved the school in the effort of hiring from a variety of sources and presented the child with an idiosyncratic teaching situation. We are fortunate that three of these televised sex education series and one 'radio-vision' (slides plus commentary recorded from the radio) were submitted to some kind of research evaluation, for it allows us to build up a fairly detailed picture of the role broadcasting can play in this area.

Chapter 14 is Granada Television's report of their series 'Understanding'. These programmes were first shown in 1966 and aimed at the 15–16 year old. Six programmes were involved each covering a specific topic (e.g. VD, Puberty). The major method of assessment was by a questionnaire sent out to a panel of schools, each programme being assessed separately. In general a very favourable response to the programmes was revealed. It is also interesting to note that 28 per cent of the schools (which presumably were more favourably disposed towards sex education than the average, as they choose to show the aids) had previously provided no regular sex education course, either in its own right or combined with other subjects. Although this is not in itself an encouraging statistic, the ability of television to penetrate schools not otherwise giving sex education attests to one major benefit of this mode of presentation.

Although some subjective reactions by the children themselves to the programmes were reported by Granada, no objective measure of effectiveness can be gained from teacher assessment alone. It is, therefore, of great interest to be able to add to the picture some research which examines the effects on the audience in terms of knowledge and attitude change. The paper by Brown (Chapter 15) does just this, showing that the programme on venereal disease resulted in marked learning and a more open and hopeful outlook. As Brown comments 'The research techniques used in the work reported on here were of the simplest sort, yet the differences [i.e. programme effects] revealed are in several cases . . . striking. . . .' This ability of paper-and-pencil tests to provide a dramatic record of effectiveness, is a powerful argument for their wider use in programme assessment.

The next Chapter (16) is Grampian Television's assessment of their 'Living and Growing' series. This consisted of eight programmes covering the major aspect of human reproduction and aimed at the 10–13 year old. The method of assessment used is very similar to that used by Granada (i.e. questionnaires completed by class teachers). One question asked of the teachers was to estimate how much of the information in each programme was known to their class before screening. From this it appears that familiarity varies very much from area to area (growth of the embryo/foetus, for example, was the least known). It is also interesting to note that, for these Scottish schools, only 28% had human reproduction as a regular part of their syllabus. Again, the power of television in this area is clearly demonstrated.

The BBC's main contribution during this period was in the primary school area. This, in many ways, is the most notable innovation of all, for parents (see Chapter 6), and schools seem less aware of the needs of children at this age group than they do for adolescents. In fact sex education in the primary school has a number of advantages:

(1) Instruction at this point may be easier than in adolescence, as the primary school child is less personally involved.

(2) The possession of an adequate vocabulary and basic working knowledge of sexuality obtained through pre-adolescent instruction may help to 'pave the way' towards more detailed information in the secondary school.

(3) With the continued lowering of the age of puberty, any attempt at preparatory instruction (e.g. telling girls about menstruation) has to be made at the primary level.

(4) The primary school child is gaining information and attitudes through his environment and it may well be easier to correct any misconceptions picked up during this learning at an early stage rather than hope to sort things out in secondary school.

Two types of aids were produced simultaneously by the BBC,[2] three television programmes and two 'radio-vision' filmstrips. These latter consist of a series of colour slides with a commentary which can be recorded from school broadcasts on the radio. The next Chapter (17) is taken from the BBC's report of the 'radio-vision' aids in use. As in the other reports by television companies, the assessment method is essentially subjective but it is very detailed and leaves little doubt as to the success of these aids. The summary of the nature of questions posed by the children is particularly interesting.

Chapter 18 deals with the impact of the BBC's three 'Merry-go-Round' television programmes which dealt with reproduction and sexual anatomy within the format of a popular on-going series. A primary school audience of 8–10 year olds was the prime target for these programmes, which in their content (which was in almost every detail explicit) and level of viewership represented something new. This factor and the general sense of public disquiet (at least as conveyed by the mass media) prompted the editor to conduct objective research into the effects of these programmes. Chapter 18 is an account of this research. Four major points stem from it:

(1) The primary school child's sexual knowledge and attitudes *can* be assessed by objective paper-and-pencil methods.

(2) The programmes resulted both in marked learning and in attitude change.

(3) The learning proved to be retained over a 3 month period.

(4) Despite the very young age of the children involved, there was a high level of parental approval of the teaching.

In the final reading, I wish to turn to the broader issue of the long-term effects of sexual instruction. It would be unfair here to claim that we really know exactly how (if at all) what is taught at school about sexuality affects the individual (and hence, society as a whole) later on. This stark admission makes sense when we come to consider the kind of research that would have to be mounted in order to make detailed pronouncements about such processes. Such a study would need to be longitudinal (i.e. studying the same individuals over time, in this case through school into later life) and to examine two matched groups, one receiving sexual instruction and the other not. As there are no more than a handful of individuals researching in this area, the chances of such data becoming available are remote and would in any event be delayed by the time it takes the sample to make the transition from childhood to adults.

In the absence of such research, we have to content ourselves with less precise techniques. These essentially consist of conducting interviews with young adults and trying to relate their characteristics at that point with their earlier level of sex education. We are fortunate here that two such studies exist, one done in the U.S.A. by Weichmann and Ellis (Chapter 19) and one which exists as part of Schofield's study in the U.K.[3] Both studies arrive at the same conclusion, namely, that sex education at school does not seem to be related to later sexual behaviour. As this conclusion has major implications, it is as well to consider whether this is a valid result. One major worry in this kind of research, is that we have to rely on the subject's ability to recall having had sex education. It is also the case that, even where recall is accurate the actual stimulus may vary vastly from subject to subject both in amount of instruction and equally important in its 'emotional tone' (matter-of-fact, deterrent, permissive etc.). In other words, the cards are stacked against discovering effects. This caveat having been given, however, it is interesting to consider what these findings mean if we take them at face value. Seemingly, teaching will neither promote nor inhibit the onset of two-person sexual activity. It may well be that this is a salutary result, suggesting that the potentialities of sex education have been over-stated and that the teacher should set himself limited objectives, either justifying knowledge for its own sake or hoping to effect quality of sexual life or to change attitudes in areas like the need for contraception. Certainly, the available data give us no reason to believe that sexual instruction of itself will either 'turn the individual on' or 'turn him off'!

NOTES

1 A readable treatment of questionnaire design and attitude measurement can be found in A. N. Oppenheim, *Questionnaire Design and Attitude Measurement* (Heinemann, London, 1968).

2 Strictly speaking the semi-autonomous School Broadcasting Council.

3 Schofield, M., *The Sexual Behaviour of Young People* (Longmans, 1965). See also Chapter 12 and Schofield, M., *The Sexual Behaviour of Young Adults* (Allen Lane, London, 1973).

14   A Report on 'Understanding'

GRANADA TELEVISION

'Understanding'

PART ONE

Preparation

'Understanding' was the first series of schools television programmes on sex education. Granada's Schools Advisory committee had previously considered transmitting the documentary 'Unmarried Mothers' in the daytime for schools, but had decided it was too adult. Instead, they asked Granada to put forward proposals for a special series designed to help teachers.

Elaine Grand, who had produced Granada programmes like 'Inside' (a sociological series on prisons) and 'Unmarried Mothers', was appointed producer. She started on this new series by talking to people working in health education in England and abroad. From this several things became apparent. First, adults do not know the questions children really want answered; they have forgotten their adolescence. All the subjects eventually covered by the series arose from questions actually asked by young people.

Second, young people are wary of being preached at by adults. So we assembled a group of 15 and 16-year-olds and invited them to ask the questions and raise the main points. We felt that our audience was more likely to listen to, understand and identify with a group of their own age.

Third, the problem of factual information. We found that most children had had lessons on human reproduction by their fourth year, but because teaching systems are so diverse, no uniform factual knowledge could be assumed. We should therefore have to give some basic instruction in 'the facts of life'.

Finally, how best to use the television medium in the teaching of human relationships? The teachers' main problems seemed to be

---

* Granada Television *A Report on Understanding,* Manchester, 1967.

overcoming embarrassment in starting the subject, establishing an easy relationship with the class, and answering questions. Television, we felt, could help: it could bring the specialist to a wide audience and avoid the necessity of the teacher introducing the subject. It could also raise controversial questions which children could discuss when the programme is finished and *before* they know what the teacher thinks. In most classrooms, a teacher's words are associated with what he believes; if children are to disagree, they have a personal barrier to break down, a barrier of admiration, dislike or fear. We felt that by using television's impersonal quality, and by showing children talking freely and responsibly to adults, the same atmosphere might be carried into classroom discussions with adults after the programme.

These ideas were discussed exhaustively with Granada's Schools Advisory Committee. But many points were still problematical. It seemed a good idea to bring a mixed group of 15 and 16-year-olds from different schools together in the studio for discussion, but would they talk? Experienced lecturers told us that children would only talk to adults they knew well, or in the company of their own classmates. Teachers feared that the programmes would be greeted by sniggering and embarrassment. The only way to settle these problems was to experiment. So the Committee asked Granada to make a pilot programme and to test it privately with classes of children.

The pilot programme

For the pilot programme, a group of 15 and 16-year-old boys and girls discussed the two subjects of 'dating' and 'shyness' with a sociologist and with a woman journalist who had a wide experience of answering readers' problems. The programme was then shown privately on closed-circuit television to three different classes in three contrasting schools. The teachers and children then completed questionnaires. Their answers confirmed that children appreciated seeing and hearing their own age group talking about these things and that such programmes could encourage responsible classroom discussion.

For example, two girls answering the question: 'had the programme helped classroom discussion?', said 'Yes, because seeing young people of my own age discussing things like this made me feel grown up and responsible', and 'Yes, it was a great help because sex did not seem so remote but more an enjoyment to be shared and talked about freely.' An overwhelming majority favoured seeing their own age group 'because they use terms we could understand, so it was easier to pick up the discussion', and 'I would like people my own age talking because I think older people make things up.' Or, as one boy put it: 'It is better with children, for adults who would be willing to talk about such matters think they know children, but I don't think they really do.'

We learnt from the faults of the pilot programme. For example, we discovered the need for an 'anchor man' to direct discussion and make sure that quieter members of the group could contribute. We reported back to the Granada Schools Advisory Committee and to the Schools Advisory Committee of the Independent Television Authority. They watched the pilot programme and gave useful criticism and advice. Finally the Committees asked Granada to go ahead with six programmes which they would see and approve before transmission.

During the preparation and production, we received patient help from teachers, and before the recordings were edited the transcripts were read by an ex-headmaster and a headmistress, who made valuable comments.

The programmes

To make the programmes, five boys and five girls aged between 15 and 16 met together for three days at the studios. One boy and girl came from a London co-ed independent school; two girls from a girls' grammar school in Lancashire; one boy from a boys' grammar school in London. Another boy and girl came from a York secondary modern school and a further two boys and one girl from a Manchester secondary modern school. Some of the children were chosen by their schools and some by the producer.

During the production of the pilot programme, a list of subjects to be covered had been compiled from questions raised by the children. These subjects were divided under six headings: Puberty, Childbirth, Unmarried Mothers, VD, The Sexual Behaviour of Young People, and Family and Marriage, each to form a separate programme. A different doctor or specialist answered questions in each, and the first two were prefaced by short diagrammatic films explaining puberty, menstruation and childbirth. Statistical information was given at the beginning of the programmes about VD and unmarried mothers, along with brief statements by unmarried mothers themselves. The remainder of each programme was a discussion between the group and the specialist, chaired by Michael Scott, a Granada interviewer.

Before each recording, the producer ran over the main subjects to be covered with the group, but there was no prior arrangement about who should ask what. All the general discussion was spontaneous, and the recording were edited into coherent programmes before transmission.

Discussion was wide. It covered such subjects as mixed v. single sex schools; dating; masturbation; intercourse; how it feels to have a baby; the differences between attraction and love; who is responsible for illegitimate children; drink and parties; the case for and against adoption; the symptoms, causes and treatment of gonorrhoea and syphilis; facts and figures about teenage promiscuity; responsibility within the family; divorce; and what you look for in a marriage partner. Neither abortion nor homosexuality were discussed as the children themselves did not raise them. A complete programme was devoted to VD because teachers reported difficulty in dealing adequately with the subject.

While production was in progress, a report came out called *The Sexual Behaviour of Young People* [1] written by Michael Schofield and sponsored by the Central Council for Health Education. A programme on it was included in the series because the report showed the falsity of the widespread impression that young people today are promiscuous. We hoped that by dispelling this myth the danger of young people drifting into promiscuity because 'everybody does it' would be lessened.

One deliberate omission from the programmes was the religious aspect of the subjects they covered. We felt that variations of belief throughout the country were so large that wide coverage might have confused children unnecessarily, while cursory treatment would have been irresponsible. We believed that the schools could best discuss these aspects themselves. We also thought that the programmes should be informative and carry their own moral, rather than moralizing.

PART TWO

The audience and opinions of the programmes

After many schools broadcasts, calls and letters arrive from the general public, praising, criticizing or complaining. No telephone calls or letters of any kind were received from the general viewing public about 'Understanding'. But correspondence from schools was very much greater than usual. More than a hundred schools corresponded with Granada itself; many of them went to great trouble to fill in detailed questionnaires both weekly and at the end of term, and to send in children's essays. Several Health Departments and Marriage Guidance Councils also expressed an interest.

Four groups of head teachers, a meeting of heads and health officials, and a Marriage Guidance Council group all invited Granada's Education Officer to talk to them about the series. The Education Officer also sat in on classes watching the programme and joined in discussion with the children. The following information is drawn from these sources. As the correspondence from schools came in at random, we may reasonably assume that it represents the general reaction to the programmes.

The schools who watched

Of the schools known to be watching, 20 per cent had sixth forms, 68 per cent were secondary modern, 4 per cent special and 6 per cent independent. At least one College of Further Education and three Colleges of Education also watched. In the Granada region, the balance between schools with sixth forms and secondary modern schools is 34 per cent to 54 per cent; so a higher proportion of secondary modern schools in the region watched than grammar schools. Of the classes watching, 22 per cent were boys, 36 per cent girls and 43 per cent mixed. Their average size was 44, though individual viewing groups varied in size from 5 to 190 children. The average of the audience was 15, but it ranged from $13\frac{1}{2}$–18.

Conditions under which children watched varied from small groups meeting in a teacher's house to several classes combining to watch in the school hall. In many cases four or five members of the staff watched too. Several classes invited local health education lecturers, the school doctor, a state registered nurse or marriage guidance counsellors to join them. Many schools went to a great deal of trouble to watch: some made sound tapes of programmes they could not see at the right time.

Eighty-eight per cent of the schools said they used television regularly. Only 50·8 per cent said that regular sex education lectures were given in their school, though another 21·5 per cent said they combined it with other subjects. But 27·7 per cent of the schools reached by these programmes had no regular instruction. After watching the series, the headmaster of a boys' ESN school said: 'It is likely that we shall continue sex instruction as a result of our experience with "Understanding".'

Several heads in mixed schools had doubts about boys and girls watching together. One headmaster said: 'In my opinion my parents would have objected to a mixed class seeing the programmes and so the boys could not see them.' In a big comprehensive school where they intended dividing boys and girls, the second television set broke down before the first transmission and the children asked if they could watch together. This worked successfully and they remained as a mixed group for the whole series.

Another senior mistress in a secondary modern school wrote:

A charming woman doctor talks to the girls, but we have found it difficult to find a suitable person for the boys. So when your series of programmes was announced I welcomed it, but with reservations. I was extremely doubtful about the wisdom of watching with a mixed group, but finally decided to make the experiment and watch the first of the series. The group selected consisted of approximately 50 boys and girls about to leave school – the most 'difficult' group we have. Two members of staff – myself and a very experienced man teacher – joined the group and each week the television session was followed by a discussion period. I am delighted with the success of the series.

And one of the boys in her class commented after the first programme. 'I knew *something* about these things before but my facts were not correct. I think boys should know what happens to girls and girls should know what happens to boys and it is a good thing that we should find out together.'

What is the right age for children to watch 'Understanding'?
We made these programmes particularly for the fourth and fifth years.

Little information was given by teachers on this subject, but many of the children's essays commented on it. The vast majority say:

I think putting it on for fourth forms is just about the right age to understand it more, because if I remember rightly I wasn't all that interested in sex in my third year.

Others said that third formers tend to treat such subjects as a 'giggle'. However, there was a strong feeling that the physical facts of puberty and childbirth should have been taught at twelve and thirteen. One tough secondary modern school found that the $14\frac{1}{2}$-year-olds 'knew it all' and were bored by the discussion, but that the $13\frac{1}{2}$-year-olds lapped it up and had long valuable discussions afterwards.

Any final decision on this matter has to be made by heads themselves, who are governed by the background of the children involved.

Parents

Many heads sought permission from parents before allowing children to watch 'Understanding'. To our knowledge only 14 children (0·4 per cent of the known audience) were not allowed to watch by their parents, and two girls asked to be excused.

Few schools have accurate figures about the number of parents who watched at home, though the figures appear to be about 144 or 4·5 per cent of the children's homes. Many more children discussed the programmes at home after school. Some watched during the Whitsun holiday or, as a 15-year-old girl from a secondary modern school told us: 'I was away ill from school for one programme. I watched it at home with my mother. Mum watched the last programme as well and when I asked her what she thought about them, she had much the same ideas as myself.'

We have not heard of any complaints by parents to schools or to Directors of Education.

In the classroom

The biggest single factor influencing the reception of the series was the attitude of the teacher taking the class and his relationship with the children. For example, in a special school where discussion is encouraged, the children 'insisted on pinching a lesson from another subject next week because our time ran out before they had finished all they wanted to say'. Other remarks by teachers illustrated how foreign free discussion on such subjects is in many schools. A teacher in a girls' grammar school commented:

The great value of the series was to stimulate sensible discussion amongst pupils and staff; to make the pupils realize that their problems were not deficiencies in the individual, but of universal occurrence. I learned that many of the children did not have opportunities to discuss *anything*, let

203

alone problems of sex, with any responsible adult. If this programme did nothing else, it enabled them to meet some adults with whom they could talk freely if they so wanted.

And a doctor visiting a mixed secondary modern school commented: 'I think there had really been very little discussion with the staff prior to these programmes.'

Seventy-two per cent of the teachers watching admitted the programmes helped discussion on subjects they would not otherwise have covered in class. VD was the one most often quoted, though masturbation, intercourse and human relations between boys and girls or with their parents, were all mentioned. A woman teacher in a mixed secondary modern school said: 'The children asked many questions about things which can "go wrong" with intercourse and childbirth. They obviously wanted information and I had not considered discussing these aspects previously.'

Signs of some embarrassment were reported from 51 per cent of classes, but in every case it apparently wore off quickly. 'The animated diagrams on menstruation and childbirth particularly caused some embarrassment with the boys, some of whom were seeing these diagrams for the first time in this particular form. It disappeared very quickly and was replaced by a keen interest in the programmes concerned.' A fourth-year girl from a girls' school wrote: 'The programmes on childbirth put a lump in my throat and made me feel embarrassed at times, but I found it very interesting and I think about the most interesting of all the programmes that I've seen.'

One difficulty children experienced was talking to teachers for the first time on these subjects. One man in a boys' school said: 'Although I detected no signs of embarrassment, I felt an easing of relationships once I had myself used some of the normally restricted terms (e.g. sexual intercourse and uterus) freely in discussion.'

Many schools commented on the value of seeing discussion by a mixed group. A boys' secondary modern school commented on the first programme. 'The relaxed, open and unselfconscious talk set the right atmosphere. It was good for boys to hear a mature woman speak in this way. A serious, sensible and matter-of-fact discussion followed.' A girls' school was 'impressed by the mature attitude of the boys to childbirth.' And a Roman Catholic boy said: 'With the aid of these programmes I was able to get the point of view of the girl.'

A variety of views was expressed on the way moral issues were dealt with. Several teachers felt that insufficient emphasis had been put on 'the fact that pre-marital intercourse is morally wrong'; others thanked us for not preaching at the children. Some teachers outlined the points they had felt it necessary to stress after programmes; these clearly showed how individual the teaching of morals is. The only comment on the religious aspects were from children at a secondary modern Roman Catholic boys' school. This quotation from one of the boys is typical of several essays: 'It is God's will that intercourse between "married" couples takes place, but very seldom if at all was God mentioned in these programmes. This is bad because God should be a part of our everyday lives and we should keep Him in our minds always.'

Contraception

Before the programmes were made, the Granada Schools Advisory Committee discussed a possible explanatory programme about methods of birth control, but felt that many Heads were not yet prepared to take the responsibility for giving children this information. So contraception was only mentioned during the programmes.

In the questionnaire sent to schools after the series, we said: 'Many young people have asked for a factual schools' television programme on contraception. Should we give it to them?' Answers were:

	%		%
Unqualified 'Yes'	38	Unqualified 'No'	39·6
Qualified 'Yes'	12·8	Qualified 'No'	4·8
	50·8		44·4

Don't know =	4·8

Opinions of the people in the programmes

The adults. On the whole the specialists taking part were approved of; for every critical remark, there is one of approbation. The venereologist came in for particular praise. Several teachers were put off by Michael Scott's manner, and almost all the essays from a class of girls, who had obviously discussed the matter with their teacher, contained remarks like: 'The interviewer, Michael Scott, didn't take these programmes seriously. He was always laughing and he always had a smirk on his face when he asked a question.' However, one lone rebel from the same school said: 'I think Michael Scott was very good in the programmes and I think he made the teenagers feel at ease in his presence.' Other sets of essays made no mention of him, and some Training College students commented favourably on his handling of the discussions. The group of children who took part in the programme with him plainly approved of his manner and were at ease with him.

The children. By and large, the children were strongly approved of, though several individuals came in for criticism. Though care had been taken to balance the group taking part, inevitably some members talked more than others, and this created an impression of 'middle-class' domination. For this reason, several tough secondary modern schools found them difficult to identify with, which probably accounts for the boredom some children felt during the longer discussions. These comments are representative of many we received:

Girls' secondary modern school: 'The class felt that the girls were very like themselves and the fact that boys took part in the discussion and talked freely without embarrassment meant that they too were willing to talk freely.'

County secondary school: 'Very like themselves – some shy, some outspoken.'

Independent girls' school: 'Surprised that questions asked were exactly what they would have asked.'

Secondary modern boys' school: 'Admired the "cool" nerve of the older boys and girls . . . the impression gained was that the children on the programme were real and "with it".'

Boys' Technical High: 'In general, the group had sensible views on the topics under discussion. They were lively and enthusiastic. However the programme was largely cornered by four of the group and we felt that the other members could have been replaced by teenagers with views to put forward.'

Secondary modern boys' school: 'The class were a little suspicious. They were rather more sophisticated than our children.'

Secondary modern boys' school: 'The general feeling was that in the main the children were from grammar schools and from the lower

206

middle-class group. The apparently younger boy, who appeared to be from a secondary modern school, was recognized as being "one of us".'

14½-year-olds in a mixed secondary modern school formed the opinion that 'the children were immature, except for a couple of children; other than that they had too many airs and graces.'

Several schools got bored seeing the same faces each week and would have preferred a change. On the other hand, one commented after the last programme that 'they had just got to know the resident team really well and felt a sense of personal loss at their departure'. A Roman Catholic boy sums up a criticism which came from several schools: 'While I was watching these programmes I noticed the boys or youths taking part did not speak very often, they left all the talking to the girls who, incidentally, spoke of what they knew and thought. This is a bad point on behalf of the boys, they should have spoken more often.' Another comment from a secondary modern boy echoes the 92 per cent of teachers who gave qualified approval to using 15 and 16-year-olds rather than adults to raise the questions. 'Boys and girls on the programme was a very good idea instead of having men and women. This is because most young people have difficulties more than others and it is no use an adult trying to explain when younger people can do it on the programme more better.'

Criticisms of the programmes

There were three main criticisms:

(1) *The time of day and months of transmissions.* Many schools who break for lunch at noon complained that 11.30–11.50 gave no time for the vital discussion afterwards. Several people who tried to get a class talking in a later lesson found it difficult. Transmission times have been put back for the broadcasts in 1967. Showing the series in May and June meant an inevitable clash with exams and with Whitsun holidays. Some schools overcame these problems by taping the programmes or by asking children to watch at home. In one city school children came back into school during the holiday to watch.

In 1967 it may be possible to have a second block showing of the series during the first two weeks of July, after exams are over. None of these arrangements makes it possible for Easter leavers to benefit from the programmes. There seems no way of helping them unless they watch at the end of their third year.

(2) *Criticism of the camera work and sound level of the programmes.* Many justified complaints were made about several children talking at once, the varying sound-level of the voices and the person talking not always being seen. These difficulties arose from the techniques used for making the programmes. Unscripted discussion with subsequent editing caused most of the problems. Some teachers also criticized the technique of showing the captions over the discussion at the close of the programme. They would have preferred a re-cap and a 'that's all for today' ending.

(3) *Criticism from people who want the subjects dealt with in a different way.* Just as no two teachers would give the same lesson, so no two people would include exactly the same information in a programme; naturally, a great deal of the criticism of the series came from people who wanted a different emphasis or balance given to it. The main request was for a more documentary approach. Thirty-one per cent of schools thought the balance between factual information and discussion was correct, but 57 per cent wanted more factual information *as well* as discussion. Only 11 per cent wanted the programmes to be entirely documentary films. We were asked for a fuller use of television's ability to bring to the classroom a film of childbirth; for a full sequence of pictures *and* labelled diagrams of the development of the foetus; for interviews with teenage unmarried mothers and fathers; for interviews with people suffering from VD or with 'bragging youngsters' with sexual experience. Some also suggested that pictures of the symptoms of VD and of the disease in an advanced state should have been shown. This desire for more information probably made some schools wish the programmes were longer.

Children's own assessment

Although these programmes were designed to help teachers, it is by their effect on children that they will be judged. We end this part of our report by quoting some of the answers a group of secondary modern children wrote to the question: 'What has the series done for you?'

'It has taught me what I did not know before and showed me that sex should be brought out into the open. It has answered a great number of my questions about sex. I feel easier in my mind now I have seen the programmes.' *A girl of* 15.

'It has made me realize that other people (teenagers and adults) are thinking on the same lines as we are. The programmes have made me understand people slightly better.' *A boy of* 16.

'Given you a feeling of not being alone. Made you understand other people.' *A boy of* 16.

'The series has enabled me to understand everything connected with sex to some extent. It has helped me to see my parents' and other teenagers' points of view. By hearing other girls' questions I now have the answers to some of the questions I would have liked to ask.' *A girl of* 16.

'Made me realize that although sex is natural it should still be kept till after marriage because it can cause a child to be born without a proper home. That it *is* true that males don't take enough responsibility.' *A girl of* 16.

And a final comment from a 15-year-old girl from a secondary modern school in the west of England:

On the whole I think the programme gave a lot of information and was very good. The young people concerned in the discussion were straight to the point and were not afraid to say what they thought. There was no embarrassment on the part of the people taking part in the discussion and so they helped us talk freely about the subjects. The subjects of these programmes are often 'put away' in the backs of people's minds, who tend to think that they should not be talked about; even my parents take this view, they have never really talked about these matters except the bare essentials. This programme was completely beneficial to all our class, and I feel if there are more programmes like this it will be a good thing.

Ninety per cent of the schools watching appear to agree with her, as they have said they will watch the series again in 1967.

Appendix A

Assessment of individual programmes

Programme 1. 'Puberty'. Introduced by Dr Zena Maxwell.
Transmitted: May 6, 1966.
Programme seen by 97 per cent of schools watching the series.
Teachers rated the amount of factual information given as:

	%
Too much	1·5
Enough	63·3
Too little	35·2

How familiar was the factual information to the children?

	%
All familiar	53
Some familiar	47

This programme was well received and was listed as the first choice by 25 per cent of schools. Another 25 per cent put it second. A few children felt the factual information was more suitable for 13-year-olds. Many other schools had to explain the technical terms, such as masturbation, and felt that rather a wide field was covered in one programme.

Programme 2. 'Childbirth'. Introduced by Dr June Lawson.
Transmitted: May 13, 1966.
Programme seen by 97 per cent of schools watching the series.
Teachers rated the amount of factual information given as:

	%
Too much	4
Enough	36
Too little	60

How familiar was the factual information to the children?

	%
All familiar	37·5
Some familiar	61
None familiar	1·5

Schools tended to place this programme second or fourth in their list of preferences.

As the figures above show, there was real need for a fuller factual film about the development and birth of a baby. We were asked for more emphasis on the part played by the husband both at conception and during his wife's pregnancy. Information on twins and deformed babies was also requested.

Programme 3. 'Unmarried Mothers'. Introduced by Mrs Pauline Crabbe.
Transmitted: May 20, 1966.
Programme seen by 92 per cent of schools watching the series.
Teachers rated the amount of factual information given as:

	%
Too much	1·5
Enough	70·5
Too little	28

How familiar was the factual information to the children?

	%
All familiar	33·3
Some familiar	65
None familiar	1·7

This programme rates about number three in order of preference.

The figures for illegitimacy shocked many children. Again, extended interviews with teenage unmarried mothers would have been welcomed. So would more emphasis on the father's responsibilities and points of view. As one teacher wrote: 'Boys felt that more emphasis should have been placed on the aspects of their responsibility although they agreed that looking in on the terrific responsibility borne by the girls made them think.'

The children's essays show that some were extremely interested in the subject. Others, particularly boys, were bored by the discussion.

Programme 4. 'VD'. Introduced by a consultant venereologist.
Transmitted: May 27, 1966.
Programme seen by 74 per cent of schools watching the series.
Teachers rated the factual information given as:

	%
Too much	7
Enough	58
Too little	35

How familiar was the factual information to the children?

	%
All familiar	15·2
Some familiar	52
None familiar	32·8

This programme is rated number one in usefulness and interest.

The figures again came as a shock to many children. Some schools asked for photographs to be shown of the disease. Many of the children's essays particularly welcomed information on a subject that is not normally discussed.

Programme 5. 'The Sexual Behaviour of Young People'.
Introduced by Michael Schofield.
Transmitted: June 10, 1966.
Programme seen by 85 per cent of schools watching the series.

211

Teachers rated the factual information given as:

	%
Too much	3·5
Enough	69·7
Too little	26·8

How familiar was the factual information to the children?

	%
All familiar	34·6
Some familiar	63·5
None familiar	1·9

This was the most controversial programme in the series. Both staff and children tended to put it either first choice or fifth choice. It was either liked very much or thought to be a waste of time.

Two children, who put it number one, said: 'Gave plenty of facts, was more straightforward and to the point. The visitor really knew and understood teenagers and discussion was good.' *Girl of* 16.

And: 'I could relate it to my own and my friends' experience easier than any other programme.' *Boy of* 15.

Others complained it was one big argument when all the children talked at once and the points were not clearly made, so there was danger of the wrong impression being given. As one teacher said: 'Weakest programme so far. Relationship of leader with the group not nearly so good as in previous programmes. Discussion could have been better disciplined, it was felt that often good points were made by the group members which may have been missed.'

Programme 6. 'Family and Marriage'.
Introduced by Professor Ronald Fletcher.
Transmitted: June 17, 1966.
Programme seen by 78 per cent of schools watching the series.
Teachers rated factual information given as:

	%
Too much	4
Enough	65
Too little	31

How familiar was the factual information to the children?

	%
All familiar	32
Some familiar	68

This programme was liked least of the series, though several teachers'

212

and children's essays mentioned the discussions about divorce and parental relationships as valuable in stimulating extensive classroom discussion.

On the whole teachers felt that insufficient facts had been given and that the discussion was based on personal opinions unsupported by experience. By this last programme many of the subjects covered had already been raised in previous classroom discussions, hence a slight sense of boredom.

Appendix B

ANALYSIS OF ANSWERS TO THE GRANADA QUESTIONNAIRE

Ninety-five questionnaires were sent out; 69 were returned. In addition, 23 schools reported weekly and detailed letters, children's essays and general comments were received from a further 6 schools in Granadaland. In all, 102 Granadaland schools corresponded with us in some way or other about the programmes.

As all the schools did not answer every question, the replies have been converted into percentages. In no case are the figures based on less than 47 replies, the majority of replies being in the 60's.

A. *Schools watching*

	%
Grammar and comprehensive schools	20
Secondary modern schools	68
Special schools	4
Independent schools	6
Colleges of Education and Further Education	2
	100

B. *Classes watching*

(1)

Boys	22
Girls	36
Mixed	43
	101

(2) Average size of class: 44 children.

(3) Average age of the children watching: 15 years.

(4) Is television used regularly in your school?

	%
Yes	88
No	12

(5) Programmes seen:

	%			%
1 Puberty	97		4 VD	74
2 Childbirth	97		5 Sexual behaviour	83
3 Unmarried mothers	92		6 Family and marriage	78

(6) Is a regular course of sex education run in your school?

	%
Yes	50·8
Combined with other subjects	21·5
No	27·7

(7) Did you regard these programmes as:

	%
(i) A complete course of instruction?	4·7
(ii) A supplement to or revision of other instruction?	95·3

(8) How many, if any, parents asked for their children to be withdrawn from watching the programmes?

Fourteen children or 0·4% of the total number of children viewing.

(9) To your knowledge, how many parents

(i) Watched the programmes?	About 144 or 4·5% of the children's homes
(ii) Discussed them with their children?	About 198 or 6% of the children's homes

Many schools had no information on this subject.

C. *The teachers' assessment of the programmes and their effect on the class*

(1) Were there any signs of embarrassment among the children during the programme?

	%
(i) A lot	0
(ii) A little	51·6
(iii) None	48·4

All the 51·6 per cent who admitted to a little embarrassment said it wore off quickly.

(2) Looking back on the programmes, have they helped you to discuss subjects with the class which you would not otherwise have discussed?

	%		%
Yes	71·8	No	28·3

(3) Would you have preferred the programmes to be factual documentary films rather than discussions?

	%
Balance between film and discussion about right	31·4
More film and a little less discussion preferred	57·3
A programme of factual film preferred	11·3

(4) What do you think of the technique of using a group of 15 and 16-year-olds to raise the main questions?

	%
Liked	64·6
Qualified approval	27·7
Disliked	7·7

(5) What did the class think of the children on the programme?

	%
All liked	46·3
Some liked	46·3
Disliked	7·4

(6) How would you rate the amount of factual information given in each programme?

| | Too much | Enough | Too little |
	%	%	%
'Puberty'	1·5	63·3	35·2
'Childbirth'	4·0	36·0	60·0
'Unmarried Mothers'	1·5	70·5	28·0
'VD'	7·0	58·0	35·0
'Sexual Behaviour of Young People'	3·5	69·7	26·8
'Family and Marriage'	4·0	65·0	31·0

(7) How familiar to the children was the factual information in each programme?

	All familiar %	Some familiar %	None familiar %
'Puberty'	53·0	47·0	—
'Childbirth'	37·5	61·0	1·5
'Unmarried Mothers'	33·3	65·0	1·7
'VD'	15·2	52·0	32·8
'Sexual Behaviour of Young People'	34·6	63·5	1·9
'Family and Marriage'	32·0	68·0	—

(8) Please number the programmes in order of preference from 1–6.

	1st	2nd	3rd	4th	5th	6th
'Puberty'	27·7	26·2	12·3	9·2	13·8	10·8
'Childbirth'	13·4	22·3	13·3	24·0	15·0	12·0
'Unmarried Mothers'	9·2	22·0	34·0	12·2	18·5	4·1
'VD'	36·7	18·3	20·0	18·3	1·7	5·0
'Sexual Behaviour of Young People'	20·5	8·5	15·1	15·1	22·0	18·8
'Family and Marriage'	3·6	9·0	12·8	27·3	21·8	25·5

(9) Will you use this series when it is shown again next year?

	%		%
Yes	90	No	10

(10) Did the programme notes tell you what you needed to know beforehand?

	%
Yes	100

(11) Many young people have asked for a factual schools television programme on contraception. Should we give it to them?

	%				%
Unqualified 'Yes'	38	Don't know	4·8	Unqualified 'No'	39·6
Qualified 'Yes'	12·8			Qualified 'No'	4·8

NOTE

1 *The Sexual Behaviour of Young People,* by Michael Schofield (Longmans, 1965). See Chapter 12.

15 Some Reactions to a Schools' Television Programme on Venereal Disease

ROGER L. BROWN

INTRODUCTION

'Understanding' was the general title given to a series of six television programmes for secondary schools produced by Granada Television. The series was designed 'to encourage responsible discussions between teachers and 15- and 16-year-old children on aspects of sex, marriage, family life and friendship'. The series was first broadcast in several areas during to Spring of 1966, and has been re-broadcast during the first half of 1967.

During the first showing, research into the impact and effectiveness of the series was conducted at a mixed comprehensive school in Yorkshire. Three classes of 15-year-old pupils, containing boys and girls of average to below average intelligence, were selected to watch the series, and information about what they thought of various aspects of each programme, and on what changes in knowledge and attitude each programme produced, was collected by means of questionnaires which each pupil completed anonymously, under the supervision of the teacher, before and immediately after each programme.[1]

The format of the programmes was roughly the same throughout the series. An expert on the particular topic being discussed was shown in conversation with a group of adolescents of about the same age as the intended audience. The same group of young people took part in each programme, and the same chairman appeared each week. In the first two programmes, introductory film inserts were used to recapitulate the basic physiological facts, though the series was not primarily intended to teach information of this sort.

The major focus of each programme was as follows:

Brown, R. L., 'Some reactions to a school's television programme on venereal disease', *Health Education Journal*, vol. XXVI, no. 3 (September 1967), pp. 108–16.

Programme 1	'Puberty'.
Programme 2	'Childbirth'.
Programme 3	'Unmarried Mothers'.
Programme 4	'Venereal Disease'.
Programme 5	'The Sexual Behaviour of Young People'.
Programme 6	'The Family and Marriage'.

THE SIX PROGRAMMES COMPARED

The first stage in analysing the data was to see which of the programmes seemed to have had a particular impact as measured by the pupils' ratings of each member of the series on a number of dimensions. Because there was a good deal of absence from the school during the period over which the series was broadcast, only 23 pupils (14 boys and nine girls) saw all six programmes; but for methodological reasons the initial comparison of the programmes was made on the basis of the reactions by this rather small group. Each of the 23 pupils rated each of the six programmes on 12 three-point scales, an average rating for each programme on any dimension was calculated, and the rating of any programme on each dimension was then expressed as a rank varying between one and six. As Table 1 makes clear, the fourth programme in the series, that on 'Venereal Disease', stood out quite noticeably from the others. On nine of the 12 dimensions, this programme came in first place.

This finding is all the more striking, because there seems to have been a general tendency for the later programmes in the series to have a lesser impact, and to be less well received than the earlier ones.

From present research, there is no means of knowing whether this tendency was due to the later programmes being actually less intrinsically interesting, or whether the novelty of watching the series just decreased progressively from the beginning to the end; but whatever the explanation, the programme on 'Venereal Disease' quite clearly reversed for that week the general downward trend. A 'halo' effect was probably operating in the way the pupils rated this programme, so that a very favourable evaluation of the new information the programme provided, or of the expert who took part (a consultant venereologist), carried over to, and coloured, the evaluation of other aspects of the programme. The general impression which the research provides is that this fourth

218

programme answered explicitly or implicitly a number of questions which were in the viewers' minds, though this could obviously not have been achieved without a clear and sympathetic presentation by the expert. The programme only came in third place in terms of interest, but this was probably due to the 'order effect' already mentioned.

TRANSMISSION OF INFORMATION

Table 1 shows that the fourth programme was placed in first place in terms of 'informativeness' and 'correcting wrong ideas'. The second programme in the series, on 'Childbirth', came in second place on

Table 1. *Ranks of six programmes on 12 dimensions*

| Dimension | Rank of programme number | | | | | |
	1	2	3	4	5	6
Interest	1	2	4	3	5	6
Informativeness	3	2	4	1	5	6
Helpfulness	3	2	4	1	5	6
Correcting wrong ideas	3	2	4	1	5	6
Worrying	4	2·5	5·5	1	5·5	2·5
Clarity	1	3	4	2	5·5	5·5
Liveliness	1	3	5·5	4	2	5·5
Expert's intelligence	3	2	4	1	6	5
Expert's friendliness	1	2	4	3	5	6
Expert's truthfulness	3	1·5	4·5	1·5	4·5	6
Expert's pleasantness	2	3	5·5	1	5·5	4
Agreement with expert	2·5	2·5	5	1	4	6
Sum of 12 ranks	27·5	27·5	54·0	20·5	58·0	64·5
Overall rank	2·5	2·5	4	1	5	6

both of these dimensions, and it is of some interest to see whether there are *significant* differences between these two programmes in these respects. In all, 60 pupils (35 boys and 25 girls) saw the second programme, and 53 pupils (33 boys and 20 girls) saw the fourth. Tables 2 and 3 show that the programme on 'Venereal Disease' was significantly more 'informative' for boys (the statistical test being inapplicable to the girls' data), and that so far as 'correcting wrong ideas' went, the same sort of difference between the two programmes

Table 2. *'Informativeness' of the second and fourth programmes*

Sex of pupils	Programme	This programme		
		told me a lot of things I didn't know	told me some things I didn't know	didn't tell me anything I didn't know
Boys	'Childbirth'	2	27	6
	'Venereal Disease'	15	18	0
			$\chi^2 = 14.30, \; p < 0.001$	
Girls	'Childbirth'	1	19	5
	'Venereal Disease'	6	12	2
			χ^2 indeterminate	

Table 3. *'Correction of wrong ideas' by the second and fourth programmes*

Sex of pupils	Programme	This programme showed me that		
		many of the ideas I had before were wrong	some of the ideas I had before were wrong	hardly any of the ideas I had before were wrong
Boys	'Childbirth'	3	11	21
	'Venereal Disease'	8	19	6
			$\chi^2 = 12.40, p < 0.001$	
Girls	'Childbirth'	0	10	15
	'Venereal Disease'	3	11	6
			$\chi^2 = 4.01, p < 0.05$	

was significant for pupils of both sexes. These findings lend added support to the suggestion that the informational content of the fourth programme made it 'stand out' from the other five.

Since the 'Venereal Disease' programme was clearly particularly stimulating for the pupils, it was thought worthwhile to analyse the reactions to it in some detail.

Because the questionnaires about the programme which had just been seen had to be completed within a half-hour period, so as to allow some time for a general class discussion of the programme before the end of the 'double period' made available within the school's timetable, and because the questionnaires administered after the first five programmes also contained questions relating to the *next* week's programme, it was only possible to ask questions about three points of information covered in each programme. Identical questions had been asked a week previously, so as to provide a 'baseline' against which to measure the effectiveness of the programme. Sixty-two pupils (36 boys and 26 girls) gave answers to the three relevant questions a week before the programme on 'Venereal Disease', and 53 pupils (33 boys and 20 girls) answered the same questions immediately after having seen the fourth

Table 4. *Changes in knowledge on three questions*

Subject of question	Sex of pupils	Before		After		χ^2	p
		Right	Wrong	Right	Wrong		
Symptom of	Boys	14	22	30	3	20·12	<0·001
gonorrhoea	Girls	9	17	19	1	17·32	<0·001
Incidence	Boys	13	23	30	3	22·99	<0·001
of VD	Girls	8	18	15	5	8·85	<0·01
Incubation	Boys	22	14	22	11	0·23	N.S.
period for	Girls	15	11	10	10	0·27	N.S.
syphilis							

programme. To make completion and scoring as easy as possible, each question was of the multiple-choice type, with four alternative answers. The three questions on venereal disease, with the correct answers underlined at the end, were as follows:

(*a*) One of the symptoms of the venereal disease called gonorrhoea is a frequent passing of water.

(*b*) The number of people with venereal disease is rising quite fast.

(*c*) The signs of the venereal disease called syphilis appear at least nine days after a person gets infected.

Table 4 shows that with one exception the programme led to a larger proportion of both boys and girls giving the right answer after the programme than before. (The totals have not been corrected for guessings.)

For both boys and girls, the proportion giving the correct answer to the first two questions rose significantly. No significant improvement was seen on the third question, but this was perhaps a harder one, and was certainly rather specific. Of course, having been asked the same question the week before in most cases, pupils would be particularly sensitive to the relevant piece of information when it occurred in the programme, but it is none the less fair to say that the programme seems to have been effective in transmitting factual information.

Table 5. *Relationship between knowledge and worry after seeing the programme*

	Boys		Girls	
Evaluation of programme	3 answers correct	2 or less answers correct	3 answers correct	2 or less answers correct
Very or rather worrying	4	11	4	2
Not worrying	12	6	4	10
	$X^2 = 5.23, p < 0.05$		X^2 indeterminate	

It will have been noted from Table 1 that the pupils found the fourth programme in the series the most worrying one. There is a slight indication in the data that for boys, though not for girls, there was a relationship between level of knowledge about venereal disease after the programme and how worrying the programme was found to be. For boys the lower the level of knowledge, the more worrying the programme was thought. This analysis is shown in Table 5. Of course, the numbers on which this finding is based are very small, but the difference here between boys and girls may be related to other differences between the sexes which will be mentioned below.

CHANGES IN BELIEF AND ATTITUDE

Besides trying to find out whether the programmes were effective in transmitting information (remembering that this was not the prime objective), the research was also aimed at discovering what changes in attitude took place as a result of watching the series.

Reactions to a Schools' Television Programme on Venereal Disease

The pupils were asked both before and after seeing the programme on 'Venereal Disease' a question on whether they thought venereal disease ought to be talked about more than it is. Here again, the effect of the programme was different for boys and girls. After seeing the programme, more boys thought that venereal disease ought to be talked about more than it is than had done so

Table 6. *Changes in attitudes to discussion of VD*

Sex of pupils	Time	much more than it is	more than it is	a bit more than it is
		VD is a problem, that ought to be talked about		
Boys	Before	20	12	4
	After	26	4	3
			$\chi^2 = 4 \cdot 18, p < 0 \cdot 05$	
Girls	Before	14	9	3
	After	12	8	0
			$\chi^2 = 0 \cdot 18$, N.S.	

Table 7. *Changes in attitudes to shame about VD*

Sex of pupils	Time	to feel very ashamed about it	to feel rather ashamed about it	not to feel ashamed about it
		People with VD ought		
Boys	Before	8	17	11
	After	3	10	20
			$\chi^2 = 6 \cdot 57, p < 0 \cdot 05$	
Girls	Before	5	18	3
	After	2	16	2
			χ^2 indeterminate	

beforehand, but this was not true for the girls. The analysis of the relevant figures is shown in Table 6.

It is interesting to put alongside this finding of a difference between boys and girls one from another question designed to tap attitudes towards venereal disease. The pupils were asked a question designed to find out whether they thought that people who contracted venereal disease ought to be ashamed about it. The effect of the programme was to lead boys to say more frequently that people with venereal disease ought *not* to feel ashamed about it, but there was no such effect as far as the girls were concerned. The analysis of these data is presented in Table 7.

Although the pupils found the programme on 'Venereal Disease' relatively worrying, what was said during it did have the effect of leading more viewers to believe that venereal disease is curable than had been the case beforehand. This was true for both boys and girls, as Table 8 shows.

Table 8. *Changes in beliefs about the curability of VD*

		If a person with VD goes to a doctor he has		
Sex of pupils	Time	a good chance of being cured	some chance of being cured	hardly any chance of being cured
Boys	Before	10	23	3
	After	28	3	2
		$\chi^2 = 22 \cdot 68, p < 0 \cdot 001$		
Girls	Before	9	17	0
	After	18	2	0
		$\chi^2 = 14 \cdot 30, p < 0 \cdot 001$		

Table 9. *Perceptions of the 'helpfulness' of the programme*

	What this programme told me will be		
Sex of pupils	very helpful to me	quite helpful to me	not very helpful to me
Boys	19	11	3
Girls	4	14	2
	$\chi^2 = 7 \cdot 16, p < 0 \cdot 01$		

In terms of beliefs about the curability of venereal disease, it may be that the programme was equally reassuring for both boys and girls; but when we turn to examine the data from a question in which the pupils were asked to rate the programme in terms of its usefulness to them, the difference between the sexes re-emerges.

Boys found the programme more helpful than did the girls to a significant extent, as Table 9 shows, and this finding may provide the best clue to the underlying reason for the differences between the reception of this programme on 'Venereal Disease' by boys and girls.

DISCUSSION

The research techniques used in the work reported on here were of the simplest sort, yet the differences revealed are in several cases sufficiently striking to invite comment and an attempt at explanation.

By the age of 15, the vast majority of adolescents will be familiar with many of the details of the physiology of reproduction, and a proportion will have had various sorts of sexual experience; but the subject of venereal disease will probably remain for many a topic surrounded by a good deal of fear and misinformation, and therefore one about which adolescents are eager for knowledge and reassurance. The Schofield report[1] makes it clear that adolescents are on the whole ignorant and misinformed about venereal disease. Eagerness for information may well have had a good deal to do with the considerable impact which the fourth programme in the 'Understanding' series achieved: the programme was certainly perceived as being highly informative *and* as serving to correct misinformation.

The programme led both boys and girls to believe more than they had done beforehand that venereal disease is curable, and on boys it had the effect of leading them to say that venereal disease ought to be talked about more than it is and that people who contract venereal disease ought not to be ashamed of the fact. Although the programme was perceived as relatively 'worrying', it may have done much to *reduce* viewers' worries about venereal disease by treating it as a curable set of diseases like many others and by bringing the whole topic out into the open. It might be argued that by reducing the fear of venereal disease too far the programme could lead towards a higher degree of promiscuity, but of course the present research cannot suggest any answers to questions of this sort. Boys particularly, it might be said, had a weight of vague worry and guilt lifted from them by the programme, and it may be suggested that it was the definite information which the programme contained which achieved this. This point of view is supported by the finding that for boys worry was negatively related to knowledge after the programme. Perhaps those boys who did not understand the programme so well as others did not have their vague fears about venereal disease reduced as much either.

It may be natural for boys rather than girls to see themselves as potentially 'responsible' for the spread of venereal disease, and this may be the underlying reason for the differential effects of this programme on the two sexes. Boys perhaps have a greater *need* to know that there is nothing particularly mysterious about venereal disease, and that it is not an inevitable concomitant of sexual activity. However, if the explanation of these findings lies in the characteristics of the male sexual role in our society, this may also suggest that girls may need to have brought to their attention the 'active' part they can play as carriers of venereal disease.

NOTES

1 Other information on reactions to the series is contained in the report produced by Granada Television. (See Chapter 14 [Ed].) The survey data described there back up the major findings of the present research concerning the relatively great impact on the fourth programme in the series.

REFERENCES

Schofield, M. (1965) *The Sexual Behaviour of Young People* (London: Longmans). (See pp. 113–18, 250–3.)

16   A Report on 'Living and Growing'

GRAMPIAN TELEVISION

'Living and Growing'

'Living and Growing' was a project in sex education undertaken by Grampian Television on the advice of the company's Schools Advisory Committee and in co-operation with primary and secondary school teachers in the North and East of Scotland. The project was based on two television series, eight programmes in school time for children of 10 to 13, and eight in the evenings for parents and teachers. Meetings and preview sessions gave teachers the opportunity of contributing their ideas to the planning of the series and preparing themselves to make the best classroom use of the programmes. A booklet for adults accompanied the series.

FORM AND CONTENT OF PROGRAMMES

It was decided that the programmes should basically give the facts of human reproduction in a style and vocabulary acceptable to 10 to 13 year olds. Although it was decided that intensive discussions of moral and social questions were inappropriate in a television series for this age, the series would try to be more than just a list of facts. 'Living' and 'Growing' would be set in the family unit and shown not only as man's greatest potential for happiness, but also as part of the process of evolution which makes each individual unique.

Programme 1

The idea of the human life-cycle is introduced. Children are made aware of their relationship to children of other age groups, to teenagers and to mature adults. Properties common to all living things are pointed out and reproduction is discussed in terms of replacement of worn out members of the species and in terms of human progress. It is shown how humans have developed the care of their young and how stability is supplied by the family unit.

Grampian Television, *Living and Growing* (Aberdeen, 1968).

Programme 2

The programme shows that every human being is unique. The idea of evolution is simply stated, showing how characteristics are selected. The need for two parents is explained to provide a new human being who resembles both, but is identical to neither.

Programme 3

A basic vocabulary of the sex organs is established. The theme of the programme is the differences between the sexes in childhood and at puberty. Mention is made of some of the 'problems' of beginning to develop, the growth of hair, spots and acne, 'breaking' of the voice, 'wet dreams'.

Programme 4

The menstrual cycle is illustrated with reassurance for girls approaching puberty. Fertilisation is explained by simple diagrams in terms of part of the relationship of affection between parents who have decided that their love and respect for each other is such that they would like to have a baby.

Programme 5

The growth of the embryo in the uterus and the size and appearance of the foetus at various stages of gestation, are described. The mother is seen in the family setting preparing for the birth of the child.

Programme 6

Labour and the birth of a baby are described diagrammatically. The cutting of the cord is shown as the culmination of the act of love 38 weeks earlier. Post-natal care and feeding are discussed. The family unit is again illustrated with the role of the father emphasised.

Programme 7

A group of children from an Aberdeen school spontaneously question Dr Dennis in the studios about some of the points which have not been covered fully in the earlier programmes. They ask about twinning, breast feeding, the possibility of abnormality at birth, etc.

Programme 8

The whole process of 'Living and Growing' is shown as a cycle. A girl child is born, grows up, marries, and has a baby—we see the live birth. The child is a boy who in turn grows up . . . and so the story goes on.

USE OF THE SERIES IN SCHOOLS

This report was prepared to give the producers some idea of the success of 'Living and Growing' and to help in the planning of future series. It may also be useful for teachers deciding to follow the repeat transmissions.

The rest of this report is based on information in:

Weekly report cards from 29 teachers
Mid-series reports from 68 teachers
End-of-series reports from 114 teachers—*(most of the detailed information is drawn from these reports) and letters from 14 teachers.*

In all, 148 teachers reported (this number includes 8 health visitors). In addition, members of the production team visited schools and spoke to parents and teachers' meetings.

Of the 148 teachers
46% were class teachers
25% were head teachers
13% were special subject teachers (6 Homecraft; 1 Parentcraft;
    4 Science; 2 English; 6 Physical Education)
10% were deputy head teachers
 6% were health visitors
 5% were unmarried males
32% were married males
29% were unmarried females
34% were married females

Age range of children in groups viewing schools series

Under 10	5%
10–11	29%
11–12	32% Suggested age range 10–13—83%
12–13	22%
Over 13	12%

Note: The youngest group included 7 year olds; the oldest 16 years olds.

Size of viewing groups for schools series

Under 20 pupils in group	13%
20–40 pupils in group	52%
40–100 pupils in group	30%
Over 100 pupils in group	5%

Note: Although viewing groups were sometimes large, discussion was usually in class units. Not all teachers have viewing figures, but we know that reports are based on reactions of over 3,800 children.

Sex composition of groups for viewing of schools series

Mixed	62%
Male	13% (5% of the total had no choice because of type of school)
Female	25% (7% of the total had no choice because of type of school)

Note: Practical conditions often determined whether viewing should be mixed or one sex.

Sex composition of groups for discussion

Mixed	33%
One Sex	67% (12% of the total had no choice because of type of school)

Note: 5 teachers said they would change from single sex to mixed groups if the series were repeated.

One teacher who kept boys and girls together thought separation would 'Defeat the whole purpose'.

Teachers who had separate sex discussions thought the questions were much less inhibited than they might otherwise have been. The emotional and physical interests of the sexes are different and so single sex discussion was more valuable. One primary school, where boys and girls viewed separately, had single sex discussions immediately after the programmes, followed later by mixed sessions.

Previous work in sex education

72% of the teachers reported that discussion of human reproduction had not previously been a regular part of their syllabus.

Preparation by teachers

45% attended preview meetings
83% watched the evening series for adults
85% used the programme notes.

Place of series in general class work

40% teachers used it as a complete course of instruction.
60% of teachers used it as part of a larger study—(2 teachers used it as revision of a previous course).

Consultation with parents

68% sent letters to parents, informing them that the series was to be followed and telling them about the adult series. A few *asked* for parents' permission.
14% held meetings to discuss series with parents. 4 girls in one school were withdrawn from the series; 2 in another school were withdrawn from programme 4.
60% of teachers thought that over half of their pupil's parents had viewed.

		Most of the information %	Some of the information %	Practically none of the information %
Programme 1	Boys	64	31	5
	Girls	69	25	6
Programme 2	Boys	6	44	50
	Girls	5	50	45
Programme 3	Boys	21	73	6
	Girls	24	71	5
Programme 4	Boys	6	32	62
	Girls	10	56	34
Programme 5	Boys	5	17	78
	Girls	5	24	72
Programme 6	Boys	3	31	66
	Girls	4	39	57
Programme 7	Boys	38	48	14
	Girls	41	49	10
Programme 8	Boys	71	29	—
	Girls	75	25	—

Notes:
1. Of the groups who already knew most of the information in the programmes, 6% were under the suggested age range of the series, 72% within the age range and 22% above the suggested age range.

2. By programme 7, many groups had had long discussion sessions and most of the questions had been answered. This programme was intended mainly for schools where little discussion followed. For the majority of schools, it was hoped to reinforce classroom work and demonstrate the possibilities of free discussion.

3. Programme 8 was a revision of the series, introducing only very few new words and ideas.

ASSESSMENT OF SERIES BY TEACHERS

Information in schools programmes known to pupils before watching programmes

Teachers were asked to estimate how much of the factual information in each programme was familiar to the children and indicate if the rating was different for boys and girls. It is recognised, that some teachers would find it difficult to determine children's previous information and this can only be an approximate assessment based on general knowledge of the children and on discussion before and after programmes.

AMOUNT OF FACTUAL INFORMATION IN SCHOOLS PROGRAMMES

Teachers were asked to rate the amount of factual information in each programme for their pupils and to indicate any differences for boys and girls.

		Too much %	Enough %	Too little %
Programme 1	Boys	8	86	6
	Girls	8	85	6
Programme 2	Boys	20	75	5
	Girls	15	78	7
Programme 3	Boys	9	89	2
	Girls	11	87	2
Programme 4	Boys	35	60	5
	Girls	23	72	5
Programme 5	Boys	7	81	12
	Girls	7	83	10
Programme 6	Boys	6	85	9
	Girls	5	86	9
Programme 7	Boys	3	72	25
	Girls	3	72	25
Programme 8	Boys	3	78	9
	Girls	7	84	9

Notes:

1. Of those for whom there was too much information in the programmes, 5% were groups under the age range, 83% within the age range and 12% above the age range.

2. The fairly high figures in the 'Too much' column for programme 4, indicate, partly, that teachers thought there were more details on menstruation (particularly for boys) and fertilisation than were necessary, but also that the programme contained too much information for pupils to absorb.

3. Many schools had already covered the questions in programme 7, and would have liked discussion at a deeper level.

Assessment of schools programmes in stimulating discussion

One of the main aims of the series was to encourage easy discussion. Using this criterion, teachers were asked to assess the programmes for boys and girls separately. Of course, the television series was only part of the process in most schools, and other factors besides the programmes contributed to the success of the discussion.

		Worked best %	In between %	Raised little or no comment %
Programme 1	Boys	19	29	52
	Girls	19	34	47
Programme 2	Boys	37	43	20
	Girls	29	55	16
Programme 3	Boys	50	27	23
	Girls	42	37	21
Programme 4	Boys	43	32	25
	Girls	67	23	10
Programme 5	Boys	65	25	10
	Girls	69	22	9
Programme 6	Boys	65	30	5
	Girls	84	15	1
Programme 7	Boys	20	44	36
	Girls	20	36	44
Programme 8	Boys	31	42	27
	Girls	31	30	39

Two schools reported that there had been no discussion after the programmes.

Notes:

1. Reports suggest that there was greater ease of discussion after the first programmes in single sex groups. Of those who found that programme 4 produced little discussion, 17% were in single sex groups,

83% in mixed. By the last two programmes there was much more discussion in mixed groups.

2. In some schools, boys were taken by men and girls by women, but in those where there was not a sex division, both men and women, married and single, reported similar ease of discussion with both sexes.

3. Head teachers and deputies were less well satisfied with programme 7 than other teachers were. Health visitors and specialist teachers found it much more successful and the majority of them rated it as the fourth most satisfying programme, although it was rated seventh by the whole group.

4. Several schools had their best discussion sessions after the earlier programmes, when 'the ice was first broken'. Others 'got better at discussion'.

5. One teacher suggests that this assessment is unreliable, as discussion branched away from the subject of a particular programme and had sometimes been exhausted before the programme specifically dealing with it was shown. Previews and advance information in booklets, however, gave teachers a good idea of the contents of individual programmes and it was possible for them to divert discussion until later programmes, if they wanted to.

Teachers' reactions to contents of schools series

53% were satisfied with the content of the series and would not have added or omitted anything.

Of the remaining 47%, several felt that programmes 1, 2, 7 and 8 were unnecessary for their pupils. Programme 7 was particularly criticised as superfluous in schools where there had been good question and answer sessions. This supports the growing theory that with particular series a teacher may choose not to take an individual programme if, from previous information, he is convinced that it would not be as effective as the rest of the series.

Although programme 7 was entirely spontaneous and un-rehearsed, a few teachers thought it sounded as if it had been scripted, while others liked the presentation of a relaxed adult/children discussion and thought it helped their pupils to talk more naturally.

Five teachers said they were unhappy about the film of the birth in programme 8, although only two schools decided against taking the programme with their pupils. Two others thought the film included too few details and would have liked more of it. Teachers of older pupils would have liked more discussion of moral and social problems. One thought the programmes should have 'pushed morality harder', another that 'there should have been more about the emotional aspects and danger of unwanted children and the dangers of VD'. As already stated, it had been decided that for the age range 10-13 this kind of discussion would come more naturally in the class room after transmissions.

3 teachers criticised the introductory music.

2 would have included more information of abnormalities.

4 would have omitted discussion of evolution.

2 would have liked more about child care.

3 thought the session on the visit to the clinic was unnecessary.

The majority of the 143 teachers had little criticism of the series.

Children's reactions to schools series

It was only possible to assess children's attitudes through their teacher's reports. Obviously this method can . provide only indications of the effects of the series and not conclusive findings.

Embarrassment

43% of teachers saw no signs of embarrassment. The others reported that programmes 3 and 4 caused degrees of embarrassment, from one girl who was obviously upset, to the majority who were mildly disturbed. In practically every case teachers said the embarrassment quickly disappeared.

There was some disturbance at the novelty of the vocabulary of the sex organs, but this soon passed. One teacher found a discussion of this embarrassment a useful way of starting talking to her pupils.

A slightly larger percentage of teachers of groups of under 20 reported embarrassment than any other group size. This may have been because of the small size of the groups, or possibly because teachers could observe more closely.

62% of all the viewing groups were mixed, but of those teachers who noticed embarrassment, 72% had mixed groups. Several teachers said that the embarrassment was caused by mixed viewing and because of this, a few changed to single sex discussion. Others, who kept mixed discussion, found no embarrassment showed during the later programmes.

35% of those reporting were head teachers or deputies, but this group made up 50% of those who noticed embarrassment. One deputy head said she thought some of the reaction came from the unusual practice for the class of not viewing with the class teacher.

Change in pupils' attitude

45% of teachers noted a general change in their pupils' attitude after the series. One or two schools found that the first reaction was in an increased awareness of the opposite sex, and consequent embarrassment. This quickly settled down to a more responsible, easier approach to discussion.

Two head teachers who had recently taken up their appointments found discussion after the programmes a useful way of getting to know their pupils. Several teachers said that their relationships with their pupils had improved. Pupils were pleased at being treated in a responsible way and responded in much freer discussion, often beyond the scope of the series.

Parents' attitude

46% reported that parents had generally shown their thanks and gratitude that a difficult job had been done for them.

Two schools reported that a few parents had expressed disapproval after the series. One of these schools had notified parents that the series was to be taken: the other had not.

Over 100 parents wrote to Grampian or to Dr Dennis. Only one was critical of the series. Typical comments are these from a father:

'It has now fallen to me the unhappy task of explaining the facts of life to my 13 year old son. I was not told any of these by my parents and my vocabulary seems inadequate to express what I want to say.'

'A closer relationship has been established between me and my son as the result of being able to discuss the programmes.'

and from a mother:

'I am a trained nurse, but still find it difficult to talk to my children.'
'First rate and sincerely hope it will be repeated for many years to come.'
'Absolutely first class.'

It is known that many parents whose children were not watching the school series followed the evening programmes.

Advantages and disadvantages of television

Practically every report thought television had advantages over other methods of teaching human reproduction. It is, of course, one of the simplest visual aids to use, and with this series, at the turn of a switch it could supply material, scripts, diagrams and film prepared

236

by experts. This was particularly useful for the 72% of teachers who had not attempted to teach the subject before, but even the most experienced teachers found it useful to have a second opinion.

Dr Dennis's matter of fact, unemotional, kindly talk was a shared experience for adults and children, which made it easier to break the ice. Many teachers spoke of the 'impartiality of television', which helped them to approach the subject of human reproduction with their pupils and talk about it on equal terms. There were disadvantages for some teachers in having to accept a 'package deal', although, of course, they could have decided to use only single programmes. A few would have preferred a longer more general course, which would not have isolated human reproduction. There was some fear that televising only the one aspect of human biology gave undue prominence to reproduction. As one teacher said, it would be unfortunate if it was thought of as a 'weekly dose'. An opposing point of view was put by the teacher who pointed out that 'health visitors usually teach human reproduction, but the television programmes have shown that it is not a specialist subject but normal procedure'.

Adult series

Teachers welcomed the opportunity to preview schools series and thought this was the most important function of the adult series. For the future, it would be helpful to show follow-up work which had been carried out as a result of the programmes and hear the experiences of children, teachers and particularly parents who had followed the series. If experts appeared, they should try to be practical and relate their discussion to the problems of children within the age range and the difficulties for parents and teachers who are introducing the children to the subject of human reproduction.

Of the teachers who sent in reports, 100% said they would take the schools series again if it were repeated.

Follow-up work

All except two schools followed up the programmes with discussion sessions. In addition, 23% undertook follow-up work other than talk and discussion. This included a wide variety of work from simple research in the library and the keeping of scrapbooks, to involved projects which extended over many subjects.

One primary school bred animals, hatched eggs, sowed seeds and studied plants, made up stories of life cycles and wrote poetry, looked at the mathematics of heredity and drew graphs of their own development and the development of a baby.

One secondary school where there were twins in a class of girls, studied twinning. They also took a census of the class members' weight at birth, time of labour, etc., in this way stimulating discussion with mothers. Girls brought photographs of themselves, showing their own development. They drew diagrams of reproductive organs, and the stages in the development of an embryo. Comparing other animals with human beings, they studied baby trout, hens' eggs in an incubator and followed the stages of development of the embryo.

Other schools carried out similar projects, involving mathematics, science, creative writing and art work.

17 'Where Do Babies Come From?' and 'Growing Up': Two Radiovision Sex Education Aids

SCHOOL BROADCASTING COUNCIL

The programmes as broadcast

RADIOVISION ('NATURE')

The filmstrips 'Where Do Babies Come From?' and 'Growing Up' were available for purchase from BBC Publications from November 1969; the commentary was broadcast on radio in mid-January 1970, at a different time and on a different day from the regular 'Nature' broadcasts. The two filmstrips consist respectively of 17 and of 14 frames of coloured, still pictures painted by an artist in a style which, while showing sufficient anatomical detail to make the meaning clear, has a non-naturalistic, decorative background to soften the impact of reality.

'Where Do Babies Come From?'

Starting with first a man and woman and then a family group, the pictures, all directed to answering the question of the title, show in sequence a nude boy and girl, then a man and woman, and a 'pregnant lady', with a later 'X-ray' picture showing the unborn child in the womb. Intercourse is indicated by a picture of the top half of a man's and woman's bodies lying close together. To answer 'How does a baby get out?' there is a picture of the birth of a baby drawn from the angle of the woman's head and with a doctor assisting the birth. Pictures of a nude baby girl and a boy follow, and the filmstrip ends, as it began, with a family group.

'Growing Up'

The pictures here show first the physiological changes as a girl grows up, ending with menstruation and the growth of pubic hair, followed by corresponding pictures of pubertal changes in boys.

School Broadcasting Council, *School Broadcasting and Sex Education in the Primary School* (BBC Publications, London, 1971) extracts.

The broadcast commentaries for tape recording and synchronised use with the filmstrips are spoken by a professional broadcaster. The vocabulary is a compromise of scientific and homely vocabulary; 'vagina', 'penis', etc., but also 'tummy' and 'womb'. The style is simple and direct.

Numbers of schools and classes using the programmes

Schools

The statistical survey shows that, of the 1,686 schools which by, January 1970 had bought filmstrips of 'Where Do Babies Come From?' and 'Growing Up', over a third had shown them to the children before the end of the summer term, and another quarter proposed to do so in 1970–1 – rather less for 'Growing Up' than for 'Where Do Babies Come From?' About 39% of those who bought the filmstrips decided not to use them, at least in the near or foreseeable future. Their reasons for this are given below. Teachers who delayed the showing of the programmes till 1970–1 did so mainly because they wanted to incorporate them in the normal work of the school, and this required rather more leisured adjustments and consultations with parents and staff. Some schools preferred to use the programmes as a revision after the television programmes. Some schools were awaiting the results of school managers' of LEA's discussions; sometimes the reasons for postponement were entirely coincidental.

However, before the end of the school year 1969–70, that is by July 1970, the numbers of schools buying the filmstrips had increased to 2,847 for 'Where Do Babies Come From?' and to 2,673 for 'Growing Up'. If all these schools (which include the 1,686 schools originally sampled) listened in the same proportions as did the earlier audience, this would give an estimated audience for the whole school year 1969–70 of about 1,000 schools for 'Where Do Babies Come From?' and 800 schools for 'Growing Up'. This rate of purchase for the whole year is approximately the same as for other radiovision programmes in the 'Nature' series.

Classes

An average of 2·9 classes per school viewed one or both the programmes, distributed unevenly over the four years of junior school life. Only 7% of the audience for 'Where Do Babies Come

240

From?' and 2% for 'Growing Up' were in the first year of the junior school (age 7–8), 25% and 19% were second year (8–9), 36% and 36% for the two programmes were in the third year (9–10), and 31% and 42% were in the fourth year (10–11). It is clear from the figures and the reports that in this introductory phase the schools were using the programmes with a wider spread than would be normal, and that, for 'Growing Up' especially, the older age-range was preferred.

Reasons for not using radiovision ('Nature')

Of the schools in the Research Officer's sample of purchasers of filmstrips, 39% said they had decided not to use the filmstrips they had bought, at least not in the near future, and in some cases, probably not at all. (We have no information about the motives of those who did not purchase the filmstrips.)

About 30% of those schools purchasing but not using the filmstrips gave no reason for their decision and it is not known whether the parents of the children in these schools were consulted.

About 15% gave extraneous reasons, for example approaching retirement, staff shortages, inability to tape the programmes. Two heads mentioned an LEA ban on the programmes.

In 12% of these schools there was no objection to sex education but staff and/or parents preferred the 'Merry-go-Round' programmes or Independent Television's 'Living and Growing' (though the latter series was for ages 10–13). The radiovision programmes were said to be 'too clinical and cold' or 'too stark' and requiring more gradual lead-in. Some disliked the style of the painting and others preferred photographs or diagrams. A few preferred their own ways of personal and incidental working and felt some resistance to even radiovision in this field where the maturity of the children was so important a factor and so varied in any one class.

12% of the non-user purchasers of the filmstrips said that the head and/or staff opposed the use of the programmes; and in another 17% parents and/or managers had joined in agreement with this opinion. In two cases, the parents petitioned the head not to show the programmes.

The remaining 14% had miscellaneous reasons often related to the time necessary to consult parents and for themselves to get used to an idea which at the time was both challenging and embarrassing.

The main sources of objection were that the school would be usurping the right of parents, that the proposed ages of the audience was too young, that no mention was made of love and marriage and that the 'mass education' characteristic, it was thought, of radiovision, was inappropriate. The kind of principles involved are illuminated by the following two quotations:

By showing these programmes to young children we are usurping the rights and responsibilities of parents. This kind of instruction should be given by the parents at the correct time. Many children are not ready for these facts as presented in the filmstrips. Each child is an individual – we recognise the need to study reading readiness, number readiness, etc – surely there must be a 'readiness' for this kind of information.

A large representative gathering of parents plus a doctor and an educational psychologist. Divided opinion on its suitability for this age group: by those against, it was said no mention is made of marriage or love in this relationship. Some [parents] felt it had helped to give them a vocabulary and were better fitted to talk to their own children. (1) Some teachers feel they could not cope with this topic as part of a series and certainly not isolated. (2) One would want to be sure that the teacher could 'carry it off', i.e. establish the proper relationship. (3) It is either 'all' or 'nothing'. You couldn't exclude children from the lessons. They would find out anyway and perhaps in the wrong way. (4) Unlike most aspects of the curriculum this, as far as parents are concerned, is controversial. Whilst some teachers could carry it through, I feel the 'climate', so far as parents of children in my school are concerned, is not right at the moment.

The reference to the prevailing unsympathetic climate was repeated by others.

Some heads felt that they needed a full measure of support from parents, even up to 100% in some cases. They had cogent reasons for this, foreseeing that even if only a small number of children were withdrawn both preparation and later work would be to some extent inhibited.

The programmes in use

PREPARATION BEFOREHAND

Consultation with parents

The replies to the Research Officer's invitation to schools using the programmes to describe any communication they had had with parents beforehand and the parents' response show that about 83% of the schools held meetings with parents and that, at practically all, the programmes themselves were shown. All but a tiny minority of the rest of the schools sent letters to parents, either seeking permission to use the programmes, often with descriptions of them, or with advice to parents to see them on the late-night showings, or expressing the head's intention to show the programmes to the children. This latter was especially so in schools where some degree of sex education was already established and the programmes were regarded as an extension of this.

Many schools held meetings on different days of the week and at different times, so that fathers as well as mothers took part. Attendances overall were good, sometimes 100%, though in a few areas parents seemed ready to 'leave the schools to it'. Parents at the meetings often acknowledged their own responsibility to give their children the necessary information, but expressed embarrassment or unwillingness, not infrequently because they did not know 'the proper words'. Some raised objections that marriage was not mentioned, but accepted the reasons for the omission, especially when foster-parents and heads of homes with children 'in care' had put their point of view. Discussions were frank and ready and, on the whole, parents were highly appreciative of the matter and style of the programmes. Some schools, both those which held meetings and those which did not, asked for written parental consent or refusal for each child to see the programmes. In the event, only a very small number of parents requested exclusion of children from the lessons in which the programmes were used; these included parents who had religious objections to their children's seeing the programmes. We have no evidence of any head not acceding to the parents' requests.

By whatever means consent was asked, the SBC Research Officer's survey shows that all the schools showing the programmes and consulting parents had at least 90% agreement from the parents and the average degree of consent was far higher than this. Many parents who decided against in the first place changed their minds later.

Perhaps the most valuable product of the exercise, commented on widely by Education Officers and by the schools alike, was the promotion of closer relationships between parents and teachers in a responsible and important part of children's education and upbringing. 'A highlight', say many; 'A most important event in the life of the school'; and time- and energy-consuming as the arranging and conducting of these meetings were, there is no suggestion anywhere that the schools found them other than worth while.

So closely had schools and parents become involved that in a few schools, including a Roman Catholic one, parents and children viewed together, in groups of parents with thirty to eighty children and members of the school staff. At other meetings the medical officer, other members of the LEA staff, or of the church attended.

Specific preparation

The schools where there was already on-going work to which the programmes were relevant, on reporting to the SBC Research Officer about their preparation for using the programmes, outlined their normal work in biology, human physiology, keeping of animals and other living things, and hygiene and health topics. The programmes were said 'to come virtually at the end of two terms' work on a project about man' and 'were used to solidify all previous work, to draw it together and tie up any ends'.

In the schools with no sex education, only a small proportion used the programmes as part of science projects, but more than a third of these said they used earlier 'Nature' programmes as preparation for 'background discussion on construction and functions of the human body, on reproduction and mating of animals'.

But for some 38% of the classes using the filmstrips the occasion was a special one and specifically prepared for by the teacher – by reminding the children of relevant previous experience with their pets, and more especially by work inspired by the notes for the teacher for the programme: collection of photographs of babies, of the children themselves at different ages, of facts of increase of weight and height, of different gestation periods of mammals and so on. The making of graphs and record books were frequent activities and, as Education Officers report, interest ran high. Sometimes there was more extended and dramatic preparation. One head pinned in the school hall a picture of himself at 18 months old, and invited staff and children to do likewise, thus awakening interest in babies, babyhood and family likeness. He also put twenty eggs, including some fertilized ones, in an incubator in the school and so deliberately provoked questions about origins of new life.

METHODS OF USE

There were no reports of the broadcast commentary being used

244

'live'. The great majority of the schools used the tape recorded programmes 'straight'. The filmstrip and tape were played together, usually without interruption, for the first showing. At the end questions were invited or arose spontaneously, and there seems always, with very few exceptions, to have been discussion of some kind. In a few cases, the teacher read the script, on one occasion because the tape recorder broke down, in other cases from choice, to make the occasion more personal. Sometimes the head or class teacher made his own commentary without the tape or script, feeling, as one said, that he could come nearer to the children's understanding and level of vocabulary in this way. Some schools report using the filmstrip frame by frame with opportunities for discussion and questions for each one.

In a high proportion of schools the programmes were repeated, often at the children's request, sometimes on the same day, sometimes later, and generally this second showing was the occasion for readier and more searching discussion. In a few cases the filmstrip was used alone for the second showing. Somewhat surprisingly a small proportion of the schools showed 'Where Do Babies Come From?' and 'Growing Up' consecutively, with only a short break between. This was usually to the older children, and one teacher at least found it too much for the children.

Many schools emphasise their efforts to make the occasion and atmosphere one of easy communication and to have arranged seating and the size of their groups accordingly. Even if large groups of two or more classes viewed together, there was generally separation into small groups afterwards.

REACTIONS OF THE CHILDREN

Education Officers watching the children observed in almost all cases great interest, with very little or no sign that the children regarded the programmes as strange or abnormal, and the reports from the schools fully confirm this. Any sniggering and embarrassment by a few quickly gave way to intense interest. Heads express great delight in the nature of the children's response which in most cases completely reassured any teachers who had formerly been hesitant.

The accumulated evidence shows that the programmes gave rise to discussion which was free, sensible and uninhibited and which indicated a new assurance in the children from the acquisition of an acceptable vocabulary. It seems as if an area of life, hitherto seen askance or with distorted vision, was suddenly no longer forbidden – a comforting and exhilarating experience. Some teachers were surprised at the vitality and range of the children's questions and observations. They speak of being 'bombarded' with questions, of the 'complete lack of embarrassment on either side', 'of the natural acceptance by the children of the facts they had been told'. 'The range of topics covered the whole field from simple biology to morals.' 'The children asked questions on every imaginable aspect with complete frankness.'

From a general survey of the many examples of questions given, one could conclude that, especially with the target age-group, the children's concern was in fact-finding, mainly on anatomical and mechanical aspects of the subject. They identified mostly with the baby, whose growth they saw in relation to themselves and that of their child relatives. Any narrowly defined sex element played a small part. They were eager to right their mistakes, for example 'that food passed solid through the umbilical cord', 'that there is danger of the baby drowning in the water of the womb', 'that the baby came out of the navel'.

Another batch of questions might be described as linguistic. They were directed at getting clear the meaning of words the children had heard, usually associated with sensational reports in the press and on television: siamese twins, multiple births, mongols, thalidomide babies and caesarian operations. But it was reported that this was not a morbid interest. Twins was a favourite topic; and some of the older children asked about 'the pill', VD, contraception and sterility. A child here and there remarked that her sister was not married but had a baby, and this raised questions of illegitimacy. More than once the problems of the creation of Adam and Eve and the birth of Jesus were raised.

The rest of the questions directly arose from the programmes – about sperm, possible pain in childbirth and menstruation, milk in breasts, pubic hair, and the meaning of the words used, sometimes contrasted with the 'rude' words which, in one school where this discussion was observed, the children seemed very glad to be able to discuss without shame.

A great many children in discussion and in writing expressed great enjoyment of the programmes and satisfaction at having been able to learn from them. 'Where Do Babies Come From?' generally

provoked more questions than did 'Growing Up' which bored some
of the boys, though the girls in older classes found it relevant to their
interests and problems and many, especially by personal approaches
to the teacher, wanted to discuss further its practical application to
their needs.

The children made some minor criticisms of the pictures, for
example that the same flowers stayed fresh for nine months! A few
were puzzled by the imaginative setting. 'People don't play with
horses and doves with no clothes on.' Some children found a few of
the pictures difficult to interpret, especially the X-ray one. But
generally the children's comments and their writing show enjoyment
of the style beyond that of some of their teachers.

Only in a very few cases was there little or no discussion – this
was sometimes in schools where previous sex education had
already covered the ground.

The evidence has been closely searched for indications of any
adverse effects on the children. In only six of the 256 classes in the
Research Officer's sample was there any suggestion of difficulty. In
each of two schools one child seems to have been unduly
embarrassed, in two others there was some nervous excitement at the
first showing, but on the second showing, thoughtful appreciation. In
another case, the children showed some signs of disgust or, quoting
their parents, said the pictures were 'rude'. One case concerned an
adopted child who for the first time realized that she must have a
'natural' mother and suffered the kind of shock she would certainly
have had to meet sooner or later. The head here expressed
considerable appreciation of the non-emotional approach in the
programme which was vital because a number of children in the
school came from a children's home. It might be noted here that in a
similar situation in the audience for the television programmes the
occasion resulted in a happy readjustment of the child to
circumstances which had previously worried her.

There is, on the other hand, some considerable evidence from
communications to heads from parents, and from the sensible
behaviour of the children, that the impact of the programmes was
thought positive and valuable. The children's writings confirm this.
In one school the head reported that two boys who had earlier
exposed themselves to startle the girls had given it up because, after
the programmes, their behaviour was received with indifference. In
the same school the occasional graffiti which had previously

adorned the lavatories subsided and then stopped. In some schools where books on bodily functions had always been available, it was observed that the books were used more frequently and there were no reports of any pictures or diagrams being defaced.

In addition to the discussions and questions which in some schools went on intermittently for some time and in some died down quickly, other work, often begun before the programmes were shown, was carried on. Much of this was of the kind suggested in the notes for the teacher, based on recording growth and development, learning about bodily functions and observing animals. Collections of pictures of babies continued and sometimes interest branched out into growth of population, heredity and life of primitive peoples.

The written work seems generally to have taken the form of a recapitulation of what the children had learnt from the programmes, sometimes with reference to their previous ideas, and quite often further work on the books about themselves and their own growth. The recapitulations that have been seen by Education Officers show an unexpectedly high degree of understanding and generally uncomplicated attitudes.

TEACHERS' OPINIONS

On the content

In response to the specific question in the survey, the teachers of over three-quarters of the classes said that the programmes covered the subject matter 'adequately'. The majority of these went much beyond this and expressed great enthusiasm. 'Excellent', 'well-planned', 'could not have done without' and similar comments were frequent. Where the matter of the programmes was criticised it was either because more details were felt to be necessary or because there was no mention of love and marriage, though only nine teachers made this point, and only two commented that the woman in the filmstrip wore no wedding ring.

On the narrator and narrative

The narrator and narrative were almost unanimously praised. A few found the narrator rather too fast, but the quality of voice and style of writing of the script evidently conveyed to most teachers sympathy, dignity and respect as well as adequate and clear explanation 'beautifully spoken' in 'a quiet natural voice'. The vocabulary, too, seems to have been generally acceptable. A few would have preferred 'woman' to 'lady' and 'abdomen' for 'tummy', though an Education Officer reports preference of 'tummy button' for 'navel'. The great majority thought that the infusion of the 'proper' vocabulary was one of the great virtues of the programmes.

On the pictures

The pictures had a more mixed reception. A very considerable majority liked them, as 'simple, uncluttered and colourful'. The colour was always appreciated. 'Beautiful, tender', 'softening any stark effects', 'tasteful and prettily shown' and so on. Many commented on the advantage of an artist's presentation of the facts. Some teachers admitted that, although they themselves were doubtful of the pictures, the children appreciated them, though some reported the children's criticisms mentioned earlier.

Where there was criticism it was directed at either the style or the clarity. 'Bit unnatural', 'decorative background distracting and unnecessary', 'style inappropriate'; and these critics (very few) would have preferred photographs or diagrams. Some teachers, like the children, found some of the slides lacked clear definition.

On the music

The music was frequently praised, often highly, for its appropriateness, emotional effect and timing, though a few teachers found it difficult to pick up the cue for a change of frame from it, and a few found it monotonous or laboured.

On the accompanying literature

On the notes for the teacher, the teachers of about two-fifths of the classes said they found them 'useful' or 'adequate', and were especially grateful to have the text of the commentary, background information and the suggestions for children's work. Many would have liked more detailed help. There were suggestions for a future booklet for teachers which would give not only more background knowledge for further teaching, but would say something of the effects the broadcasts had had on children.

The teachers of only a quarter of the classes commented on the pupil's booklet for 'Where Do Babies Come From?' Some had neither seen nor used it. A minority of those using it were generally appreciative, saying that children referred to it in the library and that it delighted some and started them thinking; but more teachers criticised it as too brief, and thought its photographic content and text uninteresting and of little value.

GENERAL NOTE

Over and above the criticisms already noted, the general impression from reading all the evidence on the radiovision programmes is of the teachers' high degree of appreciation. Among the reasons for approbation, the most frequent were that the programmes fulfilled a real need, and that they made a valuable contribution to health education. 'They are most necessary', and 'I have no doubts as to their importance.' Many say positively that parents too were grateful and pleased. One of the greatest values was said to be 'the breaking down of prejudices and awkwardnesses between parent and child'. 'The matter was presented so perfectly clearly and unexceptionably that I cannot think why there was so much protest in the press.'

The high educational and professional standards of the programmes are reflected in the fact that 'Where Do Babies Come From?' was awarded the Jury's Prize at the Sixth Session of the Japan Prize International Educational Programme Contest in the autumn of 1970. This is an annual major and much-coveted award made by an international jury of educational broadcasters.

18 The Effects of Televised Sex Education at the Primary School Level

REX S. ROGERS

SUMMARY

The effects of the BBC's 'Merry-go-ground' sex education programmes for primary schools were assessed by means of specially designed paper and pencil tests in six classes in a major urban centre. The results obtained suggest that the instruction led to marked changes in sexual attitudes and increases in various aspects of sexual knowledge – the latter gains being retained at a follow-up assessment some three months after instruction had ended. A very high level of parental approval of the instruction was also recorded. It is suggested that schools' broadcasts aimed at the younger half of the school population may have much to recommend them to the researcher.

Introduction

Despite the reluctance of some teachers,[6] the sparsity of specific training in techniques in Colleges of Education[9] and highly vocal, if minority opposition,[3] sex education is increasingly featuring in school curricula. This expansion is reflected both in an increasing quantity, if not quality, of books for teacher or pupil[7] and in a growing use of audio-visual aids.

Research into the effectiveness of sex education, however, have not kept pace with this expansion and reported evaluations,[1,4,5] with a few exceptions e.g.[2] tend to concentrate on indirect evaluation (e.g. by teacher judgement) rather than by direct measures of learning or

This paper is based on material presented to the Annual Conference of the British Psychological Society, April 1972. The research was made possible through a grant from the Television Research Committee to the Communication and Attitude Change Research Unit, Department of Social Psychology, London School of Economics. Thanks are also due to the BBC, the local educational authority concerned, and to the schools, parents and children involved. The article is to appear in a forthcoming issue of the *Health Education Journal*.

attitude change using the children themselves. This lack of research can be traced to a number of causes:

(1) There is no clear designation of responsibility within the British educational system either for research into the effectiveness of audio-visual aids or into issues such as sex education.

(2) The practical difficulties of conducting studies into controversial issues.

(3) (Not unrelated to (1) and (2).) A dearth of instruments for measuring the sexual knowledge and attitudes of children in the classroom situation.

This apparent reluctance of researchers to enter the sex education area is unfortunate on several counts. Firstly, studies in the area would seem to offer data relevant to important issues in developmental psychology (e.g. the evidence for the Freudian 'latency period'* or theories of stages in the growth of understanding). Further, although media within the school situation (schools' broadcasting and other audio-visual material) usually attracts much less attention than other mass media impinging on the child, they form a considerable and increasing part of the total media experience of young people. Indeed, because they usually have very clear objectives and are *aimed* at changing the state of the audience, they may well be a particularly interesting class of stimuli to those concerned with the effects of communications on attitudes, knowledge and behaviour. Finally, on the more pragmatic level, research findings in such areas of social concern can do much to raise the level of debate and clarify the hopes and anxieties of lay-people and professionals.

The research about to be described is an examination of techniques for studying, in the class situation, the sexual knowledge and attitudes of pre-adolescent children and how these were modified by sexual instruction – in this case, the BBC's 'Merry-go-Round' programmes and the accompanying classroom teaching. These three 20-minute programmes were ideal for such research, as they contained a great deal of information about conception and birth and also represented a major innovation in the field, both because of the very young age-group at which they were aimed (8–10 year olds) and in terms of sheer audience reach (at their first

* See Chapter 10.

showing an estimated 180,000 children of whom about 120,000 had not been instructed previously).[1]

Method

In view of the potential problems accompanying the arousal of sexual curiosity among children not to receive later instruction, the design adopted was of a simple before/after kind without control group. Except in the case of questions geared specifically to programme content, dependent measures of knowledge and attitudes were obtained both prior to programme viewing and after instruction. An attempt was made to minimise disruption of normal classroom conditions so as to provide data which reflected as closely as possible the effects of the instruction in ordinary school situations. The stimulus, for example, was taken to be programmes plus follow-up teaching and all measures at the 'after' stage were taken subsequent to after-programme discussion by the class teacher. In order to familiarise the children to being researched, assessment did not begin with the first sex education programme but a week earlier concerning a film on wild-life conservation. The tested children viewed the programmes as transmitted (June 1970) in the way normal to their school and no special seating arrangements were introduced for viewing or completion of instruments.

A discursive approach (employing pictorial, essay question, multiple choice and true/false techniques) was made to assessment in view of the age group involved, the topic and the scarcity of relevant guiding literature. As an aid to explicating results, a number of independent measures (age, sex, parental attitude to sex education, teacher ratings) were employed so that the study could yield information on the determinants of sexual knowledge and attitudes and response to the instruction. Additionally, the classes were re-assessed three months after instruction. This latter element of the design was aimed at allowing a measure of the extent to which such teaching is likely to remain salient in the long-term.

MEASURES

Teacher ratings

The class teacher was asked to perform four pre-instruction and one post-instruction ratings on each child in his/her class. All ratings were obtained on five point scales with the mid-point being the class average. The various dimensions employed showed marked inter-correlation; the dimension of 'Intelligence' (defined as '... good abstract reasoning ... rich vocabulary ... ability at peak performance ...') has been selected as representative in the results that follow.

Parental assessments

These were obtained by means of a postal questionnaire which explored: reactions to various facets of sex education; approval of their child having received instruction; estimates of their child's knowledge level before and after instruction; and, open ended comments on other effects of the teaching.

Test of sexual knowledge (This and other measures used in the classroom were developed in a pilot study. They featured extra-large type and, as an additional precaution, were read out aloud to the class.)

This test was specifically designed to meet the need for a measure of sexual knowledge appropriate to pre-instruction and post-instruction assessment. To minimise it acting as a teaching devise, no use was made of vocabulary or other verbal information. The test consisted of line drawings of male and female with instructions to name and give uses for parts of the body marked by arrows. (Examples are given in[10].) The test was scored on two dimensions, one of the correct functions, the other of correct vocabulary. The latter was split into 'vernacular' (e.g. Willie) and Latinate (e.g. Penis), as one of the features of the 'Merry-go-Round' programmes was an attempt to pass on to the child a technical vocabulary for sexual organs.

Opinion scales

Two opinion inventories were employed. The first was aimed at exposing any change in attitudes induced by the instruction and contained true/false and multiple choice items. An example attitude used was the 'naughtiness' of having no clothes on. In selecting the items care was taken to avoid material likely to disturb the child and to base items as far as possible on programme content (e.g. the showing of nudity). The second instrument consisted of simple evaluative scales for assessing reaction to the programmes.

Essay tasks

Each child completed two essays prior to the teaching and the same topics after instruction. The topics were chosen to cover the major information given in the programmes: 'How do boys' and girls' bodies change as they grow up?' and 'How babies are made and how they come into the world.'

Other measures

A number of other measures were employed in the study (e.g. a test of specific items of knowledge gained from the teaching based on content analysis of the programmes). The main one of note for present purposes was posed three months after the immediate post-programme assessment. This stated 'There was not enough time in the films (*sic*) to show you everything – what would you like to have seen that was not shown?' The objective of this measure was to tap any 'sense of omission' with particular reference to the fact that the programmes, which were elsewise candid, contained a verbal but not a visual description of sexual intercourse.

Subjects

The sample consisted of 222 children (six complete classes) from four schools in a major urban centre. The average class ages were: 8:3; 8:11; 9:5; 10:4; 10:4 and 11:5. All classes were mixed and the overall sex distribution was 109 boys and 113 girls. The classes selected had all decided to accept the programmes before being contacted and some attempt was made to avoid grossly atypical classes (e.g. those with unusual ability distributions or heavy immigrant quotas) so that the generality of the findings could be enhanced. Three class teachers were male and three female.

Results

PARENTAL QUESTIONNAIRE

Among parents who returned a completed questionnaire (122),* a very favourable reaction to the teaching emerged. To the question

---

* Data based on 122 usable returns from a mail-out of 222 raised the question of bias in our sample of 'returners', perhaps in favour of sex education. Against this possibility, we note that our results on level of approval are very similar to those of Gill, Reid and Smith.[3] Further, comparison of the children of 'returners' and 'non-returners' showed the two groups not to differ in age, sex, family size or teaching rating.

'How do you feel *now* about your child having received sex education?', the following pattern of responses were obtained:

I am very much in favour of it	49%
I am quite in favour of it	28%
I have no particular views or mixed feelings	11%
I am quite against it	9%
I am very much against it	3%

The reasons for this very positive attitude were not hard to isolate. It was clear from the responses of the parents that they both held a favourable view of the effects of sex education in general terms and as they had been shown for their particular child.

In terms of general effects, we selected ten possible results of sex education and asked the parents for their views on the likelihood and desirability of each consequence. These data are given in Table 1. As may be seen, there is a general tendency for effects seen as more desirable also to be seen as more likely and for judgements to be related to overall attitude (as measured by the question given above). It will also be noted that the most likely effects are favourably evaluated ones and that the kinds of results made much of by opponents of sex education, such as leading to 'experimenting' or giving nightmares or fears, are not seen as probable consequences.

A similar picture revealed itself in the open-ended parental accounts of how their own children had reacted. For example, we found 21% of parents mentioning a favourable effect on parent/child interaction and only 5% a negative one; again, 17% felt that their child reacted positively or neutrally to the instruction (e.g. liked it, took it like any other lesson) while only 5% reported a more negative reaction (e.g. child was embarrassed).

THE REACTIONS OF THE CHILDREN

Both the parental reports and our own informal observations of the children during and after the programme suggested little in the way of negative reactions. This impression was very much confirmed by the children's own attitude to the programmes. On a five-point scale of liking, the three programmes yielded between 85–88% of responses in the two favourable categories (like very much and quite like). This result compares with 91% approval for the previous week's 'Merry-go-Round' programme on wild-life conservation.

Table 1. *Parental estimates of the credibility and evaluation of various effects of sex education*

Effect	This effect...				If this did happen it would be...			
	is likely to happen %	might happen %	is unlikely to happen %	Correlation with overall parental attitude to sex education	a bad thing %	neither/ not sure %	a good thing %	Correlation with overall parental attitude to sex education
Leads to passing on of knowledge to other children	54	38	8	0·03	18	40	42	−0·34
Leads to 'experimenting'	11	43	46	−0·34	80	19	1	0·00
Leads to being more prepared for marriage later on	70	17	12	0·33	2	9	90	−0·19
Leads to being more prepared for how their bodies change as they grow into adults	88	8	3	0·30	0	5	95	−0·45
Causes children to ask their parents questions about sex	62	33	5	0·07	1	8	91	−0·23
Causes children to grow up in their thinking earlier	62	30	8	−0·08	15	34	51	−0·41
Makes children think more about sex	26	44	30	−0·25	30	61	10	−0·34
Gives children 'nightmares' or fears	3	16	80	−0·42	83	16	1	−0·09
Helps children grow up with strict moral standards about sex	28	46	26	0·18	7	17	76	0·01
Makes children less anxious about sex	53	33	15	0·28	3	15	81	−0·20

Notes

(1) $N = 115\pm$. (The notation $\pm$ *of a sample base* is used here and elsewhere to indicate that small deficits may occur to individual bases in the table due to subjects omitting occasional responses.)

(2) r values of $\pm0\cdot18$ significant at the 5% level (two-tailed).

Rex S. Rogers

Sexual knowledge was assessed at the pre- and post-instruction stages and again three months after instruction by means of the previously described 'Test of Sexual Knowledge'. This instrument yielded two major measures of knowledge: ability to describe

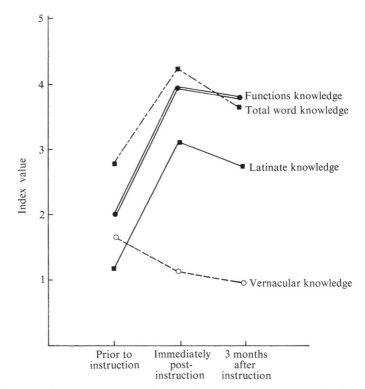

Figure 4. Sexual knowledge indices at the pre-instruction, post-instruction and 'follow up' stages

functions of sexual organs (maximum score 8) and ability to name organs (maximum score 6). The latter was usually subdivided into Latinate words and vernacular ones. In Figure 4, the basic learning statistics are given. As can be seen, the instruction resulted in gains of information both in terms of knowledge of functions (mean gain = 2·04, s.d. = 1·71, $n = 169$, $t = 15·4$ sig. beyond the

258

0·1% level) and of Latinate vocabulary (mean gain = 2·04, s.d. = 1·66, $n = 169$, $t = 16·0$, sig. beyond the 0·1% level); based on pupils completing the measure both prior and post-instruction. Further, these marked gains proved to be remarkably stable over time so that only very small losses were recorded three months later. This latter aspect of the data discourages any easy dismissal of the effects as transitory and suggests that a single stimulus, given that it is unusual and interesting, may well have considerable long-term salience with young children. Such a result may be taken as supporting the notion that early sexual instruction may have important preparatory functions.

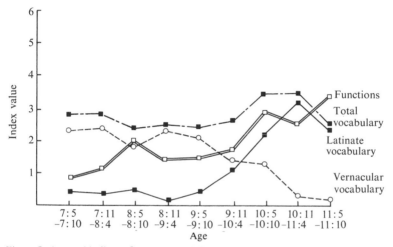

Figure 5. Age and indices of sexual knowledge prior to instruction

As would be expected, sexual knowledge proved to be linked to measures of 'cognitive maturity' such as age and teacher rated ability. These independent variables, however, were much less predictive of *gain* in knowledge, as the correlation values in Table 2 make clear.

One interesting feature of the prior knowledge levels, which reflect sexual knowledge in the uninstructed child, was the fact that overall vocabulary was very similar for all age groups. The large positive correlation between age and Latinate vocabulary being matched by an equally large negative correlation between age and vernacular vocabulary. The implication of this (the total vocabulary being too far from the maximum for the result to be an artifact of a measure that allowed only one correct name – Latinate or vernacular – per organ) is that the major effect of age on naming ability *vis-à-vis* sexual organs is not to increase the overall vocabulary but to cause the vernacular to be substituted by the Latinate. This is confirmed by a graphical plot of the variables (Figure 5). It seems then as though the younger child in our sample was characterised by a reasonable ability for naming sexual organs (albeit in his own terms) but a lack of knowledge as to what these organs did – an imbalance which was gradually corrected with increasing age.

ATTITUDE AND ATTITUDE CHANGE

In addition to a great deal of factual information, the programmes also contained a number of sequences that seemed likely to change attitudes (e.g. socially sanctioned nudity). A number of attitude statements were therefore selected and presented to the children before and after instruction. In Table 3, the major changes in attitude are considered along with the elements of content that may well have helped to bring them about. As will be noted, the amounts of attitude change are quite marked and in the direction expected from the nature of the stimulus. The changes point towards a more 'liberal' outlook in the children's view of sexuality and, with the increase in knowledge, suggest we were monitoring a very dramatic learning experience.

Faced with both changes in knowledge and attitudes, it seemed reasonable to posit a connection. In fact, for the four attitudes just discussed, correlations of degree of change with gain of either functions knowledge of Latinate vocabulary were all below $\pm$ $0.10(N = 150\pm)$. It seems, then, as though our data were compatible with the hypothesis that two separate learning processes resulted from the instruction: one the acquisition of factual information; the other that of affective information. In other words, attitude change was a direct process and not mediated by the learning of specific items of knowledge about vocabulary or sexual function.

Despite the presence of attitude change between the pre- and post-instruction stages, the test/re-test correlations for attitude items $(0.55, 0.38, 0.39, 0.44$ respectively for the quoted examples – all significant beyond the 0.1% level for $N = 170\pm)$ are high enough to make it clear that we were measuring stable judgements of the child.

Table 2. *Correlates of indices of sexual knowledge**

	Latinate knowledge			Functions knowledge		
Predictor	Before (B)	After (A)	Change†	Before (B)	After (A)	Change†
Age	0·60(196)‡	0·55(190)‡	0·08(169)	0·36(196)‡	0·32(190)‡	0·00(169)
Teacher rated	0·23(195)‡	0·14(189)§	0·09(167)	0·37(195)‡	0·39(189)‡	0·03(167)

* Decimal values in the table refer to correlation coefficients, bracketed values to sample size.
† Change $= A - B$.
‡ Significant at the 1% level.
§ Significant at the 5% level.

Table 3. *Attitude changes*

Question	Response category	% Before	% After*	Relevant programme content	Significance of shift†
How much does it hurt the mother to have the baby?	very much	33	20	Scene of childbirth in which no mention is made of pain and there are no overt cues to it	$\chi^2 - 7·2$ 1% level
	quite a lot	24	31		
	not very much	22	23		
	not at all	21	26		
How naughty is it to talk about how babies are made?	very	14	11	Basic aim of the programmes	$\chi^2 - 4·3$ 5% level
	quite	9	7		
	tiny bit	21	17		
	not at all	56	65		
How naughty is it to have no clothes on?	very	54	24	Scenes of socially sanctioned nudity – e.g. artist's models, babies in the bath	$\chi^2 - 37·0$ 0·1% level
	quite	18	19		
	tiny bit	8	20		
	not at all	20	37		
How naughty is it to talk about going to the toilet?	very	41	25	The presenter talks of excretion in making clear that birth takes place from vagina and not anus	$\chi^2 - 17·2$ 0·1% level
	quite	13	18		
	tiny bit	20	18		
	not at all	26	39		

The % distributions are based on 169± subjects who completed both pre- and post-attitude measures.
The significance of shift is assessed by testing whether among 'changers' the direct of shift is random.

Rex S. Rogers

It was, therefore, regarded as reasonable to seek predictors of attitude. As can be seen in Table 4, pre-instruction attitudes were linked to the age, ability and sexual knowledge of the child, but, interestingly, not to the attitude of his parents to sex education.

The lack of relationship between certain sexual attitudes of the child and the parental attitude to sex education is not taken as serious evidence that home-centred factors were not salient. A more likely explanation is that the parental attitude to sex education, both because most parents were in favour and because such favourability could be multi-determined, was a poor measure of the sexual 'atmosphere' of the home.

Table 4. *Correlates of the sexual attitudes of the uninstructed child*

Paraphrase of attitude	Teacher rated intelligence§	Functions Knowledge§		Parental attitude to Sex Education**
'Birth painful'	0·20†	−0·05	−0·23‡	−0·02
'Baby talk naughty'	0·30‡	0·19†	0·00	0·07
'No clothes naughty'	0·12	0·19†	0·06	−0·04
'Toilet talk naughty'	0·16*	0·23†	0·29‡	0·07

* Significant at the 5% level.
† Significant at the 1% level.
‡ Significant at the 0·1% level.
§ $N - 170\pm$
** $N - 100\pm$.

ADDITIONAL SEMI-QUALITATIVE DATA

Several of the open-ended questions we posed to the children provide additional insights into response and reaction to the programmes. For example, it was hypothesised that programme 2, which dealt with birth, would attract most negative comment. This proved to be the case, as only in the case of this programme did the question 'What did you not like about the film (*sic*)?' reveal dislikes held by over 10% of the children. However, contrary to the view that animal birth may act as an introduction to dealing with the human case, it

262

was seeing kittens born that attracted most negative comment (21%) not the human birth scene (12% mentioned as disliked).

One feature of the programmes which is obvious to an adult observer is that a visual description of sexual intercourse is not included (although a verbal one is). Our question at the follow-up stage (three months after instruction) '. . . what would you like to see that was not shown?', although not approaching it directly, was intended to tap any sense of omission – although clearly it also revealed general residual curiosity. A content analysis of responses revealed 30% of pupils mentioning some aspect of human sexual intercourse, which proved the most frequent of all content areas. This finding, together with the low level of parental or child reaction againt the instruction, seems to suggest that such exclusions from teaching aids aimed at the primary school may be unduly cautious.

DISCUSSION AND CONCLUSIONS

The major aim of the present study was to discover the extent to which the classical techniques and measures of the communications researcher can be brought to bear on the problem of how to evaluate the consequences of exposure to controversial material on a group of young children. We believe the results obtained leave little doubt as to the success obtained with such a methodology and seem to point the way towards a more thorough understanding of the role media in the school can play in influencing the child.

Looked at from the point of view of a study into teaching aid effectiveness, the results of our research provide a very favourable all-round picture of the 'Merry-go-Round' programme in action. If the learning and attitude change revealed were general for all receiving classes, then the screening of these programmes must stand as a major factor in the sexual understanding of a very large number of primary schoolchildren – particularly in view of the high level of delayed knowledge retention. This point has been stressed in popularisations of the findings[10] in the hope that a wider audience can be brought into contact with assessment by objective means rather than by *ad hoc* opinions.

The success of the specially developed measures at indexing both knowledge gain and attitude change as a result of instruction, suggests that such a methodology could well serve as a means of exploring the developmental aspects of sexual knowledge and attitudes. Some hint of what might be revealed can be seen from the

Rex S. Rogers

variations in initial knowledge and attitudes associated with various levels of age and ability. Further, our limited explorations of essay content suggest that a more directed study could prove a fruitful source of material on cognitive factors in sexual understanding.

As we noted in our introduction, the schools' broadcast sets out to affect its audience. In the case studied, it achieved this end in a quite dramatic manner. The twin factors of marked effects and a fairly objective content to which to link them suggest that research in this area could well yield data of substantive significance. Indications of this may be found in those of our data that seem to point toward separate processes of learning and attitude change. Certainly, the combination of young audience and audio-visual teaching material would appear to be a fruitful one for research.

NOTES

1 B.B.C. Publications, *School Broadcasting and Sex Education in the Primary School* (1971).

2 Brown R. L., 'Some reactions to a schools' television programme on venereal disease', *Health Education Journal*, Vol. xxvi, no. 3 (1967), pp. 108–16.

3 Gill D. G., Reid G. D. B. and Smith D. M., 'Sex education: press and parental perceptions', *Health Education Journal*, vol. xxx, no. 1 (1971), pp. 1–9.

4 Grampian Television *Living and Growing* (1968).

5 Granada Television *A Report on 'Understanding'* (1966).

6 Harris A., 'Sex education in schools', *New Statesman*, 28 February 1969, pp. 284–7.

7 Hill M. and Lloyd-Jones M., 'Sex education', *National Secular Society* (1970).

8 Little A. in *Responsible Parenthood and Sex Education* (I.P.P.F. 1970).

9 Norman Greaves J., 'Facts of life for teachers', *New Society*, 30 September 1965, pp 18–19.

10 Rogers R., 'The effects of sex education', *New Society*, 3 June 1971, pp. 949–51.

19 A Study of the Effects of 'Sex Education' on Premarital Petting and Coital Behaviour

GERALD H. WEICHMAN and ALTIS L. ELLIS*

The effect of 'sex education' on sexual behavior has been debated since early proponents attempted to include it in educational curricula. One of the oldest objections to education in human sexuality is that it would, in one way or another, lead students to 'try what they had learned'. The basic character of this argument has been phrased in a variety of different ways, and although many of the assumptions underlying this approach are tenuous, the contentions continue to exist. To offset opponents of 'sex education' in the curriculum who use this contention, proponents of sex education attempt to discount the contention argumentatively. For example, Walker identifies a seventh grade life science instructor who believes that unappeased curiosity about sex is more likely to foster adolescent 'mistakes' than would knowledge about sex.[1] A similar statement was made in the 1965 report of the World Health Organization Expert Committee on Health Problems of Adolescents: 'The fear that giving them (adolescents) information (about sexuality) will lead them into premature sexual experimentation appears to be unjustified; ignorance is much more likely to cause sexual misadventure.'[2]

Although evidence indicates that a minority of college students believe that 'sex education' causes promiscuity,[3] in the absence of research evidence argumentative opinions and counter opinions persist. This study was undertaken to determine if there was a difference in the probability of students having experienced premarital petting or coitus on the basis of variations in their exposure to 'sex education'. Specifically, two hypotheses were tested: (1) That no differences would be found in the proportion of students with premarital petting and coital experience on the basis of

Weichmann G. H. and Ellis A. L. 'A study of the effects of "sex education" on premarital petting and coital behavior', *Family Coordinator* (July 1969), pp. 231–4.

265

Gerald H. Weichman and Altis L. Ellis

exposure to 'sex education' content; (2) That, for those who had 'sex education' exposure, there would be no difference in the probability of premarital petting or coital experience on the basis of the grade level at which the college undergraduates were first exposed to 'sex education' content. For this study, the authors assumed that such terms as 'promiscuity', 'adolescent mistakes' and 'sexual misadventure' mean premarital petting and coital behavior. The, term 'sex education' is discussed in the section that follows.

PROCEDURE

An anonymous questionnaire was administered to 545 students enrolled in an undergraduate community health course at the University of Missouri in Columbia in 1967.* Demographic characteristics of the students are as follows:

Sex: 192 males and 353 females;
Age: 17-30 years with a mean age of 19·49;
Marital status: 503 single and 42 married;
Education level: 219 freshmen, 143 sophomores, 114 juniors, 56 seniors and 13 graduate students;
Religious affiliation: 331 Protestants, 102 Jews, 80 Catholics, and 32 reporting no affiliation.

The students were asked to indicate whether they had been exposed to any formal 'sex education' prior to the course in which the questionnaire was being administered. If they responded affirmatively, they were asked the grade level at which they had first received exposure to 'sex education' content. Because the term 'sex education' lacks a precise and widely accepted definition, an operational definition was used in the questionnaire by listing five social, health, and biological areas typically covered in 'sex education' courses: dating and dating behavior, reproductive anatomy and physiology, menstruation, prenatal and postnatal development, child-birth and delivery.

Finally, the students were asked to identify their premarital petting or premarital coitus experience. The instructions defined

* Acknowledgement is extended to the Department of Community Health and Medical Practice, University of Missouri School of Medicine, Columbia, Missouri for its cooperation. Gratitude is expressed to Lawrence Bee, Ed Bryant, Charles Lewis, Richard Shanteau, and Robert Hudson for helpful comments on drafts of this paper.

266

petting as any sexual contact 'from the neck down' excluding sexual intercourse (intromission).

  The data were organized for computer analysis and a frequency distribution was used to show the pattern of responses. Probabilities were estimated by the chi-square method. The statistical level of significance for testing both hypotheses was set at 0·05.

Table 1. *Percentage of those exposed and unexposed to prior sex education by premarital sexual experience and sex of respondents*

Sex education	With petting experience			With coital experience		
	Males	Females	Total	Males	Females	Total
Those exposed to sex education	93·4%	70·7%	78·8%	57·4%	17·4%	30·1%
Those unexposed to sex education	88·6%	72·3%	79·8%	55·7%	21·3%	35·6%
χ^2*	0·890	0·095	0·063	0·031	0·699	1·582
Significance level*	0·80 NS	0·95 NS	0·95 NS	0·98 NS	0·50 NS	0·30 NS
Sample size†	192	353	545	192	353	545

  * Derived from: R. A. Fisher, *Statistical Methods for Research Workers* (Edinburgh: Oliver and Boyd Ltd, 1936), Table III. A value of 3·841 is necessary to be significant at 0·05 level of confidence with one degree of freedom (NS means not significant).

  † Includes subjects without premarital petting and premarital coital experience.

RESULTS

Exposure to 'sex education' subject matter was reported by 70% of the students sampled. Premarital petting experience was reported by 79%; and premarital coital experience was reported by 32%.[4] Table 1 presents the percentages of those reporting premarital petting and coital experience according to 'sex education' exposure. Analyses of the data disclose no significant differences at the 0·05 level of confidence. The first null hypothesis was not rejected. All chi-square values computed for Table 1 demonstrated non-significance based on the 0·05 criterion. There appears to be little difference in the subjects' sexual experience on the basis of having been or having not been exposed to 'sex education' content.

  Results pertaining to the second hypothesis — that grade level of

Table 2. *Distribution of those academically exposed to sex education*

Sex education exposure	With petting experience			With coital experience		
	Males	Females	Total	Males	Females	Total
In grade school (grades 1–6)	93·9%	75·0%	84·1%	66·7%	16·7%	40·6%
In junior high (grades 7–9)	90·5%	71·7%	77·6%	52·4%	9·8%	23·1%
In senior high (grades 10–12)	93·9%	70·2%	75·5%	54·5%	21·1%	28·6%
In college	87·5%	61·9%	73·0%	31·3%	28·6%	29·5%
χ^2	5·748 NS	1·168 NS	1·873 NS	5·523 NS	6·685 NS	6·761 NS
Significance level	0·20	0·70	0·70	0·20	0·10	0·10
Sample size*	124	263	378	124	263	378

* Including subjects without premarital petting and premarital coital experience (but not the subjects without sex education exposure).

first sex education exposure is unrelated to the probability of premarital petting or coital experience – are continued in Table 2. The chi-square values in Table 2 demonstrated non-significance based on the 0·05 criterion. No evidence was found to confirm the hypothesis that petting and coital experiences are affected by the grade level of first 'sex education' content exposure.

Statistically significant support was not found to warrant rejecting either null hypothesis tested in this analysis. This suggests that any difference between the tested groups are chance differences and that the data obtained from the sample were not sufficient to reflect real differences.

SUMMARY AND INTERPRETATION

Those college students in the sample exposed to 'sex education' content prior to college were found no more or less likely to have experienced premarital petting or premarital coitus than those without such exposure. Further, petting or coital experience could not be accounted for on the basis of the subjects first exposure to 'sex education' content. Therefore, any promotional or inhibitory effect 'sex education' content exposure may have had upon premarital petting or coital experience did not become apparent in the data analyzed.

The analysis of data collected for this study does not offer support for those who categorically oppose 'sex education' on the basis that it contributes to sexual experimentation among those students exposed to 'sex education'. The data also do not support the belief that 'sex education' is useful as a mechanism of controlling premarital petting and coital behavior. A word of caution is appropriate here, however. Since there is diversity in what is labeled 'sex education', assessment of piecemeal 'sex education' content integrated in the general curriculum may not necessarily be valid for a specific course with carefully selected behavioral objectives, content, and teaching techniques. Further, the complex problems arising from terminology must be acknowledged. The term 'sex education' is not uniformly applied to a single, precisely defined subject area. The actual content of a 'sex education' course may vary not only in the material covered, but also in degree and direction of 'ethical slanting' by the educator himself. The exploratory nature of this study seems to make any attempt to theoretically explain the findings premature at this time. It should also be mentioned that the generalization of these findings is limited since the sample was not generally representative of society but was restricted to college students enrolled in a particular kind of course. These conclusions are applicable to college students in general only to the extent that the sample is representative of the college population. The possibility that the effect of 'sex education' upon sexual behavior may differ within a non-college population is in need of exploration.

This study also failed to reveal any justification for defending 'sex education' on the grounds that it will reduce the incidence of 'adolescent mistakes', 'sexual misadventures' – premarital petting and coitus. In this regard, the study was concerned only with gross rates of premarital petting and coital behavior. In view of the finding that 'sex education' does affect sexual attitudes and values,[5] it seems reasonable to hypothesize that learning quality (breadth and depth) differences and learning quantity (frequency of repetition and grade level) differences in educational experience may be crucial considerations in directing sexual behavior.

In summary, this study infers that sex education, *per se,* is not a factor which operates in a significant way to influence premarital petting or coital behavior. Since this inference carries with it many implications for educators and scientists of human sexuality, the authors recommend that more effects of 'sex education' on sexual

269

behavior be explored. More specifically, the impact of specific content areas in sex education as related to general sexual behavior or to specific types of behavior is in need of extensive investigation. Further, the influence of 'sex education' on the frequency of premarital sexual expression or the number of sexual partners is research worthy, as is the quality or the manner of sexual expression and its relationship to 'sex education' exposure.

NOTES

1 Gerald Walker, 'A new look at sex education,' *Cosmopolitan* (March, 1959), p. 61.

2 Mary S. Calderone, 'The sex information and Education Council of the U.S.', *Journal of Marriage and the Family,* 27: 4 (November, 1965), p. 534.

3 Lee A. Belford, 'Protestantism and sex education', in *Advances in Sex Research,* ed. by Hugo G. Beigel (New York: Harper and Row, 1963), p. 61; and William B. Neser and Gerald H. Wiechmann, 'Attitudes of prospective school teachers on teaching venereal disease information', *Public Health Reports,* 82: 10 (October, 1967), p. 919.

4 Frequencies of premarital coitus in this study (Males, 54% and females, 17%) are relatively consistent with data reported in a Midwest sample of college students (Males, 46% and females, 25%) by Vance Packard, 'Sex on campus', *McCall's* (August, 1968), p. 117.

5 Evelyn M. Duvall, 'How effective are marriage courses?', *Journal of Marriage and the Family,* 27: 2 (May, 1965), pp. 176-84.

Conclusion

Having considered some of the evidence concerning the need for, effects of, and practicalities of sex education, I would like to conclude by summarising what our examination seems to have revealed.

First, in the face of the extensive documentation now available of sexuality and sexual learning in childhood and the changing public attitude towards sex, the growth of sex education seems, to me at least, to be both inevitable and desirable. In taking on this task, the schools seem to have the support of the majority of parents and are increasingly assisted by the acceptance by the broadcasting companies of responsibility in this area.[1] The great ability of television to reach large numbers of classes with professional material and to take sex education into schools where it did not exist before deserves recognition by the sex educator. We now know that the success of television in sheer terms of penetration is matched by a generally very favourable reaction by teachers and by marked learning and attitude change in the classroom. However, despite this evidence of success in the short-term, the question of long-term effects, as we saw, remains problematical.

A number of major tasks seem to remain within the field of sex education:

(1) The achievement of total coverage. In other words, sex education given by every school to every child.[2]

(2) The continued evolution of teaching aids and teaching methods.

(3) The clearer definition of aims and objectives, and the explication of the issue of the content and structure of sex education schemes.

(4) The more thorough study of the effects of instruction, particularly long-term implications.

Conclusion

The main stumbling-block to the achievement of the these objectives seems to lie not in organised opposition but in the lack of any central body with specific and generally accepted responsibility within that area. As things stand at present both literature and involvement are spread across a large number of arenas and very little coordination seems to exist. The creation of a central organisation, or the acceptance by some existing body of prime responsibility would do much to improve on the present situation. Whether through the kind of body just discussed, however, or through existing channels, the basic tasks remain and I now propose to discuss some ways in which the outlined objectives could be achieved.

The goal of total coverage can be approached in a variety of ways. In view of the effectiveness of television in reaching schools which do not provide sex education, the continued expansion of this area seems a major goal. However, the ultimate success of such teaching adjuncts must depend on the willingness of teachers and the reaction of parents. To this end, we must first tackle Colleges of Education, with the aim of establishing universal courses in the practicalities of sex education. Such instruction needs to be available both to the teacher-in-training and to practising teachers. Parental acceptance, already high, can be insured only through adequate 'public relations'. In other words, by making available to the public the kind of factual material presented in this book. One area where parents need to be informed is in the rationale for instructing the pre-adolescent as there seems an assumption by the public that sex education is only relevant in adolescence.

To a large extent, the improvement of teaching aids and methods will go hand-in-hand with an expansion of this field of education along the lines just discussed. However, the role of objective research in achieving this end needs much stronger emphasis and here, in the absence of a body with specific responsibility, the task must fall on the existing research bodies and on the producers of teaching aids (the television companies with their vast resources being particularly well placed to take on such research).

The issues of aims and objectives and of long-term effects seem inextricably linked. This results both from the fact that some objectives of sex education (e.g. trying to influence later levels of sexual fulfilment) are more suggestive of long-term effects than others (e.g. success in a short-term knowledge test) and in the sense

272

that, irrespective of specific content, the time and effort devoted to instruction is likely to be a major factor in its salience and retention. Whatever the policy decisions as to content of teaching, however, the building in of evaluation into sex education seems to be the only way in which the link between aims and actual consequences can be approached. Without such feed-back, the whole process becomes an act of faith and the critics can rightly claim that the sex educator doesn't know what he is doing to his charges.

Finally, in turning to the content and structure of sex education, I am well aware of my position as an observer rather than as an active participator (in sex-*education!*) and of the dangers of prescribing and prognosticating from an 'ivory tower'. Nevertheless, this is the immediate day-to-day issue in sex education and any serious review must touch on the topic. I shall deal with two aspects (hopefully the most salient for most readers). The 'specific treatment *vs.* integration into other subjects' dilemma and the issue of future growth.

In considering the pros and cons of specific treatment *vs.* integration, two guiding principles are helpful: that we are talking of the real world and not some utopian ideal, and that, in the present system, academic relevance and social/personal relevance do not equate. The first principle forces us to recognise that because (as we have seen) many homes do not provide instruction for their children, the teacher may well find himself in the position of having to 'cram' the less knowledgeable pupils (which in practice very often means the whole class) in order, for example, to get across a working knowledge of pubertal changes to a class of ten-year-olds. Obviously, earlier instruction in the primary school might have allowed a more subtle approach in the final year but, again we know that in reality many schools do not give such earlier instruction. From working through examples such as this, where specific treatment seems the only solution it is clear that very often there is no real choice. Where there is real choice, the second principle points to another source of difficulty. If sex education education is subsumed under 'biology' in an attempt at integration, then a very real conflict occurs between the personal relevance of a topic (e.g. masturbation) and its academic irrelevance – with, in a 'real' world of restricted time, no happy solution. That the psycho-social aspects of masturbation might also be dealt with somewhere else (e.g. in 'moral education', religious instruction or 'family life education') only extends the scope of the competition between academic and social education in school time. Clearly, such issues will become increasingly pressing. This and the level of curriculum planning needed to insure adequate coverage of sexuality when presented in a 'diffused' way, provide further arguments for the establishment of some central guiding body.[3]

Turning now to the future of sex education, it is a safe bet that we are in for the kind of growth curve that sends ecologists wild! This prediction is based on the increasing extent to which sexuality is becoming a dominant mode of twentieth-century consciousness both directly (e.g. in people's lives, in advertising, in entertainment) and through its consequences (e.g. abortion, sexually transmitted diseases, population growth). The sex educator is therefore bound to find himself faced with a growing and increasingly sophisticated demand. Needs are likely to grow more subtle (as sexual information diffuses and taboos fade, a vast pool of sexual dissatisfaction and disfunction is revealed – witness the growth of sex therapy) and more technical (e.g. new forms of contraception, sex as a form of interpersonal communication). Such a pattern of growth clearly calls for specialist training along the lines of the post-graduate of post-teacher training diploma. Only through such developments, in my view, can contemporary man be helped to come to an intelligent understanding of his own sexuality.

NOTES

1 The reader may feel that too much has been made of the use of television and too little of such teaching aids as the Schools Council Humanities Project or the Nuffield Science Project. The bias is the result of an attempt to concentrate on material for which evaluations are available. No slight is intended on non-broadcast aids.

Some information on Nuffield and Schools Council programmes is given in Burke (Chapter 4). Further comments can also be found in Dallas, Dorothy, M. *Sex Education in School and Society* (N.F.E.R., Windsor, 1972).

2 Should this sound potentially dictatorial, it should be kept in mind that sex educators are just one of numerous pressure groups using democratic channels to 'ginger' the educational establishment. The 1944 Education Act, the existence of a Catholic school system, the extreme autonomy of the individual school in the U.K., the presence of competing school broadcasting systems, the wide range of sources of other kinds of teaching aids – all conspire to hold our wilder flights of sex education fancy in check!

3 Dallas, *Sex Education in School and Society* notes a further problem of the 'diffused' approach. '. . . a South London girl said she had "done" V.D. in biology, in religious instruction and in English lessons (*sic*) – and now the Local Authority Health Educators were coming in to "do" it again'.

Appendix: Statistics for the non-statistician

A number of the papers in this collection make use of statistical tests and analyses. For the benefit of the reader unacquainted with such techniques I have provided the following table which outlines the three tests employed in papers in my book, the kinds of data on which they are used and the type of question the test is employed to answer. In the final column of the table reference is made to their location in one useful introductory statistics text (M. J. Moroney *Facts from Figures* Penguin, 1956) so that those who wish may acquaint themselves further with the tests concerned.

Table 1.

Type of data	Example			Question (alternative hypothesis)	Test usually employed	See Chapters	See Moroney
Events (nominal data) e.g. people, occurrences		Boys	Girls	Do boys and girls perform differently on the test?	χ^2(chi-square) (1-tailed test)	7, 15, 18, 19	Chapter 15 pp. 249–69
	Pass	13	6				
	Fail	5	10				
Measures (ordinal data) e.g. marks, I.Q.s		Before instruction	After instruction	Does instruction affect test score?	1 sample t-test (2-tailed)	18	Chapter 13 pp. 227–33
T S Pupil no. 1		13	15	*or*			
E C Pupil no. 2		10	8	Does instruction *improve* test score?	1-sample t-test (1-tailed)		
S O		:	:				
T R		:	:				
E Pupil no. 30		7	9				
		x English Language	*y* English Literature	Are grades in English language and English literature related?	Product-moment correlation coefficient (r) (2-tailed)	18	Chapter 16 pp. 271–320
E M Pupil no. 1		38%	35%	*or*	Product-moment correlation coefficient (r) (1-tailed)		
X A Pupil no. 2		71%	63%	Are grades in English language and English literature *positively* related?			
A R		:	:				
M K		:	:				
Pupil no. 30		63%	51%				

Further reading

When I first became interested in sex education, I was made aware of the difficulties involved in the location of a comprehensive selection of relevant literature.* The following references, together with those already presented in the readings, should cover the needs and interests of all but the most specialised reader.

Benell, Florence B., 'Frequency of misconceptions and reluctance to teach controversial topics related to sex among teachers', *Research Quarterly,* vol. 40, no. 1 (March 1969), pp. 11–16.

Bjork, R. M., 'An international perspective on various issues in sex education as an aspect of health education', *Journal of School Health,* vol. XXXIX, no. 8 (October 1969), pp. 525–36.

Breasted, Mary, *Oh! Sex Education!* (Pall Mall, London, 1970).

Chanter, A., *Sex Education in the Primary School* (Macmillan, London, 1966).

Chanter, A., 'Sex education – the teacher's job', *The Teacher,* 28 (July 1967).

Coates, E. E., 'Some apparent effects of the acquisition of factual human reproductive information upon selected attitudes of upper elementary students,' Unpublished Dissertation, University of Tennessee, 1970.

Dallas, Dorothy M., *Sex Education in School and Society* (N.F.E.R., Windsor, 1972).

Dillon, Miriam, 'Attitudes of children towards their own bodies and those of other children', *Child Development,* vol. 5 (1934), pp. 165–76.

Eppel, E. M. and Eppel M., *Adolescents and Morality* (Routledge and Kegan Paul, London, 1966).

* The library of the International Planned Parenthood Foundation, 18–20 Lower Regent Street, London, is perhaps the best single U.K. source of of books and journals covering sex education.

Further Reading

Halsall, Elizabeth, 'Sixth form girls look at sex education', *Health Education Journal,* vol. xxvii, no. 4 (November 1968), pp. 179–84.

Hartley, Ruth E. and Hardesty, Francis P., 'Children's perceptions of sex roles in childhood', *Journal of Genetic Psychology,* 105 (1964), pp. 43–51.

Hill, M., 'More harm than good, the truth about sex education', *Forum,* vol. 4, no. 1 (1971).

Hill, M. and Lloyd-Jones, M., 'Sex education: the erroneous zone', *National Secular Society* (London, 1970).

Holmes, M., Nicol, C. S. and Stubbs, R., 'Sex attitudes of young people', *Health Education Journal,* vol. xxviii, no. 1 (March 1969), pp. 13–19.

Hutt, Corinne, *Males and Females* (Penguin, Harmonsworth, 1972).

Kirkendall, L. A. and Miles, G. J., 'Sex education research', *Review of Educational Research,* vol. 28, no. 5 (1968), pp. 528–44.

Morant, R. W., 'Some recent patterns of health education at the secondary level', *Health Education Journal,* vol. xxx, no. 2 (Summer 1971), pp. 52–8.

Pompian, Helen Kilmar, 'A study of the initiation of a sex education program in an elementary school. . .', Unpublished Doctoral Dissertation, Wayne State University, 1969.

Powers, G. P. and Boskin, W., *Sex Education – Issues and Directives* (Philosophical Library, New York, 1969).

Rubin, Isadore and Kirkendall, L. A., 'Sex in the childhood years', (Associated Press, New York, 1970).

Runden, Charity Eva, *Selected Readings for Sex Education* (McCutchan Publishing Corporation, Berkeley, California, 1968).

Wilson, J., Williams, N. and Sugarman, B. *Introduction to Moral Education* (Penguin, Harmondsworth, 1967).

A Handbook of Health Education (H.M.S.O. London, 1968).

'Growth Patterns and Sex Education', *Journal of School Health,* vol. xxxvii, no 5A (May 1967) (whole).

Handbook on Sex Instruction in Swedish Schools (National Board of Education, Stockholm, 1968).

Health in Education, Education Pamphlet, no. 49 (H.M.S.O. London, 1966).

Some Notes on Sex Education (L.C.C., London, 1964).

Journals: Apart from those already covered in the papers and the further references, the reader may find material of interest in:

The Journal of Human Biology
The British Journal of Sexual Medicine
The Journal of Sex Research } Both hard to locate.
The Journal of Sex Education }

Index